MOST UNCOMMON JACKSONIANS

The Radical Leaders
of the Early Labor Movement

MOST UNCOMMON

Jacksonians

The Radical Leaders
Of the Early Labor Movement

EDWARD PESSEN

STATE UNIVERSITY OF NEW YORK PRESS
Albany

Published by State University of New York Press
Thurlow Terrace, Albany, New York 12201

© 1967 by The Research Foundation
of State University of New York, Albany, New York
All rights reserved

First paperbound printing, 1970

Standard Book Number 87395-066-6
Library of Congress Catalog Card Number 67-63761

Manufactured in the United States of America

To Adele

Preface

During the Jacksonian era, an unusual labor movement emerged, composed not only of trade unions but of alleged political parties of workingmen. One of the more paradoxical features of this movement was its leadership. For these were labor leaders who in some cases had never labored, who had lived sedate lives in comfortable circumstances, even employed workers, and had spent a very short time in the movement. If these were uncommon labor leaders, they were also uncommon Jacksonians. At a time when—to the dismay of traditionalists—the mass of Americans seemed to be engaged in a frenzied contest for material gain, and increasingly optimistic about their chances, the labor leaders stood apart both from the pursuit of the main chance and from its moralistic critics.

While this book attempts to throw new light on that early labor movement, mainly by answering the questions that modern critics have raised concerning its authenticity, the major concern of the volume is with the labor leaders' views regarding American society. Although much has been written about the movement since John R. Commons and his associates wrote their pioneering volumes, relatively little has been done heretofore on the ideology of Jacksonian labor.

No claim is made here that the labor leaders were particularly original social thinkers. It is not the brilliance of their social thought, but rather its popularity or representativeness that gives it significance. The fact is that leadership had been conferred on most of them precisely because of their articulateness. While they did not speak for all laboring men, neither did they speak for themselves alone. Rather, they were the spokesmen for that significant minority which during the Jacksonian era organized a labor movement. To understand that movement we must be familiar not alone with its deeds but with its thought and feelings as well.

Part of Chapter II previously appeared in *Labor History* and is reprinted here with the permission of the editor of that journal.

I wish publicly to acknowledge my debt to two men, above all. In the two decades since I first became one of his students, Professor Joseph Dorfman has many times given me the benefit of his vast knowledge and critical scholarship. In the best Voltairean tradition, he has given me useful advice in the preparation of manuscripts for publication that were not in agreement with his own views. Professor Richard B. Morris has been my mentor and invaluable guide over the same period. It was in his seminars that I was first drawn to the Jacksonian era and its labor movement, stimulated by his ability to communicate the significance of these subjects and by his incisive and critical attitudes toward the scholarship dealing with them.

The dedication is to my wife, whose cheerfulness was balm to the spirit and whose hard work sustained our family while I was doing the research for this book.

Brooklyn, New York
January 1967

Contents

PART ONE

The Movement

1

The Emergence of
the Labor Movement

What has been called the first true American labor movement was born in Philadelphia in 1827, when skilled workers, hitherto organized in separate craft societies, combined their organizations into the Mechanics' Union of Trade Associations. In a very short time, hundreds of unions appeared in the cities and towns of the country. As in England during the same period, battalions of trade unionists seemed to spring up out of the ground, until at its height, just prior to the Panic of 1837, the movement was said to have several hundred thousand members. Another Philadelphia development also was repeated elsewhere. The last act of the short-lived Mechanics' Union of Trade Associations was the call for the formation of a new political party, devoted to the interests of workingmen. The Philadelphia Working Men's party, born in 1828, was soon followed by similar parties in every section of the country. New England's unique contribution to the era's labor movement was to be the establishment, in 1831, of the New England Association of Farmers, Mechanics and Other Working Men, in Providence, Rhode Island. This organization, which lasted until 1834, has been described as America's first attempt at industrial unionism. It may not have been that, but it was a unique organization indeed: part political party; part sounding board; part organizer of journeymen's strikes; and full-time advocate of the common interests of artisans, farmers, and factory operatives. All in all, the Jacksonian labor movement was a diverse phenomenon.

There were many causes for the rise of this movement. The programs of the various labor organizations reveal what were considered the main evils and injustices afflicting labor; they show that the American workingman lived not by bread alone. The numerous strikes waged by the unions also are revealing. Long hours, low wages, insecurity, and the threat posed by cheap labor were all considered leading issues by workers. Some developments occurring below the surface of American economic life, either ignored in the labor programs or reflected only indirectly in them, were also crucial. It is recognized today that exploitation and miserable conditions alone are not sufficient to produce a labor movement. Something else is needed. That something was not the appearance of Andrew Jackson and his party but, rather, a series of fundamental changes that transformed the American economy in the early decades of the nineteenth century.

All along the northeastern seaboard, first in such great urban centers as Philadelphia, New York, and Boston, and then in smaller communities, one way of economic life was being replaced by another. A revolution in transportation was accompanied by a rapid expansion of production, trade, and banking, resulting in the decline of an industrial system marked by small shops, limited output for a customs market, and harmony between master craftsmen and journeymen. The merchant capitalist, who sold large amounts of cheaper goods in the expanding national market, was becoming the dominant figure on the economic scene. Motivated as it was by the search for high profits through increased productivity, the new system inevitably brought with it impersonality in employer-labor relations and extreme pressure against the workingman's wages and standards. Master mechanics, heretofore members of craft societies that had been concerned with getting the highest possible price for the products made by their skilled artisans, now proceeded to desert these organizations, leaving them to the journeymen. For the masters acted increasingly as the agents of the merchants; it was the masters who actually squeezed more work out of the journeymen.[1]

In addition to its long-range effects in transforming the nation's economy and market system, the revolution in transport also created a number of immediate, aggravating problems for labor. In 1835 a group of striking New York City cordwainers—as shoemakers were then known—were convinced that the source of their difficulties lay in "the difficulty of raising the retail prices, on account of the great

---

[1] A clear account of the general economic changes of the period is provided in John R. Commons and Associates, *History of Labour in the United States* (2 vols., New York, 1918), I, chaps. i and ii. Also see George R. Taylor, *The Transportation Revolution* (New York, 1951), chaps. xi and xii.

quantity of *cheap work* brought from the Eastern States." [2] Another effect of improved transportation was the way in which it enabled employers to break strikes by advertising for men in other cities, as in the case that same year, when Philadelphia newspapers ran advertisements for two hundred men to replace cordwainers striking in New Brunswick.[3]

While the ascendancy of the merchant capitalist may have been the most important influence on the urban workingman's economic situation, other developments also affected it. For example, in the 1830 Boston congressional election, the victory of Nathan Appleton, the manufacturer who supported Henry Clay and the American System, over Henry Lee, the merchant and free trader, was widely regarded as a sign of the growing importance and influence of manufacturing capital.[4] In that city, above all, merchant princes led the way in investing an ever-increasing proportion of their capital in production rather than commerce. Many new manufacturing enterprises made their appearance during the 1830s, while old ones experienced unprecedented expansion.[5] Such rural factory towns as Lowell and Waltham, the fruits of Boston capital, were increasingly successful examples of a system that would one day replace both the small shop and the skilled artisan who labored in it.

In an age of booming capital requirements, banking and insurance companies flourished, the increase in bank capital far outstripping the increase in specie during the period. Old ideals of economy in municipal government were giving way to the establishment of a permanent debt.[6] A real estate boom was accompanied by a sharp rise in the number of state legislative acts conferring monopolistic grants on private corporations. In other words, the economy of the nation's

---

[2] The *National Trades Union*, June 6, 1835, cited in Commons, *op. cit.*, p. 440.

[3] *The Man*, June 5, 1835, cited in *ibid*.

[4] See the Boston *Courier*, November 2, 1830.

[5] Lemuel Shattuck, *Report to the Committee of the City Council Appointed to Obtain the Census of Boston for the Year 1845* (Boston, 1846), Appen. Z, pp. 44–48, 86; Edward Atkinson, "Boston as the Centre of Manufacturing Capital," in Justin Winsor, ed., *The Memorial History of Boston* (Boston, 1881), vol. IV, chap. iv.

[6] Charles P. Huse, *The Financial History of Boston* (Cambridge, 1916), p. 9; Henry P. Kidder and Frances H. Peabody, "Finance in Boston," in Winsor, *op. cit.*, p. 164.

cities was experiencing a dynamic growth of all forms of activity characteristic of an expanding capitalism. Needless to say, speculation, financial adventures, easier credit and money, all introduced a strong note of insecurity into the economic picture of the era. It is John R. Commons' conclusion that the factor that more than any other accounted for the era's trade union movement was the sharp rise in prices that resulted from the widespread use of paper money.[7]

Many contemporaries were convinced that labor was thriving under the new prosperity. In 1831 the New York conservative Philip Hone confided to his diary: "It is gratifying . . . that this city is at this time prosperous beyond all former example, and somewhat remarkable that different interests usually considered opposed to each other, are equally successful." [8] In the same year a contributor to *Hazard's Register of Pennsylvania* wrote that "as a general rule, with few exceptions, frugal industrious journeymen, unencumbered with families, may save so much of their wages, as in a few years, to be enabled to commence business on their own account on a modest scale." [9] Even more bullish were the comments of Edward Everett, the famous orator. In a speech he made later in that year in Faneuil Hall in Boston, he asked his audience: "Is it not a notorious fact that every shop is employed,—every house occupied,—every mechanic overworked,—rents and wages high and rising,—the whole community in a state of exuberant prosperity? Will any body venture to deny it?" [10]

Yet there is ample evidence that workingmen were faring poorly. In Pennsylvania, workers "shared but slightly in the general business progress of the first half of the nineteenth century," according to William Sullivan.[11] Boston's workingmen also suffered under many

[7] Commons, *op. cit.*, I, Part Two.

[8] Allan Nevins, ed., *The Diary of Philip Hone 1828–1851* (2 vols., New York, 1927), I, 41.

[9] *Hazard's Register of Pennsylvania*, VIII (July 23, 1831), 55, cited in William A. Sullivan, "The Industrial Revolution and the Factory Operative in Pennsylvania," *Pennsylvania Magazine of History and Biography*, LXXVIII (October, 1954), 476–477.

[10] From a speech delivered on October 13, before the "Friends of Domestic Industry," reported in the *Columbian Centinel*, Oct. 29, 1831.

[11] Sullivan, *loc. cit.*, p. 477; also see, by the same author, "Philadelphia Labor During the Jackson Era," *Pennsylvania History*, XV (October, 1948), 1–16.

hardships. In the years between 1825 and 1840, there was an increase in the percentage of persons too poor to pay the minimum tax.[12] A report issued by the federal government in 1833 indicated that in Boston skilled workers could be obtained at lower wages than formerly, while the extremely long hours of work put in by "city operatives" were resulting in a great increase in "turn outs" or strikes.[13] Prosperity or no, in Boston, debtors continued to go to jail in growing numbers, while the proportion of paupers in the population increased, as did the percentage of persons committed to the House of Industry, the institutional aid to paupers.[14] The records for assessed valuation of property, tax collections, and expenditures for poor relief all indicate the prevalence of poverty in the working-class wards of the city.[15] Exaggerated somewhat, but confirmed in large part by other more disinterested sources, were the complaints of the labor press that New York's workers not only found it difficult to get jobs but were so poor that they could be ruined by a brief sickness.[16]

The programs of the Working Men's parties and of the unions barely suggest the poor quality of working-class living conditions. Housing for workingmen was bad, even by the standards of that day. In Philadelphia, working-class houses "were strung along, side to side as boxcars . . . obscured from the street view. . . ." These homes usually had only one room on each floor, their tenants "huddled to the rear . . . victims of a parsimonious building policy which meant crowding, noise, inadequate sanitation, lack of facilities for rubbish removal," and—in contrast to the more fortunately situated—had

[12] Based on figures in Shattuck, *op. cit.*, p. 95.

[13] Louis McLane, Secretary to the Treasury, *Documents Relative to the Manufactures in the United States* (House Document No. 308, 2 vols., Washington, 1833), Document 3, No. 208.

[14] According to one labor journal, more than 5000 persons were aided annually as paupers in a city whose population was not yet 80,000 (*The Man*, November 27, 1834); also see Shattuck, *op. cit.*, pp. 108, 112, 227.

[15] Based on tables in *ibid.*, p. 28, Appen. JJ, p. 61. Also see *List of Persons, Co-partnerships and Corporations who were taxed twenty-five dollars and upwards in the City of Boston for the year 1834* (Boston, 1835); *Columbian Centinel*, Jan. 4, 1836.

[16] See the *Working Man's Advocate*, May 1, 8, 15, 1830; Jan. 29, 1831; Sept. 19, 1835. See also Dixon Ryan Fox, *The Decline of Aristocracy in the Politics of New York* (New York, 1918), p. 353.

none of the recently installed pumps which had been built elsewhere in the city to pipe in water from the Schuylkill.[17] Poverty, unemployment, squalor, by themselves did not evoke a labor movement. But of course they did not exist by themselves. When supplemented by the sweeping economic changes of the period, they formed precisely that milieu which galvanized skilled artisans into that kind of organized activity likely to prevent the worsening of their situation.

---

[17] Louis H. Arky, "The Mechanics' Union of Trade Associations and the Formation of the Philadelphia Workingmen's Movement," *Pa. Magazine of Hist. and Biog.*, LXXVI (April, 1952), 165–166.

2

The Working Men's Party

The unique feature of the American labor movement during the Jacksonian era was the establishment of Working Men's parties. Beginning in Philadelphia in 1828, a Working Men's movement spread throughout the country, reaching its climax in the 1830s. For the only time in American history, workers formed separate political organizations, largely independent of the major parties. Since one of the classic features of the modern American labor movement is precisely the extent to which it has eschewed independent politics, the appearance of this movement is obviously a matter of much significance. This chapter will examine some of the important aspects of the Working Men's parties, as well as some of the issues still in controversy concerning them.

If no attempt will be made here to give a blow-by-blow account of the rise and fall of the Working Men's parties, it is because it is by now a much-told tale. A fairly substantial literature has appeared since George Henry Evans and his contemporaries first chronicled the activities of the New York Working Men.[1] To this date the most

[1] George Henry Evans, "History of the Origin and Progress of the Working Men's Party in New York," in the *Radical*, 1842–1843; Hobart Berrien, *A Brief Sketch of the Origin and Rise of the Working Men's Party in the City of New York* (Washington, n.d.); Amos Gilbert, "A Sketch of the Life of Thomas Skidmore," *Free Enquirer* (New York), Mar. 30, and April 6, 13, 1834; Jabez D. Hammond, *History of Political Parties in the State of New York*, 2 vols. (rev. ed.; New York, 1850), vol II, 330–331.
For the New York area, the most recent study—and in my opinion, a most valuable and judicious volume, despite my questions about some of its interpretations—is Walter Hugins' *Jacksonian Democracy and the Working Class* (Stanford, 1960). Also invaluable is Seymour Savetsky's "The New York Working Men's Party," unpubl. Master's essay (Columbia University, 1948). Also see Edward Pessen, "Thomas Skidmore, Agrarian Reformer in the Early American Labor Movement," *New York History*, vol. XXV (July, 1954); Frank T. Carlton, "The Working Men's Party of New York City, 1829–1831," *Political Science Quarterly*, XXII (Sept., 1907), 401–415. For Philadelphia, see William A. Sullivan, "Did Labor Support Andrew Jackson?" *Political Science Quarterly*, LXII (Dec., 1947), 569–580; and, by the same author, "Philadelphia Labor During the Jackson Era," *Pennsylvania History*, vol. XV (Oct., 1948),

comprehensive, and probably still the most valuable, study remains the pioneering effort of Helen Sumner, written for Commons' *History* in 1918. In many respects it remains the basic structure on which all later works have built.[2]

The modern discussion, focusing as it has on a few major cities, has perhaps obscured what Miss Sumner's researches long ago uncovered: the ubiquitousness of the Working Men's parties. Operating under a variety of names—"Working Men's Party," "Working Men's Republican Association," "People's Party," "Working Men's Society," "Farmer's and Mechanic's Society," "Mechanics and Other Working Men," and just plain "Working Men"—they appeared in most of the states of the Union. Pennsylvania was the home of the first known group, of course, the Philadelphia party of 1828, which developed out of the Mechanics' Union of Trade Associations. Other groups in that state, some of them unknown to Miss Sumner, were organized in Phillipsburg, Lancaster, Carlisle, Pike Township in Clearfield County, Pottsville, Harrisburg, Erie, and in Allegheny and Mifflin Counties.

No. 4, 1–16; Louis Arky, "The Mechanics' Union of Trade Associations and the Formation of the Philadelphia Working Men's Movement," *Pennsylvania Magazine of History and Biography*, LXXVI (April, 1952), 142–176; and Edward Pessen, "The Ideology of Stephen Simpson, Upperclass Champion of the Early Philadelphia Workingmen's Movement," *Pennsylvania History*, XXII (October, 1955), 328–340. For New Jersey, see Milton J. Nadworny, "New Jersey Workingmen and the Jacksonians," *Proceedings of the New Jersey Historical Society*, LXVII (July, 1949), 185–198; and, by the same author, "Jersey Labor and Jackson," unpubl. Master's essay (Columbia University, 1948). For Boston and New England, see Edward Pessen, "Did Labor Support Jackson? The Boston Story," *Political Science Quarterly*, LXIV (June, 1949), 262–274; and Arthur B. Darling, "The Workingmen's Party in Massachusetts, 1833–1834," *American Historical Review*, XXIX (October, 1923), 85–86. On the Working Men's parties in general, see Joseph Dorfman, *The Economic Mind in American Civilization* (New York, 1946), vol. II, chap. xxiv; and, by the same author, "The Jackson Wage-Earner Thesis," *American Historical Review*, LIV (Jan., 1949), 296–306; Arthur M. Schlesinger, Jr., *The Age of Jackson*, (Boston, 1945), chap. xi; Nathan Fine, *Labor and Farmer Parties in the United States, 1828–1928* (New York, 1928); Alden Whitman, *Labor Parties, 1827–1834* (New York, 1943); and Edward Pessen, "The Working Men's Movement of the Jacksonian Era," *Mississippi Valley Historical Review*, XLIII (Dec., 1956), 428–443.

2 Miss Sumner wrote Part Two, "Citizenship (1827–1833)," in John R. Commons and Associates, *History of Labour in the United States* (2 vols., New York, 1918), I, 169–332.

In New York State the leading and certainly the most interesting group was organized by Thomas Skidmore and others in New York City. Brooklyn had its own organization, in which the later trade unionist John Commerford played a leading role. Parties also appeared in Troy, Albany, Rochester, Buffalo, Genesee, Utica, Salina (Syracuse), Schenectady, Geneva, Ithaca, Auburn, Batavia, Brockport, Hartford in Washington County, Canandaigua, Kingsbury, Lansingburgh, Glens Falls, Palmyra, and Saratoga. A Working Men's party convention in 1830 was attended by delegates from the counties of New York, Albany, Rensselaer, Cayuga, Oneida, Washington, Onondaga, Tioga, Tompkins, Montgomery, Kings, Cortland, and Ontario. It was reported that a number of other counties also had chosen delegates, who for some unknown reason did not attend.[3]

In New Jersey, groups formed not only in Newark and Trenton, as Miss Sumner noted, but in Hanover (Morris County), Centerville, Caldwell, Peterson, and in Orange and Essex Counties, as well.[4] Organizations, albeit questionable ones which may have been "Working Men" in name only, were started in Washington, D. C., and in Canton, Ohio. Working Men also formed in Zanesville and in Columbiana County, Ohio. In Delaware, there were branches in Wilmington, Brandywine, and Red Clay Creek, and in New Castle County.

New England had a lively movement featured by the Association of Farmers, Mechanics and Other Working Men. In addition to this group, whose members came from a number of states, Working Men were organized in Boston, Dedham, Northampton, Dorchester, and in Hampshire and Franklin Counties in Massachusetts; in New London and Lyme in Connecticut; Dover, New Hampshire; Portland and Brunswick in Maine; and in Woodstock, Burlington, Middlebury, and Calais in Vermont.

Most of our information concerning these parties comes from the pages of the dozens of journals which sprang up in this period in support of Working Men. According to the *Delaware Free Press*, one of these journals, by August, 1830, there were at least twenty news-

[3] *Ibid.*, p. 265. Based on a report in the *Farmers', Mechanics' and Workingmen's Advocate*, Sept. 1, 1830.

[4] Nadworny (*op. cit.*, f.n. 1, above) corrects Miss Sumner with regard to the New Jersey movement, for she believed that it was confined to Newark and Trenton (see *ibid.*, p. 287).

papers in a number of states that might be classified as prolabor.[5] Miss Sumner found that "some 50 different newspapers in at least 15 States" had expressed approval of the movement at one time or another between 1829 and 1832. These papers varied, naturally, in the degree of support or attention they gave to the workingmen's cause, but a substantial number of them that I have examined can properly be described as organs of the political movement, so completely were they dedicated to the Working Men's issues both in their coverage and in their slant of the news.

In the case of several of the leaders of this movement, their identification with labor consisted precisely in the fact that they edited such journals. George Henry Evans was such a figure. Another was William Heighton, an Englishman who came to this country as a youth, became a cordwainer, the founder of the Philadelphia Mechanics' Union of Trade Associations, and early in 1828, the chief editor of the *Mechanic's Free Press*, the official journal of the Philadelphia movement. This weekly has been described as the "first of the mechanics' newspapers in this country edited by journeymen and directed to them." [6] In Philadelphia, Heighton's journal prodded workers "along the path of reform and into politics," thus helping to initiate the political movement. More typical was Evans' *Working Man's Advocate* in New York City, which appeared shortly *after* the Working Men organized there. In many cases the journal followed so soon after the party that the two were practically simultaneous, as in Newark, where a Newark *Village Chronicle and Farmers, Mechanics and Working Men's Advocate* came out immediately after the political movement started.

Louis Arky's description of the *Mechanic's Free Press* could apply to numerous other papers as well: "Its pages presented a spectrum of reform, from Pestalozzian educational ideas and co-operative store suggestions to the views of free thinkers and reprints from works like [John] Gray's Lecture [*Lecture on Human Happiness*, London, 1825, a socialistic tract]." [7] In addition, the journals would carry

5 Commons, *History of Labour*, I, p. 286. Also see Edward Pessen, "*La Première Presse du Travail: Origine, Role, Idéologie*," *La Presse Ouvrière, 1819–1850*, ed. by Jacques Godechot (Paris, 1966), pp. 43–67.

6 Louis Arky, "The Mechanics' Union of Trade Associations and the Formation of the Philadelphia Working Men's Movement," p. 163.

7 *Ibid.*

accounts of workingmen's activities in other cities as well as their own, announcements of future activities, romances, advertisements, literary excerpts, and a potpourri of other material. From the point of view of the student of American labor, however, most rewarding were their editorials, the letters of contributors—so often polemical and therefore piquant as well as informative—and their listings of the demands and the programs of the Working Men's parties. Students of the history of American journalism and those who are interested in our social history also will find a treasure-trove in the *New England Artisan and Farmer's, Mechanic's and Laboring Man's Repository*, the New York *Daily Sentinel*, the Indianapolis *Union and Mechanics' and Working Men's Advocate*, and the other labor journals of the period.

If the worth of Miss Sumner's contribution endures, it is also true that the recent discussion, certainly that of the past two decades—based as it is on new evidence and reflecting new scholarly interests and frames of reference—has not only added to our knowledge but in many cases severely modified and brought into serious question her conclusions concerning important matters. In this respect perhaps the trend is similar to that in American historical writing in general: an iconoclastic revisionism which accepts no previous interpretations as sacred, inspired as it is by a relativism to which all old judgments are merely the ephemeral reflections of a forever bygone time.

It would be understatement to describe the main questions raised by the recent literature as a challenge to the traditional thesis. For these questions concern nothing less than the fundamental nature of the Working Men's movement. They ask simply: Was the movement authentic? Was it composed of bona fide wage earners battling in the interests of wage earners? Or was it spurious, consisting instead of wily politicians who wrapped themselves in the Working Men's mantle only to hide their real identity?

According to Miss Sumner the issue that divided the true Working Men's parties from the fraudulent was the tariff. For although her study expressed few doubts about the authenticity of most of the organizations which carried the title, she did believe that in some cases "advocates of a protective tariff assumed without warrant the popular name—'mechanics and workingmen.' " Adding to her suspicions was the fact that these "associations of so-called workingmen

which favored protection generally avoided committing themselves
to the usual demands of the Working Men's party." [8] But if the
organization were for free trade and in addition raised the "usual
demands," her study accepts it at face value.

In challenging the authenticity of these parties, critics have
focused on a number of issues. One bone of contention has been the
party's origins, since the way in which the organization was started,
the nature of the men involved, and the issues propelling them into
action obviously tell us whether the organization was of and for
workingmen or whether it was something else again—at least in its
infancy.

The political movement in Philadelphia grew out of a decision by
the city's Mechanics' Union of Trade Associations to enter into
politics in order to promote "the interests and enlightenment of the
working classes." The latter organization, the "first union of all the
organized workmen of any city," had been organized largely
through the energetic activity of the cordwainer William Heighton.
It included the individual unions—or societies as they were then
called—of journeymen bricklayers, painters, glaziers, typographers
and other trades, as well as the journeymen house carpenters whose
strike for the ten hour day in the summer of 1827 spurred the formation of the broader union. There can be little doubt as to the authenticity of the Mechanics' Union, whose appeal to its constituent societies rested primarily on its down-to-earth promise of financial support to journeymen on strike against their masters.[9] A few months
after it was organized, the bylaws of the Union were amended to
provide that three months prior to general elections the membership
should "nominate as candidates for public office such individuals as
shall pledge themselves . . . to support and advance . . . the interests and enlightenment of the working classes." [10] The new bylaws
took immediate effect. Several months later the *Mechanic's Free Press*
reported that "at a very large and respectable meeting of Journeymen
House Carpenters held on Tuesday evening, July 1st [1828], . . .
the Mechanics' Union of Trade Associations is entering into measures for procuring a nomination of candidates for legislative and

[8] *Op. cit.*, pp. 294–295.

[9] Arky, *loc. cit.*, pp. 155–158.

[10] *Mechanics' Gazette*, Jan 19, 1828, cited in *ibid.*, p. 162.

other public offices, who will support the interest of the working classes." Thus was born the Working Men's party of Philadelphia, in the promise by some journeymen workers to support at the polls individuals sympathetic to the working class. The most skeptical observer can hardly deny the true workingmen's character of the party, at least at the time of its birth.[11]

In New York City a Working Men's party appeared for the first time in 1829 when in the elections for the State Assembly held early in November, eleven candidates nominated by the new party made a remarkable showing. The decision to run Working Men's candidates on a separate ticket was made at a general meeting of mechanics on October 19, 1829. In addition to approving a number of other resolutions presented by the executive body, known as the Committee of Fifty, the meeting resolved "that past experience teaches that we have nothing to hope from the aristocratic orders of society; and that our only course to pursue is, to send men of our own description, if we can, to the Legislature at Albany; . . . [that] we will make the attempt at the ensuing election; and that as a proper step thereto we invite all those of our fellow citizens who live on their own labor and none other, to meet us. . . ." [12]

This Committee of Fifty had been elected at the second of two meetings of journeymen mechanics held earlier that year in the last week of April, to give leadership in the struggle to protect the ten hour day against an alleged employers' plot to lengthen it.[13] The first meeting of the mechanics, which was in fact to lead directly to the nomination of candidates—and which can therefore properly be described as constituting the first meeting of the New York Working

---

[11] William A. Sullivan, who raises a number of questions about the validity of the Philadelphia political movement on the basis largely of the candidates it was to nominate, nonetheless concedes that a long list of "economic, political and social ills" precipitated this bona fide movement of the "the Philadelphia workingmen into politics"; "Philadelphia Labor During the Jackson Era," *Pennsylvania History*, XV (October, 1948), 4. For Sullivan's suspicions regarding the "Working Men" of western Pennsylvania, see his *The Industrial Worker in Pennsylvania 1800–1840* (Harrisburg, 1955), pp. 181–193.

[12] *Working Man's Advocate*, Oct. 31, 1829; New York *Evening Journal*, Oct. 30, 1829.

[13] On the origins of the party, see the New York *Morning Courier*, the New York *Commercial Advertiser*, and the New York *Free Enquirer*, all for April 25, 1829; and the *Radical*, Jan., 1842.

Men's party—had been called in order to combat "all attempts to compel them to work more than ten hours a day." [14] It would appear then that in its origins the political movement of the New York Working Men was clearly a response of bona fide workers to an attack on their working conditions.

Seymour Savetsky, however, after a close study of this movement, which appeared to establish the intimate relationship between both the leaders and the supporters of the new movement with the Republican [or Jackson] party, concluded that "the explanation for the origin of the . . . party is to be found in the bitter internal dissensions and schisms that were wrecking the Republican Party of New York. In the fractionalization of the Republican party . . . resides the explanation for the appearance of the New York Working Men's Party." [15] While there is evidence that the emergence of the New York movement owed something to the disenchantment of some Republican (or Democratic) voters with the Tammany machine, it seems to me that it is impossible to disagree with Walter Hugins that the party's "initial impetus was economic, a protest against unemployment and a defense of the ten-hour day." [16] Even Jabez Hammond's contemporary account, while stressing the complexity and heterogeneity of the State movement, saw the beginnings of the New York City party as essentially due to the concern of mechanics in the building trade with onerous economic conditions.[17] My own research into the New York Working Men has centered on the roles of Robert Dale Owen, George Henry Evans, and Thomas Skidmore, only the latter of whom might be classified as a worker. Although these men were to steer this movement in directions determined largely by doctrinaire philosophies, this fact in no way contradicts another: the New York Working Men's party originated in a movement of journeymen mechanics to defend their position against an anticipated attack by masters and employers.

[14] New York *Morning Courier,* April 23, 1829.

[15] Seymour Savetsky, "The New York Working Men's Party," pp. 109–110. Lee Benson's *The Concept of Jacksonian Democracy: New York as a Test Case* (Princeton, 1961), accepts Savetsky's view.

[16] Walter Hugins, *Jacksonian Democracy and the Working Class,* p. 11.

[17] Jabez Hammond, *History of Political Parties in the State of New York,* vol. II, 330.

For Boston, as for Newark and other towns in New Jersey, the evidence is not clear. The program adopted by the Boston Working Men's party, the methods advocated to attain it, and the candidates nominated to represent the organization politically all raise doubts as to the nature of the movement. But according to the correspondents who reported on its first meetings in the summer of 1830, these were attended by large numbers of "men, who from appearance, were warm from their workshops and from other places of daily toil, but who bore on their countenances conviction of their wrongs, and a determination to use every proper means to have them redressed." [18]

There is much fuller information on the origins of the much more significant New England Association of Farmers, Mechanics and Other Working Men. Described by Miss Sumner as a "new type of labour organization, in part economic and in part political," this association was formed when delegates from the New England states, convening in Providence in December, 1831, agreed to hold the first convention the following spring in Boston. The advertisement for the first convention emphasized that "the object of that convention is to mature measures to concentrate the efforts of the laboring classes, to regulate the hours of labor by one uniform standard." [19] This was in fact a call for the ten hour day. It is no coincidence that the date set by the first convention for the establishment of the ten hour system—March 20, 1832—happened to be precisely the date on which the Boston shipyard workers began their strike for the ten hour day. Certainly the workers went on strike not because the Association's constitution so directed them. Rather, the Association incorporated the idea of a ten hour system, a strike to achieve it, a war chest to finance it, and expulsion of all those who would work more than ten hours per day after March 20, because of the great influence that Boston's shipyard workers and their allies had in its councils.[20] It was the defeat of the ten hour strike that led the delegates to the second convention held at Boston in September to modify the clause calling for the expulsion from the Association of those who worked

[18] Boston *Advocate*, Sept., 1830, cited in Commons, *op. cit.*, p. 291; Boston *Courier*, Aug. 11, 28, 1830.

[19] *Columbian Centinel*, Feb. 15, 16, 1832.

[20] See articles 3, 4, 5, and 9 of the Association's constitution; *Working Man's Advocate*, March 3, 1832. Also see *Boston Traveller*, March, 1832.

more than the ten hour day.[21] It appears incontestable that New
England's most important Working Men's party was organized by
workingmen to achieve—in contrast to its New York City counter-
part, which sought to maintain—the ten hour day.

The sharpest questions as to the authenticity of the Working
Men's parties have been provoked by the accumulating evidence on
the social and economic backgrounds of their members and leaders.
The organ of the Philadelphia Working Men liked to think that in
contrast to the two major parties—the Federalists, made up of lawyers and aristocrats, and the Jackson party, composed of bank specu-
lators and office hunters—"on the Working Men's ticket . . . the
candidates from first to last have been taken from the ranks of the
people." But William Sullivan has shown that during its four years
of existence the Philadelphia party nominated and supported very
few workers as candidates for office. According to his tabulation of
the party's one hundred candidates, only ten were workingmen.
Twenty-three were professional men, fifty-three were merchants
and manufacturers, eleven were "gentlemen," and three had no occupation recorded. Among these were some of the wealthiest men in
the city, including Charles Alexander, publisher of the conservative
Daily Chronicle. These facts lead Sullivan to doubt that the Philadelphia organization was a true workingmen's party.[22] Louis Arky,
on the other hand, found a high percentage of its early leaders, better
than 75 per cent, workers or artisans.[23] The contradiction may be
more apparent than real. The men who actually ran the party were
themselves workers. If the candidates were wealthy that fact was not
disconcerting to a party whose interest was confined to the views—
not the bank accounts—of its nominees.

Milton Nadworny, the leading student of the New Jersey movement, found little solid information as to the occupations or incomes
of the leaders and candidates there, although for Newark he ventures
the understatement that "undoubtedly, not all of the men in the
group were pure, unadulterated workingmen." Despite his findings

---

[21] See the letter from a Boston delegate in the *Working Man's Advocate,* Sept.
15, 1832.

[22] William A. Sullivan, "Did Labor Support Andrew Jackson?" p. 375; and Sullivan, *The Industrial Worker* . . . , pp. 178–179.

[23] Louis Arky, *loc. cit.,* p. 173.

that small businessmen and merchants often played leading parts in the movement, he nonetheless accepts it as essentially authentic.[24]

The New York City Working Men split into at least three factions shortly after their remarkable political success in the fall of 1829. There can be little doubt that the most numerous of these had little in common with true workmen. But prior to the infiltration of the party by opportunistic elements, culminating in their ascendancy over it by the time of the 1830 elections, the evidence indicates that bona fide workers were active in its ranks. Of the eleven candidates put up for the State Assembly in 1829, ten were workers. The other, a physician, got significantly fewer votes than all the rest of his colleagues in the election.[25] In its early stages, according to George Henry Evans, the party sought not only to confine leadership to workingmen but to see that these were journeymen rather than masters. That it was not successful, however, is shown by the fact that by 1830 even Evans' faction was supporting manufacturers as candidates for political office.

For that matter, Evans' definition of a workingman was rather broad. According to him, only one member of the seventy-man General Executive Committee of the New York party of 1830—a broker—was not a workingman. Evidently, to Evans, the five grocers, the two merchant-tailors, the oil merchant, the teacher, and the farmer were workers. The complete occupational breakdown for this committee unfortunately does not distinguish between masters and journeymen, but it does range over a broad category of occupations, including carpenters, smiths, masons, painters, pianoforte makers, sash makers, and porter housekeepers. Savetsky, who is not inclined to take this Party's claims at face value, nonetheless concedes that on this committee "a majority . . . belong to the laboring element in the community." His close study of the property owned by this group established that just under 50 per cent were propertyless, another 10 per cent had only personal property, while only three individuals owned property assessed at more than $10,000.[26] For the

[24] Milton Nadworny, "Jersey Labor in the Age of Jackson," pp. 58, 59–60, 75–76.

[25] *Working Man's Advocate*, Nov. 7, Dec. 25, 1829.

[26] According to Savetsky, the findings on the property holdings of the General Executive Committee members were based on a careful reading of fourteen volumes of tax rolls for the year 1830 (*loc. cit.*).

years after 1831 it has been rather conclusively shown, both by Jabez Hammond in 1846, and Walter Hugins, in 1960, that the New York Working Men included a wide variety of social and economic types.

The Boston Working Men's party did not last long, but while it lasted it showed no animus toward men of wealth. Years ago I did a study of the social position of the candidates it supported in the municipal election of 1830 and in the state congressional contest of 1831. Their mayoralty candidate, Theodore Lyman, Jr., was a wealthy shipowner, while four of their seven aldermanic candidates were among the wealthiest men in Boston. Thirty-five of their sixty choices for the State Assembly belonged to that elite group whose property was valued in excess of $2,600.[27] Since fewer than two thousand persons in a population of seventy-eight thousand had this amount of property, it would appear that forty of the party's sixty-eight nominees belonged to the wealthiest segment of the community. I must admit, however, that I am now not so sure of what I wrote then, that these figures "do not imply anything fraudulent," and that they reflect "middle class aspirations and a certain naïveté" more than they raise doubts "as to the true workingmen's character" of the Boston Working Men's party.[28] Doubts as to the actual nature of the party are indeed raised by such figures.

Doubts have also been raised by the programs of the Working Men's parties. Joseph Dorfman has not been alone in noting that some of the measures they advocated bore no relation to the economic needs of workingmen. But it is true of course that workingmen had needs that ranged beyond the economic. That Working Men's parties raised aloft a standard which included a wide variety of political, social, intellectual, occasionally even religious, as well as economic issues, does not testify necessarily to anything but their breadth of interests and hopes.

The programs of the parties were amazingly similar. For as Miss Sumner observed, "substantially the same measures were advocated by the workingmen in most of the western and southern cities, as

[27] These figures are based on the study *List of Persons, Copartnerships and Corporations who were taxed twenty-five dollars and upwards in the City of Boston for the year 1834* (Boston, 1835).

[28] Edward Pessen, "Did Labor Support Jackson? The Boston Story," p. 267.

well as in New Jersey, Delaware and New England, as were advocated by their comrades in Philadelphia and New York." [29] The program of the Philadelphia Working Men was to become the nucleus of the program everywhere. It included above all a call for a free, tax-supported school system to replace the stigmatized "pauper schools," which according to Sullivan provided a "highly partial and totally inadequate system of education for their children." The final copies of the *Mechanic's Free Press* contained on the masthead these additional reforms: abolition of imprisonment for debt; abolition of all licensed monopolies; an entire revision or abolition of the prevailing militia system (the burden of which fell most heavily on workers); a less expensive law system; equal taxation on property; no legislation on religion; a district system of election.[30] In addition, the Philadelphians intermittently protested against the unsanitary and overcrowded housing conditions of workingmen; the high cost of living; the long hours, low wages, and poor conditions of labor, as well as the low esteem in which manual work was held; the hostility of the major parties toward labor; the mistreatment of labor unions; the lottery system—"the fruitful parent of misery and want to numberless heart-broken wives and helpless children, who have beheld the means of their subsistence lavished in the purchase of lottery tickets"; the "pernicious operating of paper money"; and such down-to-earth grievances as insufficient "hydrant water for the accommodation of the poor," and "the failure of the city to clean the streets in the remote sections of the city where the workingmen reside." And earlier they had pressed successfully for the passage of a mechanics' lien law to assure workingmen first claim on their employers' payrolls. Nor does this exhaust the list; from time to time there were criticisms of the sale of liquor, of banks and banking, of charitable institutions, of conspiracy laws as used against unions, the use of prison labor, and the general complexity of the laws and of the legal system.

The Working Men of New York and of other cities did not of course slavishly follow the Philadelphia program, even though they put forward grievances and demands which concentrated on the

[29] *Op. cit.,* p. 296.
[30] Cited in Sullivan, "Philadelphia Labor During the Jackson Era," pp. 9–10.

same essentials.[31] In New York City, for example, Thomas Skidmore early won the Working Men over to support of an "agrarian" program calling for "equal property to all adults," a plank which was supported until the expulsion of Skidmore from the party at the end of 1829. Later, Robert Dale Owen, George Henry Evans, and their supporters championed a unique educational system known as "State Guardianship," under which working class children not only were to receive an improved education under a tax-supported program but were to board out in the new public schools as well. At one time or another, the party also stressed anticlericalism, compensation for jurors and witnesses, direct election of the mayor, smaller electoral districts, the payment of certain political officials (for the classic reason later emphasized by the English Chartists, that otherwise only wealthy property owners could afford to hold office), reduction of salaries in some cases, civil service reform, abolition of capital punishment, pensions for Revolutionary War veterans, a single municipal legislative chamber, and free trade. With regard to the half dozen or so issues which were most emphasized, the mastheads of the labor journals which proclaimed them could have been interchanged without notable difference. On many occasions the New York *Working Man's Advocate* and the Philadelphia *Mechanic's Free Press* carried precisely the same slogans.

Some programs, as has been indicated, were related to local problems and issues. The New England Association reflected its rural composition by calling for a reform in land tenure laws, and its sympathy with factory operatives by insistence on factory legislation. The Working Men of Boston advocated a reduction of the fees charged by professionals, while calling also for decreases in what were considered exorbitant expenditures of the state government. And in Cincinnati the Working Men added "improvements in the arts and sciences" to the classic appeal for equal universal education and the abolition of licensed monopolies, capital punishment, unequal taxation on property, the prevalent militia system, and imprisonment for debt.

There is no question but that this was a broad program, substantial portions of which were supported by men and groups having noth-

---

[31] For a useful and comprehensive modern discussion of the New York program, see Hugins, *op. cit.*

ing to do with labor. Imprisonment for debt, for example, was opposed by many people outside of the Working Men's movement, on broad humanitarian grounds, in some cases, and on grounds of economic inefficiency, in others. Its victims were not always the "laboring poor." Yet it would be an economic determinism of a very rigid sort, indeed, to insist that authentic labor organizations confine their programs to economic issues advantageous only to workers.

Much of the Working Men's program was in fact concerned with the economic interests of labor. Workers did of course seek a larger slice of the pie. But they also sought improved status in society, and some of them organized in order to support the perfectionist demands put forward by their idealistic leaders as the means of achieving this status. The programs of the Working Men's parties reveal them to have been champions of social justice and a truer democracy, as well as critics of every kind of social abuse.

Still other questions as to the authenticity of the Working Men have been raised over the alleged closeness of their relationship with the Jacksonian party. Where Arthur M. Schlesinger, Jr., sees a coalition between the two movements, some critics of his thesis have interpreted the same evidence as indicating the essential fraudulence of the Working Men's parties, which were thus only front organizations for the Democrats. It is perhaps a source of comfort to these critics that their charges are similar to those made one hundred and thirty years ago by some National Republican leaders and publishers.

With regard to this issue, as with others, the evidence is either inconclusive or too complex to permit of black and white generalizations. Assuredly, from time to time and with regard to certain issues, the two movements behaved as one. The organ of the Newark Working Men, the Newark *Village Chronicle and Farmers, Mechanics, and Workingmen's Advocate*, admitted in April of 1830 to its sympathy with the Jacksonians. And there seemed to be more than coincidence in the decision by the two parties in New Jersey that year to hold their nominating conventions for the state legislature in the same small town on the same date. It it not surprising that after the fall elections critics denounced the collusion between the two parties. Five years later the Newark Democrats still evidently depended to a large extent on the political support of the Working Men, while in 1836 the two groups jointly supported a number of legislative candidates. The leading student of the New Jersey Work-

ing Men concludes that they consistently supported the Democrats
and their candidates.[32]

In New York City the striking political success achieved by the
Working Men in 1829 seems to have been the result largely of a shift
in the voting habits of people who ordinarily voted for the "Republican" or Jackson party.[33] The New York party broke into several
splinter groups shortly after the 1829 election. The so-called *Sentinel*
or *Advocate* wing, named after the journals published by Robert
Dale Owen and George Henry Evans, supported much of the Democratic program, especially its antimonopoly features. In fact, according to Savetsky, this faction was simply absorbed or assimilated into
the New York Jacksonian organization after its defeat in the elections of 1830.[34]

In New England the decision in 1833 of the New England Association to support as their gubernatorial candidate, Samuel Clesson
Allen, erstwhile supporter of Andrew Jackson and opponent of the
Bank of the United States, led more than one Whig journal to de-
nounce the unholy alliance of Working Men and Jackson men. The
same fact is the basis for Schlesinger's conclusion that at this time the
Massachusetts Working Men increasingly threw themselves behind
Jackson's monetary program.[35] Yet this same New England Association convention urged the formation of a pro labor national political
organization. When the Association again nominated Allen for Gov-
ernor at its last convention in September, 1834, at Northampton, it
simultaneously urged rejection of the candidates of the major parties
for state office. A close study of its programs, conventions, resolutions, and actions indicates that from its birth in Providence in
December, 1831, until its demise not three years later, this organization was little concerned with, let alone sympathetic to, the Democratic party. As for the Boston Working Men's party, it showed no
support whatever for the Jacksonian party. Its slate of candidates

---

[32] Nadworny, *loc. cit.*, pp. 55, 68–69, 75.

[33] This is the conclusion of Savetsky, according to whom the Working Men
were essentially Democrats grown disenchanted with Tammany (*loc. cit.*, pp.
110, 115).

[34] *Ibid.*, p. 60.

[35] *The Age of Jackson*, p. 158.

for the Board of Aldermen and the State House of Representatives included a goodly number of National Republicans.[36] Although its mayoralty candidate, Theodore Lyman, Jr., had worked for Jackson's victory in 1828, he had broken with Old Hickory's party well before the 1830 municipal elections. The nonsupport of the Democrats by the poorer wards in the 1831 elections provoked David Henshaw, Jackson's appointee to the strategic collectorship of the port of Boston, to charge that Boston workingmen were the enemies of the Democratic party. (The evidence indicates that workmen were no great friends to the Working Men's party either.)

In New York City not only Skidmore but Evans, Owen, and their supporters as well, regularly voiced their opposition to both major parties. Despite their occasional agreement with the Democrats on a particular issue, their press warned that Jackson had no interest in important reform. If old Hammond can be believed, the men who "flocked to the standard of the Workingmen" in New York were "opposed to the Albany Regency and the Jackson party." [37]

The Philadelphia Working Men had no objections to supporting candidates of whatever social background or political persuasion. Yet their journal saw no contradiction in denying any connection with either of the major parties. In fact, it stressed the danger represented by the Democrats, "for as most of us are deserters from their ranks they view us with the same sensation as the mighty lord would the revolt of his vassals: there cannot be so much danger from the Federalists as, generally speaking, we were never inclined to trust them." [38] In the elections of 1829, the one year in which the Philadelphia Working Men achieved an outstanding success, they combined with the anti-Jacksonians in support of eight local candidates, while endorsing only one Jackson supporter. Sullivan has concluded

---

[36] Two of its seven candidates for alderman were National Republicans, according to the Boston *Courier*, Dec. 9, 1830, and the Boston *Daily Advertiser and Patriot*, Dec. 11, 1830. Fifteen of the sixty state candidates were also nominated by the National Republicans, while a number of the remainder were prominent members of the party, according to the *Columbian Centinel*, May 7, 1831.

[37] Jabez Hammond, *op. cit.*, p. 331.

[38] *Mechanic's Free Press*, April 12, 1828, cited in Sullivan, "Did Labor Support Andrew Jackson?" p. 571.

that "an analysis of the [Philadelphia] Working Men's Party reveals that both in its composition and its predilections, it was amazingly regular in its support of the anti-Jackson forces." [39]

Even for New Jersey the situation was more complex than the allegations of some National Republicans would make it appear. The original platform of the New Jersey Working Men refused to align the group in support of Jackson. As the Working Men of Morris showed in 1834, they had no compunctions about nominating a Whig to office. His success goaded the Democrats into charging that the Whigs used the Working Men as tools! The following year an election rally of Newark's Working Men's party expressly stated that it preferred neither of the major parties. And although in 1836 there was a degree of cooperation between the two groups, before the year was out there was evidently a falling out that may have been due to the Working Men's resentment at being used by the Jackson party.[40]

Two points need to be stressed. The programs of the Working Men's parties called for reforms that in most cases went unmentioned by the Democrats, whether on local, state, or national level. This would indicate that the organizers of the new movement were motivated precisely by the failure of the Democrats—not to mention the National Republicans—to work toward goals that were regarded as of the highest importance. Something new in the form of a Working Men's party was added because it was believed it was needed. In addition, despite the attempt by some historians to treat the political issues and the major parties of the era in striking ideological terms, as though they represented diametrically opposed social and class viewpoints, the facts are otherwise. As Charles Sellers, Glynden Van Deusen, Bray Hammond, Richard Hofstadter, and others have shown, the major parties had similar views on many important issues, differing more in tactical approaches than in fundamental objectives, with neither party dedicated to a drastic alteration in the fabric of society. Of course there were Democrats and Democrats. But Jackson himself and the leaders of the Democratic party in most of the states, were practical men of pragmatic temper. All of which is to say that it is to misinterpret the nature of the Democratic state machines

[39] Sullivan, "Philadelphia Labor During the Jackson Era," p. 13.
[40] Nadworny, *loc. cit.*, pp. 67, 69–73.

or the national Democratic party of Andrew Jackson's day, to believe that so loose, opportunistic, all-inclusive, and eclectic a coalition would devote itself to the kinds of reform urged by the Working Men.

What is to be concluded concerning the relationship between the Working Men—led by radicals who often sharply criticized the Democratic party—and Jacksonian Democracy? To the extent that it, too, opposed aristocratic privilege and monopoly, the Working Men's movement may perhaps be interpreted as part of a broadly defined "Jacksonian Revolution." But neither organized nor unorganized workingmen became a fixed part of a Democratic political coalition. And if the Jacksonian movement was in fact a movement primarily devoted to achieving a freer competitive capitalism, the Working Men clearly had demands which went far beyond that objective.[41] Yet, according to the large view which seeks to impose a pattern on an era, reforms of varied character, championed by diverse groups, each seeking the achievement of its own objectives, somehow merge in a broad, all-embracing reform movement. It is only in this general sense that the Working Men of the Jacksonian era can be said to have been a part of a large, sweeping movement, toward whose political expression—the Democratic party—they often displayed indifference, if not actual hostility.

Examination of the various controversies concerning the authenticity of the Working Men's parties establishes one thing clearly: it is impossible to generalize about the movement, as though its constituent parts were alike in all particulars. The origin of some Working Men's parties was obscure; of others, dubious. Some arose out of economic struggles; others, out of concern for status. Some came to be dominated by opportunists, others by zealots. The only safe generalization perhaps would be that no two parties experienced precisely similar careers.

Yet it is also clear that despite inevitable differences in their circumstances and behavior, these organizations, arising more or less simultaneously and calling for like reforms, had much in common.

---

[41] See Richard Hofstadter, *The American Political Tradition* (New York, 1948), p. 56; Bray Hammond, *Banks and Politics in America from the Revolution to the Civil War* (Princeton, 1957), *passim;* Joseph Dorfman, *The Economic Mind in American Civilization,* II, chap. xxiii; Richard B. Morris, "Andrew Jackson, Strikebreaker," *Amer. Hist. Rev.,* LV (Oct., 1949), p. 68.

Common to the Working Men's parties in the major cities was their authenticity—at least for part of their history. By authenticity is meant that they were formed by workers or men devoted to the interests of workers, explicitly sought workers as members or at least supporters, devised programs promoting the causes and welfare of workers, and entered politics in the hope of goading the major parties to concern themselves with important reforms heretofore ignored. The authenticity of the party was not compromised when, evincing no interest in their social status or the size of their bank-rolls, it backed candidates who promised support of the Working Men's program or important elements of it. Nor was there anything suspect on those occasions when nonworkers gave their support to portions of the party program.

The origins of the Working Men in Philadelphia, New York City, Newark, and the cities of New England, revealing as they do either the working class backgrounds or aims of the founders, strengthen the belief that the parties were not misnamed. It is true that these parties contained many men who by present definitions would not qualify as workers. But the definition of that earlier day was much more flexible. The prevailing concept was that all who performed "honest toil" were workingmen. Even to such a radical as George Henry Evans, only lawyers, bankers, and brokers could be designated as persons not engaged in the kind of useful occupation qualifying them for membership either in the Working Men's party or the working class. (It is interesting testimony to the growing con-servatism of the New York City Working Men that a resolution incorporating Evans' sentiments was defeated as too restrictive. In the fall of 1829, on the other hand, there was strong support for the principle of confining leadership in the party to journeymen and, in Evans' words, denying a vote to any "boss who employed a large number of hands.") Additional light on this issue is thrown by the similar discussion that arose among the Philadelphia Working Men. According to the *Mechanic's Free Press*, early in the party's history, in the summer of 1828, it was decided that while employers might be present at meetings, they could not hold office. Yet one year later its Ricardian Socialist editor, William Heighton, could write: "If an employer superintends his own business (still more if he works with his own hands) he is a working man. . . . If this view of things be correct, shall we look with a jealous eye on those employers who prefer being considered working men? Who are willing to join us in obtaining our objects?" Not only for political candidates but for mere membership in the party, as well, the important issue evidently had become simply whether the man would join in "obtaining our objects."

It is also true that at a certain point in its career the New York party seemed to be in the hands of men who had little sympathy with its expressed program. But these elements infiltrated the party only after its dramatic success in the 1829 elections; and they succeeded in taking it over only by the use of money, intra party intrigue, extra legal tactics, and newspaper excoriation, accompanied by continuous lip service to reform. The New York Working Men underwent a *transition* that shows that in its heyday it was not only an authentic but also an impressive organization, even frightening to some politicians. Perhaps nothing more dramatically suggests that this and other Working Men's parties were bona fide than the opposition, to put it mildly, they inspired in Democratic and National Republican politicians alike, and above all in most of the press. The Boston *Courier* was not alone in arguing that "the very pretension to the necessity of such a party is a libel on the community." The underlying thought of the editors, the Buckinghams, was that rich and poor, publishers and lowly typesetters alike, we are all workingmen: therefore, what need was there for a separate Working Men's party?

In the nation's cities a Working Men's party did appear. It burst forth on the political community like a meteor, either electing its candidates or achieving a balance of power on its second try, as in the City of Brotherly Love, or immediately after putting forward its original slate, in other cities. In New York City, for example, a ticket nominated for the State Assembly less than two weeks before the election, elected one and came near to electing several other candidates, amassing better than 6000 out of 21,000 votes cast. And yet in this, as in other cases, the political success was decidedly ephemeral. Decline set in almost immediately, culminating in a few brief years in the party's demise and disappearance.

What accounted for the almost immediate downfall of the Working Men's party? From that day to this, attempts at explanation have not been lacking. Some Philadelphia leaders bitterly blamed workers themselves both for their blindness to their own true interests and for their lack of courage. Other sympathizers attributed party failure to the mistaken policy of supporting wealthy candidates personally sympathetic to monopolies.[42] Thomas Skidmore, himself cashiered out of the New York party for his radical views and his uncompromising way of fighting for them, charged that the party's doom was sealed by its permitting rich men to take over, men who had no business in the party. His onetime opponent Evans later came to agree with him.[43] Hammond also noted that the New York State party contained within its ranks men who made their living doing what they professed to criticize, not excluding banking. By his view, "this party, if it deserves the name of a political party, was too disjointed and composed of materials too heterogeneous to continue long in existence." [44] New York friends of the Boston Working Men's party, on the other hand, attributed its pathetic political showing to preoccupation with issues, such as religious infidelity, that were not properly the concern of a workingmen's political organization.[45]

In her summary of causes for the failure of labor parties, Miss Sumner listed "changes from industrial depression to prosperity which turned the workers' attention from politics to trade unionism"; dissension—"legitimate" when resulting from heterogeneity, "illegitimate" when started and nurtured by "professional politicians of the old parties, who worm themselves into the new party"; the inexperience of the leaders in regard to the practical problems in managing a political party; the hostile activities of open enemies of the party; and "the taking up of some of its most popular demands by one of the old parties." [46] The authors of the most recent literature tend to confirm many of her judgments. For New York, both Hugins and Savetsky before him stress the way in which Tammany and the Democrats absorbed the program, especially its antimonopoly features. Savetsky also calls attention to the lack of dynamic and energetic leadership such as might have been provided by a person

[42] The columns of the *Mechanic's Free Press* for 1830 and 1831 carry many of these post mortems.

[43] The *Working Man's Advocate*, March 6, and April 17, 1830; *Free Enquirer*, March 20, 1830; the *Radical*, Jan., 1842; the *Friend of Equal Rights*, April 14, 1830, cited in the *Working Man's Advocate*, April 17, 1830.

[44] Jabez Hammond, *op. cit.*

[45] See *Working Man's Advocate* for May, 1831, especially the issue of May 11.

[46] *History of Labour*, I, 326.

like Frances Wright—erroneously designated by contemporary opponents of the party as its high priestess, with an eye toward tarring it with the same infidelity brush that was applied to her. Arky emphasizes the Philadelphia party's inept machinery: "For political purposes the movement was clumsily organized." Sullivan stresses the lack of class consciousness of its members, threats made by employers against those who supported it, and above all, the very nature of the party and its candidates. It is the provocative conclusion of Arthur Schlesinger, Jr., that the Working Men disappeared because "their own parties were engaged in kindhearted activity on the periphery of the problem," on such issues as education, imprisonment for debt, and clericalism; whereas the Democrats stressed the core issues that really counted. Thus, "during the Bank War, laboring men began slowly to turn to Jackson as their leader, and his party as their party." [47] Not the least questionable feature of this interpretation is its assumption that the Working Men's parties and "laboring men" were one and the same thing. If most laboring men did not vote for Jackson, it is also sadly true that, apart from a few exceptional cases, at no time did they vote even as a significant minority for the parties organized in their behalf.

It is hard to disagree that their own political ineptness and inexperience, internal bickering, heterogeneous membership, and lack of funds, together with infiltration of their ranks by men interested only in using them, the opposition of the press, and the shrewdness and adaptability of the Democrats, all played an important part in bringing about the downfall of the Working Men. Several related points might also be mentioned. Better than the major parties then or now, the Working Men's party represented the Burkean definition of a political party as a group of men united in behalf of certain political, social, and economic principles. Its membership may have been broad, but the party's program was not all things to all men, a grab bag designed primarily to win office for those who professed to support it. In the American society of the Tocqueville era such clarity of program worked against the chances of success at the polls.

When the Working Men's party did open its lists to individuals of opposing viewpoints, it failed to shake the following of the tradi-

[47] Schlesinger, Jr., *The Age of Jackson*, p. 143.

tional parties, which were much more adept at practical politics. Perhaps by this stratagem the party that presumed to speak out for labor fatally blurred its image—at least in the eyes of workingmen.

Speak out the Working Men did, in a message that was idealistic and radical. As the message became clearer, an American public seeking the main chance and increasingly optimistic about its possibilities lost interest in the nay-saying of the radical dissenters who formulated the Working Men's program. It may well be, then, that a reform party was doomed to failure in an American society bemoaned by James Fenimore Cooper—a society in flux, whose characteristic members quivered in anticipation of material fortunes to be made. Such optimism when shared by workers is the stuff that kills off ideological politics.

A final assessment of the Working Men's parties cannot fail to note their significance, notwithstanding their failings and their ephemeral vogue. Immediately after the remarkable showing of the New York Working Men became known, the Democrats promised to pass the lien law that the new party was agitating for. Nor was it a matter of a lien law alone. Even in the short run, the Democrats, in New York and elsewhere, hastily showed greater concern than ever before for the various reform provisions of the Working Men's program.[48] Thus, one of the factors that helped accomplish their disappearance as a separate political entity also was an indication of their strength. If it is the function of radical parties in America to act as gadflies, to goad and influence, rather than win elections, then the Working Men succeeded admirably.

Of course the degree of success they enjoyed is hard to measure. The Working Men were not alone in championing public education, abolition of imprisonment for debt, banking reform, reform of the militia system, factory laws, general incorporation laws, recognition of labor's right to organize unions, shorter hours of work for labor— to name some of the leading issues. It is impossible to fix with precision their contribution in comparison with that of other individuals

[48] Walter Hugins sees a smashing victory accomplished by the New York State Working Men in 1834, several years after they had formally disbanded as a separate party. In his words, "though forced by circumstances to disband as a political party, the Workingmen had reached the climax of their power and prestige. The party of Jefferson and Jackson had seemingly embraced the principles (antimonopoly) of the party of 'Mechanics and Working Men' "; (*op. cit.*, p. 35).

and groups who supported one or another of these measures. But there would seem to be no question that the role of the Working Men's parties was an important one, in some cases even greater than is usually believed. In the struggle for the creation of a public school system free from the stigma of charity or pauperism, for example, it has long been the fashion, certainly since Frank Carlton pointed it out, to accord much credit to the Working Men. Yet, as Sidney Jackson has shown, not only did the Working Men agitate for the establishment of such a system but they also advocated sophisticated qualitative measures that seem remarkable for their prescience. Among the changes they sought were an improved curriculum, less concerned with pure memory and "superannuated histories," less emphasis on strict discipline, better physical conditions for children, better trained and better paid teachers, and better equipped schools, free of clerical influences.[49] In sum, Helen Sumner's generous estimate does not seem overdrawn: "The Working Men's party, in short, was a distinct factor in pushing forward measures which even conservative people now recognize to have been in the line of progress toward real democracy." [50]

It has been suggested that one of the factors working against the long-run popularity of the Working Men's party was a radicalism not congenial to opportunistic Americans. But on the other hand, the party's relative popularity, brief though it was, suggests that some of their contemporaries were receptive to the voice of protest. That a Thomas Skidmore, who favored a redistribution of property, could win acceptance as a leader of the New York party, or that the program of the "conservative" Cook-Guyon faction, which came to dominate this party, continued to pay lip service to radical reform, indicate not only that an important minority in the Jacksonian era were disenchanted with their society and its institutions, but that it was considered politic by some astute men to cater or defer to this mood. A final significance then of the Working Men's party lay in the testimony its career afforded that the United States of the Jackson era was not altogether devoid of the sense of alienation that in England and on the continent provided fertile ground for the spread of Owenite, Chartist, Fourierist, and other socialist doctrines.

[49] Sidney Jackson, "Labor, Education and Politics in the 1830's," *Pennsylvania Magazine of History and Biography*, LXVI (July, 1942), 282–284.

[50] *History of Labour*, I, 332.

3
The Trades' Union Movement

During the decade that followed the organization
of the first trades' union in Philadelphia in 1827, hundreds of thousands of workers formed themselves into unions, the greatest spurt
occurring in the early and middle 1830s, almost immediately on the
heels of the Working Men's party decline. This movement thrived
until the Panic of 1837. The cessation of business activity and the
unemployment that followed in the wake of that debacle made it
impossible even for the enthusiastic and energetic unions of that
era to continue. Organizations which had pressed aggressive demands, waged hundreds of strikes, and talked hopefully of creating
a national movement proved unable to withstand the business cycle.

Concerning the authenticity of this movement, little important
controversy has taken place. Because of the very quantity of strikes
and the character of membership—essentially journeymen workers—
the movement's *bona fides* was never in doubt. Argument has been
confined to such issues as the number of strikes waged and the results of strikes in particular places.[1] There has been no such heated
discussion as has swirled around the Working Men's parties.[2]

Retelling the story in detail is unnecessary at this late date, but
there should be value in reassessing the movement in the light of new

[1] For example, William Sullivan has shown that there were many more strikes
in Pennsylvania in the early and middle 1830s than were known to Edward B.
Mittelman, the author of the section on trade unionism in Commons' *History
of Labour in the United States*. He has also shown that in Pennsylvania the
ten hour movement was not quite so successful as had been believed. See Sullivan, *The Industrial Worker in Pennsylvania 1800–1840* (Harrisburg, 1955),
chap. vi, *passim*. Walter Hugins has presented fuller evidence than heretofore to
indicate that there was little connection between the political and the economic
movements of workingmen during the era, in his excellent chapter on New
York unionism; Hugins, *Jacksonian Democracy and the Working Class* (Stanford, 1960), chap. iv. A close study of the Massachusetts evidence, in my opinion, reveals that, in contradiction to the assertion in Commons, the ten-hour
movement in that state was not a complete failure. But these are, if not small
matters, certainly not views which require any fundamental recasting of
thought concerning the Jacksonian union movement.

[2] See the previous chapter.

evidence. At the very beginning, a word about usage is in order. Why were they described as *trades'* unions rather than *trade* unions? Then as now the fundamental unit in the structure of the workers' organization was composed of men in a given community, village, or city, who were engaged in the same craft. What is called a *local* today was in those days known as a *society*. When the different societies of a city merged or combined into one larger body, the latter was known as a union of the societies, a union of the trades, or a trades' union. The trades' union thus was an amalgamation that might be referred to today as a City Central.

Scores of new societies emerged in the 1830s. A transformation was taking place in many of them, concern with the personal distress of individual members, or "benevolence," giving way to preoccupation with economic issues of the group, such as wages and hours. Most significant of all, however, was the joining together of societies into trades' unions, on a scale unprecedented then and impressive even today.

Societies had been organized by skilled workers in dozens of trades in the nation's cities and towns during the 1820s. Although they were concerned with broad and humanitarian issues that in some cases had little or nothing to do with the conditions of wage earners, these groups concentrated on what today would be called bread-and-butter demands: a shorter working day and, above all, higher wages. The most effective method they used was the "turn-out," or "stand-out," as the strike was then known. Already in this earlier period a few trade societies had seen the wisdom of amalgamation. Thus the organization out of which grew the first Working Men's party, the Philadelphia Mechanics' Union of Trade Associations, at its height included at least fifteen societies joined "to assist each other in cases of emergencies" and no longer to leave "the advantage . . . entirely with masters during a stand-out." [3] It is a matter of some interest that the larger union was then evidently unable to attract the "older, more substantial, incorporated journeymen" to its membership, relying to a large extent on newly founded organizations among the tobacconists, ladies' cordwainers, printers and compositors,

---

[3] Louis Arky, "The Mechanics' Union of Trade Associations and the Formation of the Philadelphia Working Men's Movement," *Pennsylvania Magazine of History and Biography*, LXXVI (April, 1952), 153, 155–156.

blacksmiths and whitesmiths, leather manufacturers, saddlers and harness makers.[4] (By the 1830s established trade societies had lost any hesitancy they may have earlier felt toward organizing or becoming associated with trades' unions.) As to the decline of the societies of the 1820s, it has been attributed to labor's growing interest in politics (the last act of the Philadelphia Mechanics' Union, it will be recalled, was to urge its members to organize politically); the discouraging effect of six conspiracy trials; and above all to the depression of 1828–1831.[5]

The upsurge of unionism in the 1830s seemed to flow from the sharp price rise that accompanied the return to prosperity, on the one hand, and the attacks on the skilled journeymen's position that resulted from the rise of the merchant capitalist, on the other. These attacks took the form, among other things, of attempts at wage cutting, the splitting up of trades with a consequent sharp decrease in the time required for training apprentices, the devaluation of skill, a reliance on female, child, and even convict labor, and the use of improved methods of transportation to hire cheap labor from distant places or even to break strikes.[6] A case can be made too for the view that the decline of the political movement in the early 1830s helped precipitate the economic movement—the rise of the trade societies and unions of the 1830s—just as a short time earlier, the decline of the unions and trade societies of the late 1820s helped pave the way for the formation of Working Men's parties.[7] For Pennsylvania it has been found that although factory workers were in a distinct minority the Trades' Union of Pennsylvania they organized in 1833, while short-lived (it lasted only from September to December), nevertheless provided the "impetus for the great trade union movement of the 1830s" that was to center about Philadelphia.[8] And throughout the

[4] *Ibid.,* p. 159.

[5] Joseph G. Rayback, *A History of American Labor* (New York, 1959), p. 75.

[6] See John R. Commons and Associates, *History of Labour in the United States* (New York, 1918), vol. I, Part Three, chap. i.

[7] One of the recommendations made by the failing New England Association of Farmers, Mechanics and Other Working Men at its third convention, in October, 1833, was for the establishment of trades' unions composed of societies of "working men of every description." Four months later such a union was formed in Boston. See *The Man,* February 20, 1834.

[8] Sullivan, *The Industrial Worker. . . .*

country the growth of cities provided the milieus most conducive to the rise of the youthful unions.

In response to new conditions that threatened both their status and their standard of living, journeymen in the early 1830s began to organize trade societies, at first by the dozens, and by the mid-1830s, by the hundreds. In Philadelphia, Boston, Baltimore, Newark, and New York, in the east, and then in Buffalo, Louisville, Pittsburgh, Cincinnati, and St. Louis in the west, journeymen formed together to "control the prices to be paid them," to oppose the misuse of unskilled, cheap, and apprentice labor, and to secure a shorter working day. Carpenters of every variety, bakers and soap makers, printers, cabinet makers, masons and bookbinders, house painters, comb makers and brushmakers, tailors and hat makers, weavers, jewelers, blacksmiths and machinists, rope makers and sail makers, carvers and gilders, shoemakers and chair makers, and dozens of other occupations, formed societies.[9]

Almost simultaneously the craftsmen who had created their journeymen's trade societies saw the value of merging their societies into general trades' unions and they proceeded to do so. For they understood that "trade societies alone were not sufficient," that organizations confined to working men of the same craft were "too small to cope with employers single-handed." [10] New York City, which witnessed the birth of the first trades' union, on August 14, 1833, was followed before the end of the year by Baltimore, Philadelphia, and Washington, D.C. Other cities which organized trades' unions by 1836 included Newark, New Brunswick, Albany, Troy, Schenectady, Boston, Pittsburgh, Cincinnati, and Louisville.

The unions concerned themselves with many reform issues having little or nothing to do with conditions or wages of work. They were interested in the general improvement of society. They thus gave a willing ear to, in some cases they even conferred leadership on, men who not only belonged to none of their constituent trade societies but who had never actually worked with their hands. Since many journeymen doubtless continued to aspire to becoming master me-

[9] See Commons, *op. cit.*, Appendix I, pp. 472–477, for a listing of the trade societies organized in New York, Baltimore, Philadelphia, and Boston in the years 1833 to 1837.

[10] *Ibid.*, p. 357.

chanics, it is not surprising that in the Boston Trades' Union the membership included masters or employers as well as journeymen workers.[11] But broad interests notwithstanding, these organizations were concerned primarily with down-to-earth issues: higher wages, shorter hours, an improved standard of living for their members, job security. Their characteristic activity was the strike.

For they had been established in order to achieve for their members an economic strength they otherwise lacked. Typically, the something new represented by the union—in contrast to the individual societies which comprised it—was a war chest in the form of regular dues contributed to the general union treasury by each member of the constituent societies. This fund was available to the needy members of a society out on strike with union approval; and at such a time dues were usually drastically raised. Thus, during the strike of the New York society of journeymen tailors in 1836, union dues were raised from six and one-quarter cents a month to twelve and one-half cents a week, in order to provide the striking tailors with adequate funds. The money was to go for supporting strikes, helping unemployed members, and defraying expenses incurred in the course of such activities as resisting employers' associations, securing a ban on prison labor, and defending the union in the courts. Funds were to be spent practically, not lavishly. Typical limitations confined benefits to fully paid-up members of a society that had belonged to the union for a prescribed period of time, and who were engaged in a strike that was supported by the union. After 1835, when strikes had become a commonplace, such support was by no means granted automatically but, instead, usually followed investigation by the union of both the causes of an impending strike and whether attempts at reconciliation had been made and resisted by employers. The boycott was another practical activity undertaken by unions. Access to thousands of workers and their families, and to the public at large,

---

[11] See the *Working Man's Advocate*, June 14, 1834; or the new journal published by George Henry Evans, and adopted by the New York City Trades' Union, *The Man*, for March 7 and 12, and May 30, 1834. On the other hand, for evidence that some journeymen in the Boston union were highly critical of having masters in the membership, see the journal adopted as the unofficial organ of the Boston Trades' Union, the *New England Artisan*, for July 19, 1834.

which could be reached through its own organ or a sympathetic press, gave the union a power in this regard far greater than that possessed by any one trade society. But the most important union activity of the period was the strike.

The pattern of strikes followed closely the course of the business cycle. The temporary economic setback of 1833–1834, traditionally attributed in large part to Nicholas Biddle's policy of retrenchment, was marked by a handful of strikes. But with the spirited economic upsurge of 1835 and the investment and speculative boom of the following year, the trickle of turn-outs became a flood. Across the length and breadth of the country, thousands of society and union members, and in some cases unorganized and even unskilled workers, turned out in hundreds of strikes. The issues were higher wages, the maintenance of wages, the ten hour working day, and the closed shop. The expenditure of money and energy in these strikes makes quite clear what the unions of the Jacksonian era were about. Broad or humanitarian issues were peripheral. The central purpose was to assure the journeyman craftsman the highest price he possibly could get for his labor, a minimum degree of leisure, and the assurance that attempts to undercut his position, especially by the use of cheaper labor, would not be tolerated. The purpose of the closed shop, for example, was not to achieve an abstract power but simply to prevent the employment of cheaper labor.

The great success of the strikes for the ten hour day made 1835 the turning point in the history of American labor's effort to reduce its working day. Even before they organized into unions, workingmen had opposed the "sunup to sundown" working day, a carryover from agriculture, and a tradition in which labor was permitted only those privileges employers chose to grant. A statement put out by the master carpenters of Boston in opposition to the ten hour movement, in 1825, referred to the long working day as "that which has been customary from time immemorial." The journeymen house carpenters in response struck against a working day whose length was so clearly "derogatory to the principles of justice [and] humanity." The failure of that strike was due in part to the opposition of the merchant capitalists, who not unexpectedly attributed it to sinister foreign influences while bemoaning the moral consequences of an excess of leisure that was sure to promote drunkenness.[12] Also contributing to the defeat of the strike, were the master carpenters. In opposing the reduction of hours they appealed to the ambition of the striking journeymen: one day they too would become masters; what would they think then of the shorter working day? Seven years later the ship carpenters and caulkers, masons, painters, slaters, and sail makers joined the house carpenters of Boston in another assault on the traditional working day, strengthened by support from striking workers in South Boston, Taunton, and other suburbs of the city. In view of the little that has been written about it, it is instructive to examine the causes of the failure of the 1832 strike.

The Boston press, owned by wealthy conservatives, such as Hale of the Boston *Daily Advertiser and Patriot*, the Buckinghams of the *Courier*, and Adams and Hudson of the *Columbian Centinel*, consistently attacked the strikers.[13] And this time the master mechanics not only criticized the striking journeymen with words. In addition to offering their allegiance to the merchants, they appealed to strike-breakers, backing up their appeals with money.[14] Large sums were supplied by shipowners and merchants who in addition organized a committee to defeat the strike, holding regular meetings for that purpose. (On the roster of the merchants' committee was the name of Lot Wheelwright, a former candidate of the Boston Working Men.) The strike in Boston appears to have been crushed, although there is some evidence—in contradiction to the findings in Commons' *History*—that in a few places and for a few trades a reduction in the working day was accomplished.[15]

It is ironic that despite their several struggles for the ten hour day, the workers of Boston alone among workingmen in any major city

[12] One of the signers of the anti-ten hour resolution was Samuel Perkins, erstwhile candidate of the Boston Working Men in 1831!

[13] The only exceptions to this policy were the Boston *Morning Post* and the Boston *Transcript*.

[14] The *Morning Post*, May 23, 1832; The Boston *Daily Advertiser and Patriot*, May 23, 28, 29, 1832. One of the strikebreaking masters was Leach Harris, earlier a candidate of the Boston Working Men's Party.

[15] See the *Working Man's Advocate*, April 7, 1832; "Notice to House and Ship Owners," in the Boston *Post*, May 18, 21, 1832. If Seth Luther can be believed, the hours of work of shipwrights, caulkers, gravers and some founders had been reduced; Luther, *Address to the Working Men of New England* (3rd edition, Philadelphia, 1836), Appendix 6 and 7, pp. 36, 37.

failed to achieve it during the Jackson era.[16] Adding to the irony is the signal contribution made by Boston unionists to the success of the great Philadelphia ten hour strike in 1835. The workers of Boston struck again in that year, once more unsuccessfully, but a fiery pamphlet they put out had an electric effect on strikers in over a dozen northeastern cities and towns. The failure of the 1835 strike brought down with it the short-lived Trades' Union of Boston.

The Boston Trades' Union was to a large extent a child of the ten hour movement, specifically the unsuccessful strike of 1832. The first convention of the New England Association of Farmers, Mechanics and Other Working Men had been convened precisely on that date in 1832 which had been set aside for launching the carpenters' strike. The resultant failure compelled the association on the one hand to put aside the ten hour issue and on the other to support the recommendation made by Boston's workingmen at the third convention in 1833 that a trades' union should be organized in Boston the following year. Early in 1834 representatives of sixteen trades convened to form the Boston union.

In addition to including masters in its membership, this union devoted much time to such broad issues as the prevalent militia system and imprisonment for debt, which were not, strictly speaking, wage earners' issues. It seemed to go in heavily for speechmaking by men who had not the remotest connection with manual labor, one of its top leaders, in fact, belonging in that category. It lasted only a few months more than one year, a short life even for this period of relatively ephemeral labor organizations.

At its height the Boston Trades' Union was believed to have over four thousand members.[17] The structural organization of at least one of its societies was regarded as a model by skilled workers elsewhere, who were seeking to form a journeymen's society of their own.[18] Its very existence aroused the furious opposition of New England con-

---

[16] William Sullivan, however, uncovered evidence that the carpenters in Pittsburgh and some craftsmen elsewhere in the state had not yet achieved the ten hour day by as late as 1836 (*The Industrial Worker* . . . , p. 143).

[17] *The Man*, Feb. 20, 1834.

[18] When the New York City masons were forming their own society they patterned their organization after the Boston Operative Masons' Society of the Boston Trades' Union (*The Man*, June 11, 1834).

servatives in the pulpit, the law, and good society, in general.[19] The antimasonic leader Benjamin Hallet attacked the union as a secret and illegal conspiratorial organization which practiced unusual cruelties on its members.[20] But even its harshest critics had to acknowledge the brilliant success of its imposing Fourth of July parade in 1834, widely regarded as the most splendid in a city which took its holiday celebrations very seriously. Contingents from each of its sixteen societies, following in the wake of colorful banners; elaborate floats; and a mighty ship built especially for the occasion, which was pulled by twenty-four white horses, combined to make a most impressive appearance.[21] In Seth Luther and Charles Douglas the union had two of the best known and most able leaders of the era's labor movement. Its membership was responsive to fiery oratory.[22] But it was not radicalism in general that the workers wanted to hear: their interest was in the shorter working day.

On May 20, 1835, in a speech he delivered before Boston workingmen, Theophilus Fisk urged them to fight, not for the ten hour, but for the eight hour day—"eight hours for work, eight hours for sleep, eight hours for amusement and instruction is the equitable allotment of the twenty-four." [23] The striking carpenters, masons and stone cutters, who turned out at the beginning of May, would have settled for the more modest objective of the ten hour day. In July they were joined by the journeymen housewrights, who showed their enthusiasm by marching through the wealthy wards of the city chanting the *Marseillaise*.[24] Nevertheless, like the others before it, this strike ended in defeat, despite the fact that a special committee set up to enlist support for the strikers outside the city met an enthusiastic

[19] Arthur M. Schlesinger, Jr., *The Age of Jackson* (Boston, 1945), pp. 165–166.

[20] See the sarcastic replies to these charges in the *New England Artisan*, May 31, June 21, and October 25, 1834.

[21] *Columbian Centinel*, July 5, 9, 1834; Boston *Post*, July 7, 1834; *New England Artisan*, July 12, 1834; *The Man*, August 6, 1834.

[22] See the speech made by the Democratic legislator Frederick Robinson, "An Oration Delivered Before the Trades' Union of Boston and vicinity," reported in the *New England Artisan* for July and August, 1834.

[23] "Capital Against Labor," an address delivered before the mechanics of Boston, May 20, 1835, and reported in the *Working Man's Advocate* for July 25, 1835.

[24] *Working Man's Advocate*, July 25, 1835.

reception wherever it traveled along the Atlantic Coast. Nor could the trenchant pamphlet prepared for the union by Seth Luther, Levi Abell, and A. H. Wood help the Boston strikers, for all of its influence elsewhere. In Philadelphia, "the effect [of the circular] was electric," according to the union leader John Ferral. Reprinted and distributed by the union there, it became "the absorbing topic of conversation." [25] Inasmuch as it has only been briefly alluded to in the Commons' *History* and elsewhere, a few words on the contents of this "Ten Hour Circular" may be of value.

It contained a fair share of class rhetoric. "We claim by the blood of our fathers, shed on our battle fields in the War of the Revolution, the rights of American freemen, and no earthly powers shall resist our righteous claims with impunity," it thundered at one point. "The God of the universe has given us time, health and strength. We utterly deny the right of any man to dictate to us how much of it we shall sell . . . !" it declared at another. It effectively refuted the old canards about the alleged debauching effects on working men of shorter hours of work, when it inquired as to why employers felt no concern about these effects during the slack winter months when lack of work (caused by employer unwillingness to expend the fuel necessary to provide light in the season of little daylight) left men with whole days of free time.[26]

By the end of the year, however, with the possible exception of the plasterers who, according to one Philadelphia labor paper had secured the ten hour day, the Boston strike ended in failure. But if John Ferral's estimate of its influence was accurate, the Ten Hour Circular was a most significant document, indeed, since before the year was out, the ten hour day had become the rule for "most of the city mechanics who worked by the day." [27] The "sun to sun" system had been replaced by the "six to six" system, which provided two breaks of one hour each for breakfast and for lunch. At the end of the decade the Van Buren Administration was to extend the latter system to government works. In view of this achievement, John Ferral's letter to Seth Luther is understandably enthusiastic

[25] See the communication from John Ferral in *ibid*.

[26] *The Man,* May 13, 1835.

[27] Commons, *op. cit.*, p. 393.

when it refers to the success of the Philadelphia ten hour strike.[28] The shorter working day represented the outstanding achievement of the era's labor movement.

More than two-thirds of the better than two hundred strikes of the period were for higher wages. In 1836, the single year which had the greatest number of strikes, high wages were the goal of all but a handful of them. Not only were wages low, even by the standards of that day, but prices were skyrocketing, during the inflationary boom that marked the era.[29] In addition to the problem of trying to maintain the balance between the price of labor and the price of necessities, the worker also had to worry about being paid in a fluctuating currency whose face value all too often had little resemblance to its actual worth. An age which paid skilled journeymen from roughly one dollar to something less than two dollars daily and which provided him a most modest living at the rates, was understandably marked by numerous turn-outs. A high proportion of the strikes was successful; at least the masters granted the price demanded—either for labor or for the goods the journeymen made. These gains, unfortunately, were to be ephemeral. For following the Panic of 1837 not only were tens of thousands of workers thrown out of work, but wages and the price of labor were substantially cut as well.

Apart from strikes, one of the more significant developments of the era was the attempt on the part of at least five trades to organize societies or craft unions on a national scale. Responding to impersonal developments, above all, in transportation, which by bringing cities closer together, sharpened the competition between them, in 1836, journeymen house carpenters, handloom weavers, comb makers, cordwainers and printers took steps to create national societies which would uphold uniform prices and wage standards won by agreements, and thus give real meaning to strike or bargaining successes. Most of the information we have with regard to these attempts concerns the cordwainers and the printers. In the case of the former, it has been explained that "perhaps no other trade at this

[28] The letter, written on June 22, appears in *The Man*, June 29, 1835.

[29] Edward B. Mittleman's observation that food prices doubled between 1833 and 1836 is not backed up by the figures he cites. See Mittleman, Part Three "Trade Unionism," in Commons, *op. cit.*, I, 396.

time was so completely in the hands of the merchant-capitalist." [30] Representatives from sixteen cities and towns assembled in New York City in March of 1836 essentially to oppose strikebreaking and to adopt a standard bill of prices for the product of journeymen labor throughout the country. The printers, who met at the same time in Washington, D.C., to found the National Typographical Society, were responding to a revolution in the newspaper industry which had already drastically worsened the conditions of journeymen and threatened in the near future to undermine them even more. The rise of the daily paper in the nation's cities had meant the replacement of the "practical printer" by the capitalistic publisher who knew more about marketing and how to tap sources of income than he knew about printing. Such a one was Duff Green, for a time Jackson's favored printer, who depressed wages by using inadequately trained apprentices, and in general hiring the cheapest labor he could get. In this industry journeymen showed as much interest in a uniform apprenticeship system, therefore, as in a uniform price list. But in the absence of the requisite conditions for the existence of national labor organizations, these were indeed "premature national trade unions," as Edward Mittelman describes them.[31]

The most interesting development of the period was the organization on a national scale of one union of all the trades' unions. It was a failure, perhaps inevitably so, but a significant and striking failure. The judgment of many modern observers is that this so-called national union was altogether ineffectual, confining itself to the passage of harmless resolutions that were either too broad or too general, that it lacked an efficient structure, represented few workers, and essentially served only to provide a forum for the speechmaking proclivities of a few activists.[32] The evidence, however, permits other interpretations.

To anyone familiar with the internal arrangements of the modern American Federation of Labor and the Congress of Industrial Organizations, certainly the structure of the National Trades' Union was—to use understatement—a loose one. Having no experience whatever

[30] *Ibid.,* p. 441.

[31] *Ibid.,* p. 438.

[32] For example, see the discussion in Foster Rhea Dulles, *Labor in America* (2nd rev. ed.; New York, 1960), chap. iv.

with a national organization of all the trades, the men who responded
to the call of the New York City Trades' Union for a convention,
in the summer of 1834,[33] simply improvised. To be on the safe side,
they obligated the unions they represented to very little. The function of elected officers was essentially to preside over meetings.
Financing was to be left to the individual unions and placed on a
voluntary basis. Action was confined to the expression of opinions
or to the suggestion that opinions be made known to government.
Nothing was binding, nothing was done to give continuity or to
assure that the organization would function between conventions.
In fact the main practical result of the first convention seemed to be
the calling of a second. Evidently few unions had been contacted,
since only six northeastern cities were represented at the first convention, and four states—New York, New Jersey, Pennsylvania and
Maryland—at the second (although three carpenters from Boston
were also permitted to sit in, in view of the disappearance of that
city's trades' union).

Yet commencing with the second convention which again was
held in New York City, in October of 1835, steps were taken to
tighten up the structure. These steps were modest, to be sure, yet
they represented both improvement and a sign that the Union's
leaders were aware of the need for it. Individual trade societies could
now be represented where no union existed. A treasury was established. A committee of correspondence was to maintain contact
among members between meetings. A commission consisting of a
representative from every trades' union was to devote itself to estab-
lishing either craft societies or unions of the trades throughout the
country. The third convention, held at Philadelphia toward the end
of October, 1836, tightened up the system of representation by re-
lating it to the size of a society's membership rather than, as in the
past, allowing equal representation for any society regardless of its
size. Regular dues were now to be required of each member of a
member union or society, with forfeiture of membership the punishment for nonpayment. Most important of all, it provided that thereafter decisions of the national union were no longer to be merely
advisory but rather were to be binding on all members. Although the
number of delegates at this third convention declined slightly from

[33] *Working Man's Advocate*, May 17, 1834.

what it had been at the second, much greater significance attaches to the fact that many more cities and sections sent delegates than ever before. For now, in addition to New York, Newark and Philadelphia, Reading, Pittsburgh, Washington, and Cincinnati were also represented.

There is no question but that the National Trades' Union provided a sounding board for a relatively small number of union leaders, men in some cases who represented little or no union membership, themselves. The third convention, for example, gave a place to Charles Douglas, by then an individual with no union base whatever, who represented New England at large. This may have been a weakness, but it accorded with the spirit of that era's unionism; for the societies and the city trades' unions of craftsmen, as well, were willing to give a respectful hearing and even leadership to gifted individuals of whatever vocation, so long as they seemed to be dedicated to the interests of labor. What such leaders as Ely Moore, William English, John Ferral, Levi Slamm, and John Commerford had to say at these conventions, throws further light on what American labor was thinking during the Jackson era.

Perhaps the greatest significance of the National Trades' Union—at least to the historian—is what it reveals of American labor's state of mind. The debates, the contents of the organization's constitution, its many resolutions, all make clear that while the national union was indeed concerned with broad reform issues, it did not stint with regard to matters of direct concern primarily to wage earners. Not that it is a weakness, in my judgment, for a labor movement to show an interest in reform in general, or what the labor historians of the Commons generation might call "citizenship." Powerful and successful modern unions do not confine themselves to bread-and-butter issues. And what has become all too clear today, when the line between pure business unionism and either dubious or corrupt union practices is often a very fine one, is that idealistic dedication to social reforms of every kind is not only one of the most attractive features of a labor movement but perhaps a necessary sign of its integrity. Certainly in this regard the gravest charge that might be directed against the National Trades' Union would be that it was ahead of rank-and-file members in positions it took on some issues. It favored an "equal, universal, republican system of education." It supported free public lands to actual settlers, on the basis of its belief that under such a policy, surplus labor would be drained off while the wages of the remaining workers would rise. The prevalent factory system was damned for its threat both to skill and to the conditions of journeymen, as well as for its alleged inhuman characteristics. Support of a selective and moderate protection of "the mechanic arts" was motivated more by a concern for high wages than an abstract interest in tariffs. Speculation was opposed for its depressing effects on the value first of money and then of wages, rather than for any moral laxity it betokened. Keeping young females out of factories showed a decent respect for American womanhood, but it also showed a wish to maintain the jobs and income of adult males who worked in shops.

Most of the National Trades' Union's program had to do with the needs and interests of workers and unionists. It sought the establishment of unions "in every part of the country," "to unite and harmonize the effort of all the productive classes of the country." [34] Child labor was to be abolished. Prison labor was to be strictly regulated to assure that it did not compete with free labor. Unions were to be given legal recognition, as were the strikes or boycotts they supported. The Congress should fix the ten hour day in all government workshops. Wages must be brought up to match prices, which had more than doubled during the past half-decade. For that matter, there should be a uniform—and high—price of labor for each trade in the country, the task of the unions being to enforce adherence to this price. The down-to-earth character, as well as the militant radicalism of the organization, is suggested by a resolution approved by the second convention, which urged a general strike in support of any movement by a city union or trade society whose attempt to bring its wages up to the approved standard was resisted by a combination of employers. If when the English Chartist leaders spoke of a general strike they had in mind by that measure something closer to socialism than to a mere rise in wages, nothing so extreme was in the mind of the National Trades' Union and its leaders. Yet a concerted strike, for whatever purpose, was militant enough. For that matter, although the word socialism was foreign to the Union's leaders, the idea of producers' co-operatives appealed to a number of them as a topic worthy of the closest examination by workers.

The trouble with this program was not its impracticality. The dif-

---

[34] *The Man*, September 2, 1834.

ficulty arose rather in carrying out or translating into action the measures approved in convention. The National Trades' Union turned out to be a short-lived organization for the same reasons essentially as were its member unions. Workers were divided, with the skilled fearing the unskilled. The transportation revolution and changing technology were undermining the traditional ways of labor and of rewarding labor. Unity remained a vague or distant ideal in the absence of a truly connected national market or industrial system. The hope of becoming a master or employer, nourished by the era's spirit of speculation and optimism, turned the thoughts of the potential unionist in other directions. In addition, the national union faced special problems, for where a local society offered direct and immediate aid to its specialized craftsmen members, the national group represented only one more dues collection in behalf of what many men must have quite understandably thought of as vague promises. Such promises were morally worthy and may have been in the actual interests of labor, but working men were neither better nor more altruistic than their fellow Americans of other classes in the age of speculation. A trade society operated directly on its members, whereas the national union's controls were remote. In all likelihood, however, it was the Panic of 1837 and the resulting economic stagnation that did in the national union. It vanished in the same wreckage that claimed its union constituents.

In discussing the causes of the decline of the Jacksonian union movement, it is impossible to avoid mention of the great depression that followed the Panic of 1837. The unions were too frail to be able to resist a cataclysm that was estimated to have put one-third of American workers out of work and reduced another substantial fraction to part-time work in the course of one year, while depressing wages by 30 to 50 per cent within two years.

Other factors also explained the downfall of the unions. Employer and capitalist hostility to unions undoubtedly weakened them. It ranged from a persistent abuse and denunciation that identified unionism with foreign agitation, atheism, tyranny, immorality, and, of course, drunkenness, to effective organizations designed to meet fire with fire.[35] Journeymen's organizations were opposed by associations of masters. Merchant capitalists organized, as they did in Bos-

---

[35] William Sullivan, *The Industrial Worker* . . . , p. 89.

ton, and had the wherewithal to make themselves felt; in some cases making unsubtle threats against striking unionists.[36] Blacklists were employed. And there was always the press, most of which could be counted on to attack unions and strikes as illegal, immoral, or both. The law, too, was used as a bulwark against labor organization. Contriving new variations on the old common-law theme that strikes and boycotts were illegal conspiracies, employers fell back on the courts in a number of significant cases.[37] Although the indicted workers were not found guilty in most of these, the sweeping decisions against boycotts, unions in general, the closed shop, and even (in two New York cases) concerted action to raise wages, had a sharply negative impact on trade unionism. In the 1835 case of the Geneva shoemakers, who were charged with striking against a master because he employed a man at less than the price scale agreed to by the journeymen, the Chief Justice of the Supreme Court of New York had asked, "if journeymen bootmakers by extravagant demands for wages so enhance the price of boots made in Geneva, for instance, that boots made elsewhere, in Auburn, for example, can be sold cheaper, is not such an act injurious to trade?" This logic challenged not only the closed shop but unionism itself. One year later the striking journeymen tailors of New York City were found guilty of conspiracy in a trial in which the judge relied on the Geneva decision, as he stigmatized unions as illegal combinations. However, a storm of protest followed the decision and the imposition of fines on the union leaders. The liberal New York *Evening Post* joined the publishers of the *Union* in condemning the proceedings. One of the consequences of this case was a turn toward politics. Many of the workingmen and their friends among the middle classes now identified themselves with the Loco Foco movement within the Democratic Party, and later that year helped to form the Equal Rights Party.[38] Although in Philadelphia and Boston, as in New York, some trade unionists began to advocate either greater political activity by labor or the creation of separate political groups divorced from the

[36] See the *New England Artisan* of October 25, 1835, for an example of this.

[37] See John R. Commons and Associates, *A Documentary History of American Industrial Society* (Cleveland, 1910), vols. IV and V, for descriptions of the major cases and trials of the period.

[38] Frederic Byrdsall, *History of the Loco-Foco or Equal Rights Party* (New York, 1842), p. 67; Hugins, *op. cit.*, chaps. iii and iv.

major parties, the decline of the Jacksonian union movement has rarely been attributed to politics or to a wrongheaded decision by unionists to enter politics.[39]

Aware as they were that the political views of their journeymen memberships were varied, the unions of the Jackson era for the most part steered clear of politics. Formed not to achieve utopia or doctrinaire political goals but improvement in the economic situation of skilled journeymen, they acted accordingly. At the first convention of the National Trades' Union, a lively controversy developed before it was finally agreed that the views of the body should not be expressed on the "political" conditions of the laboring classes. According to Charles Douglas, however, if workers were supporters neither of Jacksonism or Clayism nor any other ism but *workeyism*, this meant not that politics as such were harmful, but rather that the politics of subordination to the major parties was to be avoided.[40] He agreed with John Ferral that ultimately it was only through legislation and by carrying "their grievances to the polls" that workingmen could achieve their rightful place in American society. Most of the prominent labor leaders of the time agreed with them.[41] It is a measure of their statesmanship that in their role as trade union leaders they put aside their strong beliefs in political action, in order to maintain the harmony and effectiveness of the unions. But even statesmanship could not avail the trades' unions of the Jackson era—organizations whose time had not yet come.

[39] Arthur M. Schlesinger, Jr., however, writes that "a main cause of the decay of the [Boston] Union was the enthusiasm with which the workingmen were turning to politics" (*Age of Jackson*, p. 167). Schlesinger was not critical of this alleged decay, since, by his interpretation of the era, the Jackson Administration's programs were much more to the point, and therefore deserving of labor support, than those of the union; in allegedly ditching the union for the Democratic party, the workers were acting wisely and in their own interest. In my opinion, a better explanation of the fall of the Boston Trades' Union would emphasize the defeat of the crucial ten hour strike of 1835 and the power of the master mechanics, the merchant capitalists, and the newspaper publishers who combined to defeat it.

[40] *The Man*, Sept. 6, 1834.

[41] See chapter eleven.

PART TWO

The Leaders

4
An Introductory Profile

When we speak of the labor movement today, we mean by it trade unions composed of men who work for wages, led by men who have risen from the ranks after careers as wage earners. Middle-class reformers, no matter how sympathetic, are not considered part of that movement. It was otherwise in the age of Andrew Jackson. Then, a number of labor groups were led by men who had not themselves been workers.

The fact that they themselves were not workers is only one of the paradoxes in the backgrounds of some of the early leaders. A number of them had only brief ties with labor groups. Others did little more than publish journals sympathetic to labor. Some were unusually well-educated craftsmen, with little personal experience of working in shops, but much experience in the propagation of grandiose schemes. Even in the case of some men whose hands were calloused from years of the "honest toil" they were fond of praising, the impression is strong that they had used their labor experience as a springboard to political careers. And perhaps the unusual nature of this early labor movement is best illustrated in the fact that among its leaders were men who had employed the labor of others. One of them, Thomas Brothers, was not only a hat manufacturer but at one point in his career had to answer the charge that he paid his journeymen less than did other employers! In the second issue of his journal, under the heading, "Aspersions Answered," he wrote:

> I have just been informed that some place-hunting fellow, with a view, no doubt, to injure this paper, has asserted that I do not give to my journeymen the best prices. I deny this. . . . I have actually been giving more than double the price of napping the same kind of hats than has been given by the big manufacturers. All of which I can, and will prove, if necessary.[1]

Labor organizations consisting largely of skilled artisans fearful of being replaced by cheap or unskilled labor, and who were as much

[1] *The Radical Reformer and Working Man's Advocate*, June 20, 1835.

concerned with opportunity, education, and social prestige as with bread-and-butter issues, had no difficulty in conferring leadership on men of varied background. Regardless of their backgrounds, however, the men whose careers and ideas are examined in this book were leaders of authentic labor or workingmen's organizations. Their leadership might be manifested by election to office or by some other means, but it was never self-appointed: in all cases, they were regarded by their memberships as leaders or spokesmen of their organizations. I stress this point in order to make it altogether clear that this study does *not* deal with reformers who had no direct or formal ties with labor groups. Such prominent reform figures, for example, as Theodore Sedgwick, William Gouge, William Leggett, Condy Raguet, and Samuel Clesson Allen, whatever they may have been, were not labor leaders. Nor would other reformers or faddists or politicians qualify as labor leaders, even by the broader standards of that time, merely because they occasionally agreed with labor. The era's labor movement may have been broad, but it was not that broad. The leaders may have been unusual, but they did meet one criterion: they were leaders of actual labor organizations.

When I conceived the idea of this study I proceeded to draw up a list of the labor figures who seemed to be most ubiquitous, influential, and representative. Gradually, a list that began with more than thirty names was pared, as I deleted those men who seemed in no important particular to be unlike other—but more articulate—figures. For I must be frank: I find the social ideas of silent men impossible to get at. Of course their beliefs might be inferred from their acts; but why bother, when similar things were done by men who had no compunctions about explaining themselves? A Frances Wright was considered and rejected. That contemporary opponents of the Working Men's party delighted in referring to it as the creature of "Mad Fanny" did not make it so; any more than it made this charming and eloquent woman the caricature depicted by the press. The interesting Philadelphia leader William Heighton was omitted because his ideas have been examined by another writer, elsewhere.[2] Finally, I reduced the list to the leaders who are dealt with in these pages. In their place of birth, social background, occupation, relationship with a labor

[2] See Louis Arky, "The Mechanics' Union of Trade Associations and the Formation of the Philadelphia Working Men's Movement," *Pennsylvania Magazine of History and Biography*, LXXVI (April, 1952).

organization, period of time in the movement, and in their beliefs, these men in my judgment represent a balanced and representative cross section of American labor leadership during the Jackson era.

An unusual number of the leaders were editors or publishers, men whose leadership consisted precisely in their putting out of labor journals. For others, the lure of printers' ink was irresistible, even where printing or publishing was not their primary occupation. These men were brimming over with things to say.

The relatively comfortable backgrounds of some of them show that it was not their own social or economic difficulties that drew them to the cause of labor. The social conscience of Robert Dale Owen, well-to-do leader of the New York Working Men, was shaped not by his own misery but by the suffering of others. He tells us that as a child he could not erase from his mind the picture of children crippled and deformed in the factory, an image that haunted his dreams. His contemporary Thomas Skidmore was not a rich man, but he believed that it was not his personal experiences but his reading of the old Jeffersonian journal the *Aurora*, "when yet a boy," that planted radical ideas in his mind. Seth Luther was very much influenced by his travels across the country and the numerous examples of human misery he witnessed. Thomas Brothers was stirred by the writings of Paine. These men became workingmen's leaders because of their evident sensitivity to social inequity. In this sense they were as much social reformers as anything else. If some of them remained in the labor movement only a short time, they had no compunctions about it. They were only passing through, on their way, perhaps, to other noble causes.

In the two chapters that follow, I deal with the labor careers, first, of the Working Men's leaders and then of the trade unionists. I have made no such separation in treating their social beliefs, however, for the good reason that there seem to be no substantial differences in the viewpoints of leaders of the one or other kind of organization. True, the Working Men's leaders tended to write comprehensive volumes on society's ills and how to cure them; the unionists more typically authored pamphlets and newspaper articles, or simply made speeches. But while their literary formats might differ, it will be seen that their ideas were similar.

5

The Leaders in
the Working Men's Parties

What manner of men were the Jacksonian labor leaders? Were they authentic leaders, particularly in view of the unusual backgrounds and ephemeral labor affiliations of a number of them? This chapter and the next will attempt to answer these questions, not with lengthy biographies but by brief examination of their careers in the labor movement. Although some of the Working Men's leaders, particularly Robert Dale Owen, George Henry Evans, and Stephen Simpson, have not failed to attract scholarly notice, their biographers for the most part have focused on those aspects of their diverse careers that had nothing to do with labor, or that occurred long after that movement declined.[1] In this sense, the discussions that follow help fill out the general historical record, while providing indispensable information on the *practice* of these men whose *theory* so interests us.

Thomas Skidmore was the most original and provocative of what was a strongly non-conformist group. As the undisputed leader of the original New York City political movement and the author of a striking volume affirming the right of all men to property, he has not

---

[1] For Owen, see Richard Leopold, *Robert Dale Owen* (Cambridge, 1940); and Elinor Pancoast and Anne R. Lincoln, *Robert Dale Owen, the Incorrigible Idealist* (Indiana, 1940). For Evans, see Lewis Masquerier, *Sociology or the Reconstruction of Society* (New York, 1877); and Helene Sarah Zahler, *Eastern Workingmen and Public Land Policy* (New York, 1941); both of which deal with Evans' career after 1840 as a land reformer. For Simpson, see Arthur M. Schlesinger, Jr., *The Age of Jackson* (Boston, 1945), pp. 201–202; Broadus Mitchell, "Stephen Simpson," in *Dictionary of American Biography*; Joseph Dorfman, *The Economic Mind in American Civilization* (New York, 1946), vol. II, 645–648; Philip R. V. Curoe, *Educational Attitudes and Policies of Organized Labor in the United States* (New York, 1926), pp. 45–47, which discusses Simpson's original educational theories.

been completely neglected.[2] Yet significant facts concerning his labor career have either been omitted or misinterpreted.

Hardly anything in Skidmore's early life indicated that he would become a labor leader. Born in rural Connecticut at the turn of the century, he began to teach in that state when he was but thirteen. For the next several years he taught in Princeton, Bordentown, and Richmond, and at Edentown and Newbern in North Carolina. During the next phase of his career, spent in Wilmington and Philadelphia, he threw himself into chemical and mechanical research, and worked on a number of inventions, ranging from attempts to improve the manufacture of gunpowder to papermaking.

The remainder of his life was spent in New York City. He came to the metropolis in 1819, married two years later, worked as a machinist, and emerged from obscurity only three years before his death. In 1829 he played a decisive role in the formation of the Working Men's party of New York, and also wrote his provocative treatise on property. Thereafter he was a center of controversy until his death during the cholera epidemic in the summer of 1832.

The leading facts pertaining to Skidmore's participation in the New York City labor movement were brought to life first by his colleague George Henry Evans and in the more recent past by Frank T. Carlton and Helen Sumner.[3] According to the standard account, he dominated the organized workingmen's movement which arose in April of 1829 as a protest against an alleged employer's plot to lengthen the working day. Under his influence the first meeting of the "mechanics" resolved not only to defend the ten hour day but

[2] John R. Commons and Associates, *History of Labour in the United States* (New York, 1918), vol. I, Part Two, chap. iii; Frank T. Carlton, "The Workingmen's Party of New York City, 1829–1831," *Political Science Quarterly*, XXII (Sept., 1907), No. 3, 401–415; Joseph Dorfman, *The Economic Mind* . . . , II, 641–645; Joseph L. Blau, ed., *Social Theories of Jacksonian Democracy* (New York, 1947), pp. xxv, 355–364; Herbert Harris, *American Labor* (New Haven, 1938), p. 30; Willard Thorp, Merle Curti, and Carlos Baker, eds., *American Issues* (2 vols.; Chicago, 1944), I, 233–241; Walter Hugins, *Jacksonian Democracy and the Working Class* (Stanford, 1960), *passim;* Edward Pessen, "Thomas Skidmore, Agrarian Reformer in the Early American Labor Movement," *New York History*, XXV (July, 1954), 280–296.

[3] George Henry Evans, "History of the Origin and Progress of the Working Men's Party in New York," in the *Radical*, 1842–1843; Carlton, *loc. cit.;* Helen L. Sumner, in Commons and Associates, *History of Labour*, I, 234–245.

also criticized the existing division of property.[4] A second meeting, held a few days later, elected a "Committee of Fifty" to give leadership to the new movement. Skidmore's domination of this committee is revealed in the nature of its "agrarian resolutions" presented for the approval of the membership at a meeting on October 19, 1829. At other meetings held later in the month, he was one of eleven candidates nominated by this new Working Men's party for the State Assembly, and in the balloting held during the first week of November received over 6,000 votes, barely failing of election, together with most of the other labor candidates.[5] This near success frightened conservative editors and politicians, a number of whom now joined the party with the obvious intention of taking it out of Skidmore's hands and orienting it in a more sober direction. They succeeded so well that at a meeting held on December 29, 1829, the Committee of Fifty was dissolved and Skidmore was forcibly prevented from taking the floor.[6] Too proud to stand such treatment, Skidmore quit the organization and formed a new party, "the original working men," which consisted of a small number of his loyal followers. Thereafter his influence steadily declined. He published a short-lived newspaper, the *Friend of Equal Rights*, and utilized the lecture platform and the letter columns of the New York City press to keep his theories in the public eye, but his death on August 7, 1832, was mourned by only a few.[7] A standard opinion about the sig-

[4] According to the first historian of this movement, Skidmore had shrewdly proposed the resolution on property as a means of frightening the "aristocratic oppressors" of journeymen laborers into relinquishing their attempts to lengthen the working day (Evans, in the *Radical*, Jan., 1842), Skidmore's complete dedication to the idea of thoroughgoing change in the means of distributing property suggests that he favored discussion of "the nature of the tenure by which all men hold title to their property" for its own sake, simply because he would not overlook any opportunity to raise the issue. Before the year was over he published his book *The Rights of Man to Property! Being a proposition to make it equal among the adults of the present generation; and to provide for its equal transmission to every individual of each succeeding generation, on arriving at the age of maturity. Addressed to the citizens of New York, particularly, and to the people of other states and nations generally* (New York, 1829).

[5] *Working Man's Advocate*, Nov. 7, 14, 1829; the *Radical*, Jan., 1842, pp. 8, 11, 18; New York *Evening Journal*, Nov. 9, 1829. He received 6,143 votes, only 23 votes less than Ebenezer Ford, the one mechanics' candidate who was elected.

[6] *Working Man's Advocate*, Jan. 16, 1830; *Free Enquirer*, Mar. 20, 1830.

[7] See the *Free Enquirer*, Dec. 26, 1829; Jan. 9, 23, and March 6, 1830; July 2, 1831; and Aug. 18, 1832; *Working Man's Advocate*, Feb. 13, 1830; July 28, and

nificance of his activity in the labor movement is that it "furnished the opponents of the labour movement during many coming decades with a telling catchword whereby to deprive it of a hearing before the public." [8]

Skidmore's program, calling as it did for an immediate and total renovation of society, was of course ahead of his own and possibly any later time. After his expulsion from the original party, most of the workingmen by their actions showed their indifference to the message. The fact remains, however, that some of the harsh conclusions drawn by contemporaries and later scholars alike about the negative role played by Skidmore, are not always warranted.

It has been said, for example, that he "split the party" of workingmen because he would not tolerate within it any deviation from his views. Specifically, he has been charged with opposing the plan for reorganization of the party's internal structure, put forth in November and December, 1829, by a number of insurgents. Backed by men who were critical of Skidmore's philosophy, this new plan had the dual merit of overthrowing the power of Skidmore and the Committee of Fifty, while providing for stronger and seemingly more democratic local organizations within the party. It called for committees within each ward of the city to run the party and control the executive committee. Skidmore was accused of opposing the plan only because he felt he could more easily dominate a more amorphous organization.[9]

Actually Skidmore was not opposed to ward committees. He favored a system in which committees for each of the wards would serve as the basic units of the organization, with power to supervise local matters and select all candidates. He also believed, however, that the Committee of Fifty should continue to function side by side with the smaller committees for the purpose of calling general meetings and corresponding with "other parts of the union." What probably caused some of his contemporaries to misinterpret Skidmore's

---

Aug. 11, 1832; *Daily Sentinel,* Feb. 26, 1830; and *Sentinel and Working Man's Advocate,* Aug. 7, 1830.

[8] Commons and Assoc., *History of Labour,* I, 245; Philip S. Foner, *History of the Labor Movement in the United States* (2 vols; New York, 1947 and 1955), I, 135-136.

[9] See the *Working Man's Advocate* and the *Free Enquirer,* November, December, 1829, January, 1830; Commons, *op. cit.,* p. 242; Foner, *op. cit.,* p. 134.

position as blanket opposition to ward committees was his idea that the Committee of Fifty should be elected at large, city-wide meetings, rather than at small assemblages, which he feared might be dominated by enemies of the workingmen.[10] As it turned out, even one of his harshest critics later became convinced that Skidmore's fears in this respect had been justified.[11]

The charge has been made that it was Skidmore who split the party of New York Working Men "when he and about forty of his followers organized what they called the Poor Man's Party" on December 29, 1829. At the mass meeting called by the Committee of Fifty on this date, Skidmore was prevented from addressing the group by the faction in control. Such behavior by the dominant group indicated that so far as they were concerned there was no room in the organization for Skidmore.[12] In his later history of the Working Men's party, Evans, who in 1830 had himself been critical of Skidmore's quitting of the party, now justified it on the grounds that by stifling discussion, preventing Skidmore from taking the floor, and by causing the adoption of an address of "milk and water character," the recently infiltrated conservative faction was responsible for Skidmore's departure from the party.[13] He did not split but, rather, was read out of the party.

On setting up his new group Skidmore argued that "the rich" had taken over the Working Men's party. In a letter to the *Daily Sentinel* he charged that nineteen members of the new executive committee were rich men who had no business in the party. For a man who saw society sharply divided between laboring poor and oppressing rich, whose sympathies were so decidedly with the former that he could not accept the right of employers or wealthy men to participation in the new movement, the altered social composition of the party's new leadership was a matter of high principle about which he could not compromise.[14] An opponent who at first criticized Skidmore's organ-

10 See the letters by Skidmore, writing as "Marcus," in the New York *Evening Journal*, Nov. 25, 27, 1829.

11 Evans, "History of the Origins and Progress of the Working Men's Party in New York."

12 *Working Man's Advocate*, Jan. 16, 1830.

13 Evans, *loc cit.*

14 See the *Working Man's Advocate*, March 6, 1830; *Free Enquirer*, March 20, 1830; the *Radical*, Jan. 1842, p. 8. In the first issue of his *Friend of Equal*

ization of a new party, later conceded that a number of the new leaders of the Working Men were in fact "aristocratic." [15]

A standard criticism recently directed against Skidmore's program is that it was foisted upon the Working Men and was not actually understood by them.[16] To conservative contemporaries the idea that large numbers of New York workingmen could agree to such principles as the right of the great mass of the community to "equal participation" in the "enjoyments of a comfortable subsistence," was not worthy of consideration. Convinced that "such principles [as were approved by the April meeting of the organized workingmen] would lead to the dissolution of society into its original elements," men who valued the rights of property comforted themselves that "the people at the meeting meant no such thing. *They could not have understood their own resolutions.*" [17]

This interpretation, that the Working Men who for many months supported Skidmore's radical social program did not know or understand what they were supporting, was soon being echoed by some of his colleagues in the New York City labor movement, interested in replacing his doctrines with theirs.[18] Even Frances Wright—"Fanny Wright, the high priestess of Beelzebub" and the apotheosis of agrarianism to the commercial press of her day—thought his program overzealous, preparing "reforms . . . beyond what the public mind can accurately appreciate." [19] Robert Dale Owen, who had been elected secretary of the New York Working Men's party at the very meeting which unanimously endorsed a radical statement on property drawn up by Skidmore and the Committee of Fifty, soon after-

---

Rights, April 14, 1830, Skidmore came out in favor of "drawing a line between rich and poor"; see *Working Man's Advocate,* April 17, 1830; *Free Enquirer,* March 20, 1830.

[15] *Working Man's Advocate,* April 17, 1830.

[16] Commons, *History of Labour,* I, 245; Foner, *op. cit.,* pp. 134–135.

[17] New York *Commercial Advertiser,* April 25, 1829. Italics mine.

[18] Robert Dale Owen and George Henry Evans, the leaders of the dissenting faction, regarded education rather than radical reform of inheritance laws as the way to fundamental reform. Editors of New York's leading pro labor journals of the time, they at first went along with Skidmore. However, when a movement against his leadership arose within the party, they coalesced with the dissidents, and soon were attacking his views.

[19] *Free Enquirer,* Nov. 21, 1829.

wards tried to convince the conservative press that things in the labor party were not what they seemed to be. In stating his objections to Skidmore's program, Owen argued that New York workingmen had not fully understood it when they voted to support it, and that he, Owen, had only "casually attended" the meeting, "ignorant what were the objects of those who called it, what were the measures to be proposed, or who the individuals who were to propose these measures; and . . . heard the resolutions at the meeting for the first time."[20] Whether Owen's disclaimer is valid is an open question, in view of his early acceptance of these ideas he now found it politic to criticize. His statement that Skidmore's program was not understood, however, was made without substantiation. It was the biased verdict of an interested party, rather than an accurate appraisal.

It is significant that before he tried to convince the New York press that he was not an agrarian, Owen had written that he thought the "agrarian" resolutions "would do much good . . . by calling public attention to crying abuses." And the recently organized Association for the Protection and Promotion of Popular Education, of which Owen was a leader and moving spirit, had at its first meeting passed a resolution that "in the opinion of this meeting . . . any peaceful and effectual measures which shall tend permanently to equalize the possession of landed property, and of all other property, will prove eminently useful to society."[21] This was almost pure Skidmorism and indicates that Owen himself as well as a number of his supporters understood quite well the nature of the program they later criticized as not understandable. Yet despite the absence of supporting evidence, this partisan evaluation was later accepted by scholarly authorities.[22]

Between the time of the organization of the New York City Working Men's party in April and the elections in November, 1829, the followers of that party supported the leadership of Thomas Skidmore. In view of his open proclamation during that time of his agra-

[20] Robert Dale Owen to editors of the N.Y. *Commercial Advertiser*, Oct. 26, 1829; also see the *Free Enquirer*, Oct. 31, and Nov. 7, 14, 28, 1829.

[21] *Free Enquirer*, Nov. 7, 14, 1829.

[22] Helen Sumner uses language very similar to Owen's when she writes: "Only a small minority of the Working Men's party ever actually endorsed with full understanding the division of property idea which the political dreamer, Thomas Skidmore, endeavoured to foist upon them" (*op. cit.*, I, 245).

rian theories and the favorable way in which resolutions incorporating his ideas were received, the conclusion seems unavoidable that those who voted in favor of Skidmore's program did not do so blindly. The contrary view expressed by Owen and others was an interesting but interested judgment, based not on fact but on intuition.

The facts themselves suggest that Skidmore's role in the New York labor movement was not quite so negative as his contemporary critics would have it believed. With the Working Men's movement apparently a success, forces from without and within its ranks determined to wrest leadership from him. They succeeded, but at the same time they accomplished the real destruction of the party as well as of its influence at the polls. When this was done they attributed the deterioration of the movement to Skidmore's policies, despite the fact that the movement's only success came during the period of his leadership.

Skidmore's personality also caused offense, for according to his critics he was an arrogant man, overbearing and high-handed toward opponents. More sympathetic observers referred to an attractive personality but a steadfast one which would not permit him to deviate from views he believed to be absolutely correct.[23] "All else is quackery," he said of views which differed from his own.[24] His death was mourned by a small number as the passage of a man of great integrity. Evans, who at first had felt that all Skidmore sought was notoriety, but who had gradually come to feel for him a grudging respect, wrote on this occasion: "Thomas Skidmore had virtues for which many friends will remember and regret him. His open candor, his independence of spirit, his fearless contention for his own rights and the rights of the poor man, together with his benevolent feelings, acute responsibility, and talented mind, will not allow Skidmore's name to pass without a notice of regret."[25] Another admirer predicted that a future time would show great interest in Skidmore, such as is "always felt for the neglected, abused benefac-

---

[23] Amos Gilbert, "Thomas Skidmore," in the *Free Enquirer*, March 20, 1834. See the *Working Man's Advocate*, May 8, 1830, for a denunciation of the editor by Skidmore.

[24] Thomas Skidmore, *Moral Physiology Exposed and Refuted* (New York, 1831), p. 52.

[25] *Working Man's Advocate*, Aug. 11, 1832.

tors of the age in which they lived," as well as for his theory, "in spite of its errors, when thousands of the popular publications of the day shall be forgotten." [26]

Robert Dale Owen, son of the famous socialist reformer of the early nineteenth century, was another leading figure in the New York Working Men's movement. He early served as secretary of the party, was the leader of an important faction and edited several pro-labor newspapers during the movement's heyday in 1829 and 1830. Denounced by conservatives as wild-eyed radicals, Owen and Skidmore nonetheless detested each other and engaged in bitter polemics on several occasions. The tendency of some contemporary doctrinaire radicals whose theories differ only slightly, to reserve their worst abuse for each other rather than for the "class enemy" they are so fond of denouncing, each in his own way, is clearly not a new characteristic in American life.

An interesting figure whose public career continued for almost a half century after the fall of the Working Men, Owen has been described as "one of the most versatile figures in an age of versatility . . . editor, educator and labor leader . . . politician, diplomat, a man of letters . . . legislator, feminist and champion of a new religious faith . . . advocate at one time or another of all sorts of reforms ranging from birth control to Negro emancipation and . . . author of all sorts of books from theological disputes to treatises on architecture and plank roads." [27]

Born in Glasgow, Scotland, in 1801, he was brought up in a comfort made possible by his father's industrial profits.[28] As a young man he knew a "refined, aristocratic and semi-isolated life on a country estate," marked by private tutors and the blessings of membership in the rising industrial aristocracy.[29] The greatest influence on his adolescent mind was his experience at the von Fellenberg school in Hofwyl, Switzerland. Progressive education *circa* 1818, this college, which drew its students solely from the wealthy classes, provided not only a broad curriculum which included gymnastics, agriculture and mechanics as well as the classic liberal arts, but it also exalted the process of formal education as the surest means of correcting social

[26] Gilbert, *loc. cit.* Also see the *Radical*, April, 1841, p. 52.

[27] Richard Leopold, *op. cit.*, pp. vii, viii.

[28] See Chapter 1.

[29] Leopold, *op. cit.*, pp. 6–7.

wrongs, a notion that was later to become the core of Owen's social thought. The faint traces of paternalism and condescension that were later to permeate his thinking were probably due in part to the lesson taught by Fellenberg that "extremes of wealth would always exist," and his hope that "the poor would learn to respect the rich and the latter, to appreciate the dignity of manual labor." [30] On the other hand, liberal philosophical principles were inculcated by his father, who taught the perfectibility of man and the necessity to gear social institutions to human requirements, and by the eminent Jeremy Bentham, who confirmed the elder Owen's teaching that "utility is the test and measure of virtue." [31]

Owen came to this country in 1825 to help his father found a pioneer communitarian society at New Harmony, Indiana.[32] He became the editor of the New Harmony *Gazette*, the journal published by the community, and used its columns to criticize "every irrationality in society." His fundamental social beliefs for this period were clearly expressed in a series of lengthy articles he published in four consecutive issues of the *Gazette*. Entitled "Wealth and Misery," they dealt, as the title indicates, with that dilemma which has always plagued civilized society, and they offered the young Owen's explanation of the causes of social inequity, as well as the panacea for their cure.[33] During this phase of his career he met Frances Wright, a woman of great vigor, reforming zeal, and charm, entering into a close relationship with her that lasted for a decade. In his own words, "this new acquaintance mainly shaped, for several years, the course and tenor of my life." [34]

After a brief period in which they worked as co-editors of the

---

[30] *Ibid.*, pp. 11–13.

[31] Robert Dale Owen, *Threading My Way* (New York, 1874), p. 201, *et passim*. This was an autobiographical account, written when he was seventy-three, of his early years up to the eve of his participation in the Working Men's movement. It is a most useful volume, though the reader must always keep in mind that these are reminiscences put down long after the fact.

[32] See Arthur E. Bestor, Jr., *Backwoods Utopias* (Philadelphia, 1950), for a good account of the New Harmony and the other nineteenth-century communal experiments.

[33] New Harmony *Gazette*, Nov. 8, 15, 22, 29, 1826. These articles were later reprinted with Owen's consent in the *Working Man's Advocate* of May 1, 8, 15, 1830, with some additional observations appended.

[34] On Miss Wright's great influence on young Owen, see *Threading My Way*, p. 296.

Gazette, and co-operated in the establishment of an experimental community in Nashoba, Tennessee, aimed at re-educating manumitted Negroes—a project that turned out to be a great disappointment—Owen and Miss Wright came to New York together. After first setting himself up in most comfortable and fashionable quarters, Owen proceeded to throw himself into a number of reform causes.[35] He and Miss Wright became joint sponsors of perhaps their most successful enterprise, the *Free Enquirer,* a journal that gained much notoriety and some admiration for its attacks on social distress, inequality, ignorance, hypocrisy, and organized religion. It was while they published the *Enquirer* that Owen was drawn into the Working Men's movement. Almost from its infancy the new party was castigated by the conservative press as the "Fanny Wright party in politics." [36] Actually, although Miss Wright devoted some of her stirring public lectures to a discussion of the plight of labor, she played no direct part in the Working Men's movement.[37] But it was conceived to be good strategy by the party's opponents to smear it by any means that came to hand. And how could it be more effectively embarrassed than by identifying it with this notorious woman?

At a "numerous meeting of mechanics" in New York City on October 19, 1829, Owen was called on to act as secretary of the group.[38] Thus began his formal career as a leader of the Working Men, an episode which closed a little more than one year later, following the decisive defeat of his faction in the 1830 elections. Almost immediately, as has already been indicated, Owen tried to detach himself from the "agrarian" resolutions of Skidmore, which that meeting had unanimously endorsed. After the meeting he lost no

[35] *Ibid.,* Leopold, *op. cit.,* pp. 71–72.

[36] See the New York City press, especially the *Courier,* the *Evening Journal,* and the *Commercial Advertiser* for 1829 and 1830.

[37] Seymour Savetsky not only finds no trace of Miss Wright's having participated in the movement, but it is his judgment that had a woman of her ability and zeal done so, it would have been a much more effective force than it was; see *"The New York Working Men's Party,"* unpubl. Master's essay (Columbia Univ., 1948), p. 129. That Miss Wright could stir audiences is amusingly revealed by the conservative Philip Hone, who confides to his diary that he was charmed against his will by the magnificent person and the eloquent rhetoric of this firebrand; see Allan Nevins, ed., *The Diary of Philip Hone 1828–1851* (New York, 1927).

[38] The *Free Enquirer,* Oct. 21, 1829.

time in assuring the New York press of his hostility to such measures, as he began to work to undermine Skidmore's influence.[39] Ironically, despite Owen's disclaimers and his attempt to ingratiate himself with conservatives, they never ceased attacking him as a "fanatic visionary" in his own right. Smearing him with the brush of infidelity, they charged that on the one hand he was a secret agrarian and on the other hand that he was a hypocritical rich man who only pretended to be a friend of labor.[40] To his fellows in the new movement, his criticisms of Skidmore's resolutions were much more circumspect, emphasizing their "bold and novel nature," their impolitic character, the bad publicity they were likely to receive. In view of these things, Owen suggested, the workers might well have given more careful consideration, perhaps even deferred their support of the program. Why enter a wedge with the blunt end foremost? [41]

It was not the redistribution of property but the reorganization of the educational system that Owen favored. (The failure of New Harmony helped account for this new belief.) Shortly after the 1829 elections Owen helped organize the Association for the Protection and Promotion of Popular Education, as an adjunct to the political movement. For he meant what he told conservatives when, in an editorial entitled "To the Conductors of the New York Press," which was part of his campaign to free himself from the taint of agrarianism, he assured them that he and his colleagues "propose no equalization, but that which equal national education shall gradually effect." [42] Skidmore was wrong in believing that "the unequal distribution of landed property is the chief source of the calamities of the poor," since "if property were at this day equally divided among all our country's citizens, in one single year, we should probably again be plunged into all the evils of riches and poverty." [43] Where earlier

---

[39] *Ibid.*

[40] See, for example, the *Commercial Advertiser*, Oct. 23, 26, 1829; and the account of such attacks in the *Free Enquirer*, Nov. 7, 1829. Usually an attack on Frances Wright also cited her friend Robert Dale Owen.

[41] *Free Enquirer*, Oct. 31, 1829. When it seemed clear that he was likely to remain anathema to the New York press, he advised workers not to be so prudent as to reject "heterodox assistance merely by way of purchasing a fair character from their enemies" (*ibid.*, Nov. 14, 1829).

[42] *Ibid.*, Nov. 28, 1829.

[43] *Ibid.*, Oct. 31, 1829.

Owen had leaned toward a program of immediate and drastic social reform, he had now come to agree completely with Frances Wright that "until equality be planted in the mind, in the habits, in the manners, in the feelings, think not it ever can be in the conditions." The system of national republican education, or "state guardianship" as it popularly came to be known, was the means by which the necessary equality would be planted.

This plan called for children to be taken from their homes and placed in national schools under a system of state "guardianship [which] would . . . furnish to all the children of the land equal food, clothing and instruction, at the public expense." The curriculum would be a broad one, incorporating agricultural and mechanical, as well as intellectual subjects. (Shades of the von Fellen-berg school!) Through such a system, first individuals would be regenerated, and then ultimately the society itself. And all this without violence. This was the program Owen now began to urge, in the pages of the *Enquirer* and also the *Sentinel*, a daily which came out early in 1830.[44]

After the expulsion of Skidmore, Owen joined with Evans—the first publication of whose *Working Man's Advocate* he enthusi-astically applauded when it came out in October—in a collaboration that for a short time, early in 1830, promised to place the State Guardianship group in control of the party on a state level.[45] But it was not to be. An open break occurred in the party in May, 1830, when by a narrow vote the party's executive committee denounced and rejected the Wright-Owen education plan, charging that it would break up the home and family, as well as undermine religion. The Owen supporters retaliated with the charge that the dominant faction, headed by Noah Cook, an editor of the *Evening Journal*, was made up of schemers, Clayites in Working Men's clothing, who had entered the party only to control it and misuse it for their own sordid purposes.[46] The party's new split was widened in August when the

[44] *Ibid.*, Jan 16, 1830; *Daily Sentinel*, April 8, 9, 10, 12, 13, 14, 1830. This paper later in the year merged with the *Working Man's Advocate*.

[45] The *Working Man's Advocate* supported the educational program of Owen and Miss Wright.

[46] See the *Free Enquirer*, June 5, 1830; *Sentinel and Working Man's Advocate*, June 16, 1830. For a clear and concise account of this phase of the New York party, see Hugins, *op. cit.*, chap. i.

state convention, now dominated by the Cook faction, refused to seat the "Sentinel" delegates. Separate slates of Working Men's candidates were presented for the state elections in the fall. The Owenites suffered a severe defeat, their candidates receiving slightly more than two thousand votes, only a little over one-third of the total of the previous year, whereas the Cook faction got better than seven thousand votes. The disillusioned Owen (and Evans) now counseled mechanics to devote themselves to self-improvement instead of politics.[47] As for Owen himself, the crushing defeat of his program in effect ended his career as a Working Men's leader. He was now to throw himself into a number of reform causes, including the education of the poor in the uses of contraceptives, that initiated a new phase of what eventually was to be a career of more than a half-century of general reform, lecturing, politics, and, ironically, religious propaganda.[48]

George Henry Evans was the other member of the triumvirate that dominated the New York Working Men's movement at the very beginning of its career. Evans was the publisher and editor of the most popular labor journal of his day, the *Working Man's Advocate*. From the time of the first issue, when Evans denounced the politicians of both major parties as men who only talked of the people's rights while actually they "made and multiplied laws only to promote their own interests," his weekly came to be accepted as the official publication of the new movement.[49] He continued to edit this journal until 1836, long after the Working Men's party had collapsed. In 1834, when a formidable trades' union movement appeared in New York City, Evans edited a new daily journal, *The Man*, which acted as an official organ for the cause. The numerous periodicals he put out early in the 1840s indicate that the printers' ink he had absorbed early in his life never completely left his blood.[50]

[47] *Working Man's Advocate*, Nov. 13, 1830.

[48] Near the end of his life, the onetime infidel and socialist was writing that "the secular school can never prevail against the spiritual. It has nothing to offer but this world, and that is insufficient for man"; (*Threading My Way*, p. 296).

[49] The *Working Man's Advocate*, Oct. 31, 1829; May 8, 1830.

[50] In 1841 he put out the *Radical*, a monthly which lasted for five years. In 1844 he came out with *People's Rights*, in addition to a new *Working Man's Advocate*, which the following year became *Young America*.

Evans' contribution to the Working Men's cause was not confined
to editing. He threw himself into a number of organizational activities, and, as has been indicated, was an active collaborator of Robert
Dale Owen in trying to convert the party to support of a particular
educational system. He was active participant rather than passive
observer. Similarly, the journals he edited were passionately partisan,
never confining themselves to an objective chronicling of the news.

Evans' main claim to fame, however, rests not on his exertions in
behalf of the New York Working Men, but rather on his career after
1840. For from that time until his death in 1856, he devoted his life
to the cause which he had come to regard as the universal cure of all
social ills: Land Reform. Evans' name became synonymous with the
movement that regarded national policy on public lands as the most
important of all problems, and the equal distribution of virgin soil
as its solution. "Vote yourself a farm," became his slogan.[51]

There is no doubt that Evans' ideas about land and land policy
were very much influenced by his experiences with the Working
Men. In fact he credited Skidmore's bold theories with causing him
to reflect on the inequity of the system by which land was owned.[52]
This, then, was one of the most important and influential reformers
of the nineteenth century, whose career with the New York
mechanics and their friends provided him his first practical experience as a social reformer.

Evans was born in rural Herefordshire, in England, in 1804. His
father had been a British commissioned officer while his mother's
family were well-to-do. He came to this country when he was a
child. His family having settled in central New York, Evans, while a
youth, was apprenticed to a printer in Ithaca. Until early manhood
he worked in the newspaper craft in "country printing offices where
he might be at once editor and delivery boy, pressman and com-
positor." [53] His intellectual history for this period is obscure, but evidently some fermentation was taking place. For in 1829 he arrived

[51] Helen Zahler's *Eastern Workingmen and Public Land Policy* remains the
best study of this movement. Lewis Masquerier's *Sociology or the Reconstruction of Society* contain the interesting personal reflections of one of Evan's
land-reform collaborators.

[52] *Working Man's Advocate*, March 6 and May 22, 1830. Also see the *Radical*,
April, 1841, p. 52; April, 1843, pp. 51–52.

[53] Zahler, *op. cit.*, p. 19.

in New York City and almost at once became active in the rising labor movement. In September he organized a debating society for "mechanics and other working men" of the Fifth Ward.[54] He also helped organize the New York Association for the Protection of Industry and for the Promotion of National Education, and was rewarded by being elected chairman of this new organization. Evans had met and become an enthusiastic admirer of Robert Dale Owen, his senior by several years, who had also just recently come to New York. The two exchanged articles in their respective journals and by the spring of 1830 collaborated in the editing of the merged *Sentinel and Working Man's Advocate*. Instances of disagreement between the *Free Enquirer* and the *Working Man's Advocate* are very rare.

One of the things that probably drew Evans to Owen was the fact that Owen seemed to know at any particular moment precisely what was wrong with society and what was needed to correct it. For throughout his life Evans seemed to be attracted to one cure-all or another, and to an extent, therefore, to the individuals who conceived them. He had an enthusiasm for panaceas.

Moreover, he could entertain several enthusiasms simultaneously. For example, he was at first so taken with Skidmore's program that the first issues of his *Working Man's Advocate* proudly ran on its masthead the slogan: *All children are entitled to equal education; all adults to equal property, and all mankind, to equal privileges.*[55] But with the third issue of the paper the slogan on the masthead was changed to read: *All children are entitled to equal education; all adults, to equal privileges.*[56] He had now been converted to the theory propagated by Miss Wright and Owen that educational reform alone was the key to a solution of social problems. He assured his readers, however, that he continued to believe "that all are at birth entitled to equal means to pursue happiness; and among these are food, clothing, and shelter . . . which we call property." But since children are incapable of using property, what is required instead is an equal education. At such time as they become adults, Evans continues to believe they are entitled to equal property.

[54] *Free Enquirer*, Sept. 30, 1829.

[55] See the issues of Oct. 31 and Nov. 7, 1829.

[56] *Working Man's Advocate*, Nov. 14, 1829.

Thereafter if unequal skills result in disparities, so be it.[57] In effect, then, like Henry George, at a later time, who hoped through the mechanism of the Single Tax to accomplish the same results as socialism, but with less disturbance and at smaller social cost, Evans now hoped through the milder method of Equal Public Education to accomplish the beneficial results sought by agrarianism.[58] That he never completely lost his sympathy for the redistribution of property is shown, among other things, by the relative fairness and lack of rancor he showed Skidmore in later years, despite his clear differences with him.[59]

Before his career as a New York labor leader ended, Evans developed a number of new enthusiasms. At one point he was the ardent champion of what he called a co-operative system which would reward men in direct proportion to what they contributed to society in useful labor.[60] That in 1834 he became the vice-president of the Working Men Opposed to Paper Money was only logical, for at that time he was in the throes of his conviction that "the abolition of the Rag Money System [the paper money issued by banks] and other Licensed Monopolies" was the fundamental reform.[61] And before failing health in 1836 forced him to depart for a farm in New Jersey, where he was to spend five years in rest and in preparation for the career of land reformer that lay ahead, he had been converted to a new faith: "Three fourths . . . of all the vice and misery existing in the United States," he wrote, "might be eradicated by the just and practicable measure of allowing every necessitous individual to cultivate (without charge) a portion of the uncultivated land under such restrictions as would prevent any further *monopoly* of it." [62]

[57] *Ibid.*

[58] Henry George, *Progress and Poverty*, Modern Library Edition (New York, 1939), pp. 328, 403–405; cf. George R. Geiger, *The Philosophy of Henry George* (New York, 1933), pp. 130–131.

[59] *Working Man's Advocate*, Jan. 16 and May 8, 1830; the *Radical*.

[60] An early expression in favor of co-operative associations as a temporary expedient appears in the *Working Man's Advocate*, Feb. 20, 1830. For his more fully thought-out ideas, cf. *ibid.*, April 14, 1832; *The Man*, Feb. 18, 1834.

[61] *The Man*, May 7, 17, and Aug. 2, 1834.

[62] *Working Man's Advocate*, June 14, 1834. Over a year before, Evans asked that the public lands be used as a safety valve, by being made available to unemployed workers (*ibid.*, Jan. 26, 1833). Also see the issues of March 2, 1833, and especially of May 9, 1835.

He was now launched on his final career, in which he would become the "heart, soul and voice" of the mid-century movement for land reform.[63]

The picture painted by several of his contemporaries indicates that Evans was universally liked as well as widely admired by those in and out of the Working Men's movement. Where Skidmore was considered arrogant and Owen patronizing, Evans is described as possessing "great evenness of temper, . . . mild and courteous in his intercourse with others; he made no parade of oratory, but spoke in a plain and clear manner—direct to the point. He was patient in argument, and never allowed himself to arise to a passion." [64] The historian of the Loco Focos wrote, "there lives not a more unpretending and incorruptible man." He adds a charming vignette:

Honest George! we can see him in our mind's eye, in his murky office at Thames Street, editor, compiler, printer, etc. of his daily and weekly papers. There he was close [?] at his desk, attending to and contending for all the rights and interests of the working masses of mankind, but neglecting his own rights and interests in money matters. Like all such men, he had his full share of difficulties, and yet he made up his excellent newspaper. . . .[65]

Some modern interpreters of social thought attribute the behavior of important figures either to environmental or philosophic influences. Can it be that in the case of George Henry Evans the tolerance and magnanimity he showed opponents, were due less to the fact that their ideas were not too unlike his, than to his simple good nature and emotional balance?

Stephen Simpson, the son of a Philadelphia bank cashier, was the Congressional candidate of the Working Men's party in the 1830 elections.[66] His acceptance of that party's support, together with a volume he wrote the following year, purporting to analyze the ills of society from the worker's viewpoint, comprised the substance of his identification with the labor movement.[67] The unusual nature of

---

[63] Zahler, *op. cit.*, p. 38.

[64] Masquerier, *op. cit.*, p. 99.

[65] FitzWilliam Byrdsall, *History of the Loco-Foco, or Equal Rights Party* (New York, 1842), pp. 14–15.

[66] *Mechanic's Free Press*, Oct. 2, 1830.

[67] Stephen Simpson, *The Working Man's Manual, A New Theory of Political Economy on the Principles of Production the Source of Wealth, Including an*

the early American labor movement is nowhere better illustrated than in the fact that so tenuous a connection gained for Simpson the reputation of a major labor leader.[68] In fact, his admirers, impressed by the radicalism of his views and his eloquence in expressing them, called him the "American Cobbett," after the fiery English reformer and anticapitalist.[69] A recent critic describes Simpson as the "leading spokesman of the Philadelphia Working Men's party of 1828–1831." [70]

Simpson was born in Philadelphia in 1789 of relatively well-to-do parents. As a young man he worked for a short time as a merchant and also in the Philadelphia bank of Stephen Girard (as had his father before him), and he developed a keen admiration for the eminent capitalist in the process.[71] He was, however, far more interested in literary pursuits. He edited a number of short-lived newspapers and literary journals, wrote poetry and newspaper articles, including some for the liberal *Aurora*, and he belonged to an esoteric society which discussed contemporary literary trends.[72]

He was also interested in politics. An early admiration for Jackson, first formed when Simpson, who had volunteered to fight in the War of 1812, served under the General at New Orleans, turned sour after the election of 1828 when Simpson's hopes for a position in the new Administration were disappointed. Thereafter Simpson became an ardent anti-Jacksonian. His antipathy toward Old Hickory did not

---

Enquiry into the Principles of Public Credit, Currency, the Wages of Labour, the Production of Wealth, the Distribution of Wealth, Consumption of Wealth, Popular Education, and the Elements of Social Government in General, as they appear open to the scrutiny of common sense and the Philosophy of the Age (Philadelphia, 1831).

[68] See the *Working Man's Advocate*, Sept. 3 and Oct. 8, 1831.

[69] See Thomas Brothers, *The United States of North America as They Really Are* (London, 1840), p. 119; Joseph Dorfman, *The Economic Mind*, II, 645. On Cobbett, see G. D. H. Cole, *The Life of William Cobbett* (New York, 1926). By this time Cobbett had moved far to the left, by perhaps 180 degrees, compared to the views he had expressed decades before, as "Peter Porcupine," the Federalist champion.

[70] Arthur M. Schlesinger, Jr., *op. cit.*, p. 201.

[71] Stephen Simpson, *Stephen Girard* (Philadelphia, 1832), pp. 110–115, *passim;* also Simpson, *The Working Man's Manual*, p. 75.

[72] Stephen Simpson, "Literary Clubs," in *The Author's Jewel* (Philadelphia, 1823), p. 79; Broadus Mitchell, *loc. cit.*

prevent him, however, from co-operating with the youthful Working Men's party, nor did it prevent him from embracing a radical social program.

Simpson had earned a reputation as a critic of the exploitation of labor by capital, and was widely known as a champion of a democratic public education system. Like Working Men elsewhere, the Philadelphia party felt no qualms about naming a candidate who was not himself a mechanic and who had already been nominated for office by another party. In 1830 they nominated Simpson to Congress, despite the fact that he was already the candidate of the Federal Party for Congress from the first Congressional district.[73] That he was not a workingman by the ordinary definition of that term was regarded as no contradiction by a party which at its birth had made clear that in choosing candidates for office it would be concerned not with their social standing but with their views. Simpson accepted the nomination with alacrity.[74]

Following the failure of his Congressional race and the subsequent decline of the Working Men's party early in 1831, Simpson began in August of that year to publish a new paper, the *Pennsylvania Whig*. This organ supported the National Republicans on most issues, poured much abuse on the Jackson Administration, and among other things, defended many of the policies of the second Bank of the United States.[75] Simpson's support of the bank brought on him the scorn of former admirers in the labor movement, who accused him of having discarded his earlier sympathy for labor.[76]

Actually these criticisms of Simpson did not do him justice, for it is not true that "all of his previous opinions were forsaken." His approval of the bank's policies, for example, was by no means unqualified. In fact, he wrote that in the absence of the inflationary and irresponsible policies pursued by the numerous small banks, there would have been no need for the national bank. In addition, he believed that notwithstanding its useful functions—a view with which such modern authorities as Bray Hammond and Walter B. Smith

[73] *Mechanic's Free Press*, Aug. 25 and Oct. 2, 1830.

[74] Commons, *History of Labour*, I, 192, 228.

[75] *Pennsylvania Whig*, Aug. 24, 1831.

[76] See the *Mechanics' Free Press* and the *Working Man's Advocate*, Sept. 3 and Oct. 8, 1831.

would have much sympathy [77]—its charter should have been amended
to assure smaller dividends, the prevention of proxy voting, and the
earmarking of excess profits for appropriations "to the cause of public education." [78]

In September of 1831 he published his *Working Man's Manual*.
Described by Simpson as a "plain elucidation of some of the leading
principles of the working men," this volume demonstrates that its
author continued to believe in 1831 as he had in 1830 that idle capitalists profited at the expense of industrious labor.[79] A modern critic,
who thinks Simpson wrote the book "to insinuate himself into the
confidence of the growing labor movement"—a charge which if true
would indicate that Simpson continued to identify himself with this
movement and hoped to play an influential part in it, whatever his
motives—nonetheless concedes that it was an effective and powerful
statement of the Working Men's position.[80]

Simpson may thereafter have continued to believe in a radical general philosophy, but in practical affairs he devoted himself to the
pursuit of self interest. His later years were characterized by oppor-
tunism, specious financial enterprises (in 1839 he was charged with
conspiracy to defraud depositors out of their hard-earned savings in
a savings fund started by Simpson and a friend earlier in the year),
and dubious attempts to curry favor with the Democratic party.[81]

John Commerford of the Brooklyn branch of the New York
Working Men, William English of the Philadelphia party, Seth
Luther and Charles Douglas, both of them leaders of the first New
England Association of Farmers, Mechanics and Other Working
Men, although active in these political movements, actually are
most important for their trades' union activities and will therefore

[77] Bray Hammond, *Banks and Politics in America* (Princeton, 1957); Walter
B. Smith, *Economic Aspects of the Second Bank of the United States* (Cambridge, 1953).

[78] See the *Pennsylvania Whig*, May 2, 1832.

[79] Mitchell (*loc. cit.*) describes Simpson as an important anticipator of Marx
on the basis of the views expressed in the *Working Man's Manual*. For the
judgment that this is not the case, that such attribution is due more to the
coloration of Simpson's words than to their meaning, see the discussion in
Part Two, below.

[80] Schlesinger, *Age of Jackson*, pp. 201–202.

[81] Dorfman, *The Economic Mind*, II, 647–648.

be discussed in the next chapter. The fact of their participation in both the earlier and later periods of the movement does indicate a kind of continuity between its political and economic phases.[82] And the fact that Commerford, English, and Luther were workingmen themselves, as had been Skidmore, further illustrates that some Working Men actually were or had been workers.

The prominence of Skidmore, Owen, Evans, and Simpson was due primarily to their doctrines or theories. The Working Men's movement awarded leadership not to the rank and file mechanic or journeyman but to the relatively well-educated individual who knew or thought he knew how to cure the ills of society. Although this movement was concerned with workers, whom it regarded as the main victims of a society imperfectly and inequitably arranged, it did not attempt to organize itself along functional or working class lines. It sought, it welcomed, the support of men of whatever class, so long as they seemed in favor of the reform of society. Some division of opinion had arisen, especially when the parties were first organized, as to whether membership or administrative posts should be filled by men who were not "working men." The usual resolution of this issue had been to broaden rather than narrow the base of a party which having little voting support for the most part, needed all the membership it could get. But so far as its top leaders went, there was never real dispute. All that the party-sympathetic-to-workingmen cared about was whether these men believed in its reform program. This, Owen and Simpson, as well as Skidmore and Evans, clearly did. Moreover, they were true leaders in the sense that instead of merely following the programs of others, it was the particular programs or schemes that they advocated and originated that were taken up and supported by the Working Men.

[82] Hugins makes an impressive argument for the view that in New York the trades' union leaders did not for the most part come from the Working Men's movement (*op. cit.*, p. 76).

6

The Trades' Unionists

The labor movement was born in Pennsylvania in 1827 and came alive there again during the trades' union upsurge of the 1830s. One of the most unusual figures to play a leading part in the latter movement was Thomas Brothers. He was a hat manufacturer who had been accused of underpaying the labor he himself employed in his own establishment! [1] This complex individual was also a critic of democracy, an anti-semite and altogether one of the most uncommon of an uncommon group of labor leaders. Born in a small village in Warwick County at the close of the eighteenth century, by the time he left England for this country, in 1824, he already had become a manufacturer.[2] Emigration to the United States had been his dream since boyhood, when an enthusiastic reading of Thomas Paine's *Rights of Man* had convinced him that an aristocratic system of government and society was responsible for the grinding poverty that was increasingly prevalent in his native land. By the time he departed for America he had come to regard the capitalistic system's financial operations, in addition to aristocracy, as the root causes of social misery. In the "far-famed republic" he sought not only to make his fortune but to find the embodiment of his political and social ideals.[3]

Somewhat startled by the disparity between actual conditions in America and what he had been led to expect, Thomas Brothers settled down in Philadelphia to the business of advancing his personal fortune. During these first years he gave little time to anything but business. While founding a hatmaking establishment which employed journeymen workmen, he only dabbled in reform activities. With the passage of time, however, he became more active in outside

[1] See Edward Pessen, "Thomas Brothers, Anti-Capitalist Employer," *Pennsylvania History*, XXIV (Oct., 1957), 323.

[2] Thomas Brothers to William G. Lewis, Esq., July 8, 1839, in Brothers, *The United States of North America as They Really Are: Not as They are Generally Described: being a cure for radicalism* (London, 1840), p. 1.

[3] *Ibid.*, pp. 3–4, 11.

affairs.[4] In the spring of 1835, against a background of a resurgent labor movement, he began to publish a weekly pro labor journal, the *Radical Reformer and Working Man's Advocate*. By that time Brothers was a confirmed champion of the movement. In the midst of the struggle then being waged by Philadelphia workers for the establishment of the ten hour day, Brothers played a leading part at a large public meeting called to support the striking workingmen.[5] He saw no irony in the advice he continually gave workingmen, that to secure their objectives they should depend on their own efforts alone and reject the aid proffered by well-meaning employers. Obviously he did not come under his own injunction. And he had nothing but contempt for that "place-hunting fellow" who had suggested that Brothers' great love for the working class in general was not evidenced for the few workers he himself employed.[6]

Though he held no posts in any labor organization, his journal served as the unofficial mouthpiece of the Philadelphia trades' union movement.[7] Besides Brothers' own contributions, it carried stories and articles of interest to labor, excerpts from the fiery William Cobbett's *Penny Register*, and the speeches and writings of such prominent labor figures as William English and John Ferral. In fact, Ferral, who was a leader of a number of labor organizations, was an agent for the distribution of the *Radical Reformer*.[8] The paper was dominated by Brothers' own writings. During this period his ideas were not simply prolabor but extremely radical, taking the form oftentimes of diatribes against the existing order. The violence of some of

[4] See the *Working Man's Advocate*, Feb. 1, 1834, for an account of a town meeting held in Independence Square, Dec. 31, 1833, at which Brothers delivered a long address attacking the second Bank of the United States.

[5] According to his account, some old-time "office-holders and office-seekers" objected to his chairing of the meeting. He gave in to them only on the advice of his friend William English, the Secretary of the Philadelphia trades' union; described in the *Radical Reformer and Working Man's Advocate*, June 13, 1835, pp. 6–7, 9–10.

[6] See the sharp response in the *Radical Reformer*, June 20, 1835. For a critical view of Brothers, see Joseph Dorfman, "The Jackson Wage-Earner Thesis," *American History Review*, LIV (Jan., 1949), p. 298.

[7] It gave up the ghost in October of 1835, but during its brief existence its relationship to the union movement was analogous to that of the *Mechanic's Free Press* to the Philadelphia Working Man's party several years earlier.

[8] An advertisement listing Ferral's home address as a center for the paper's distribution appeared regularly in its issues.

the language he used in denouncing the wicked men and institutions allegedly responsible for labor's plight was due more to his emotionalism than to the strength or logic of his views. For he was a highly unstable man, one who only a few short years after the decline of the labor movement not only rejected many of his former notions but turned bitterly against radical reform.

It would seem that his intellectual history is but another illustration of the classic biographical cycle: from radicalism in youth to conservatism in maturity. Actually the changes in Brothers' thinking were rather more complicated and not reducible to so convenient a formula. His earlier radicalism contained within it the germs of his later conservatism. When he returned to England in 1838, after the panic of the previous year had almost ruined him financially, he had become a critic of democracy, "most reluctantly obliged to acknowledge the fallacy of self-government, believing that it [had] . . . no existence in the nature of things." [9] His American experience had completely undermined a belief in political reform that had been frail to begin with, though it left unshattered his sympathy for the underprivileged. Disillusion transformed the agitator for the rights of workers into a champion of reform through aristocratic benevolence. The change was punctuated in 1840 with the publication of his *The United States of North America as They Really Are*, a book which mingled bitter comment on social inequality with abject subservience to political toryism. It was primarily a source book of glaring social evils in this country, for with much zeal Brothers had collected materials on cruelty in the prisons, atrocities against slaves and abolitionists, the general deterioration of manners in society, the duplicity of politicians, and the suffering of the poor to document his new thesis that democracy was inevitably a failure. "Under what is called self-governments," he wrote, "there may be as much oppression, poverty and wretchedness, as under any other kind of government." [10] Recalling his American experience, Brothers warned the English Chartists that democratic opportunists, promising all things, "will tell you as many flattering tales as a simpering bawd would:

[9] Brothers to Lewis, *op. cit.*, p. 2.

[10] Brothers to the Chartists (II), Sept. 5, 1839, and Brothers to his sons, *ibid.*, pp. 245, 121.

their motive, like hers, would be to plunder you to the utmost extent." [11] This argument is only a variation on a theme he had played in his Philadelphia days, that politics in a democracy is full of sound and fury, signifying nothing of importance to the laboring poor.

Rather than depend on themselves or on hypocritical politicians, Brothers now advised workers to place their faith in God and in the ancient class of aristocrats.[12] At least in those days prior to "reform," when that class had been powerful in England, no man in need had been allowed to suffer or go without community support, nor was poverty considered a disgrace. Yet certainly Brothers knew that social abuses had been rampant in this bucolic society he now professed to admire. An unhappy personal experience in the United States, his hatred for financiers and monopolists—to him "the vilest race that ever infested the world"—and his inability to adjust his thinking to the dynamic economic developments in America and England, combined to transform his political philosophy. Like other raidcals who followed him, he no longer believed that democratic politics was the path to reform; but unlike them, neither did he counsel independent workers' action. Instead he retreated to a position that would place responsibility for society's welfare in the hands of the patricians.

Yet, in a sense, he had not strayed far from the promise he had made in his original prospectus for the *Radical Reformer and Working Man's Advocate*. Then he had said, "for my own part, no exertion of mine shall be wanting to protect the defenceless in all cases, against the powerful. . . ." [13] But where earlier he had urged the poor and the workers to fight for themselves, he now advised them to rely on the conservative well-meaning. He had replaced class struggle with *noblesse oblige*, ostensibly to achieve the same ends. Unable to reconcile himself to an expanding commercial society, with its shattering effect on all things traditional, Thomas Brothers at first engaged in a movement in behalf of those whom he conceived to be its main victims. When this proved unavailing, and after he himself experienced severe personal losses, he turned his back on all

[11] Brothers to the Chartists (I), Aug. 9, 1839, *ibid.*, p. 224.

[12] Brothers to Thomas Atwood, July 15, 1939, *ibid.*, pp. 52–53.

[13] *Radical Reformer*, June 13, 1835, pp. 1–2.

its works and attempted to restore a romantic past of his own creation.

A very different type of figure in his origins, his way of making a living, his role in the labor movement, and in the period of time he devoted to that movement, was John Ferral (sometimes spelled Ferrall or Farrel). A handloom weaver whose role in creating a trades' union movement in Philadelphia after 1833 was second to none, he was also one of the outstanding and best known leaders of the national labor movement.[14] At the third convention of the New England Association of Farmers, Mechanics and Other Working Men, held in Boston in October, 1833, he was the only non-New Englander admitted as a member, attending in order to gather information "in relation to the working classes in New Haven." His later election to the highest offices in the National Trades' Union clearly was due to the fact that his contacts with labor movements outside of Pennsylvania had made him well known, and to the universal respect in which he was held. He was indefatigable. Late in 1833 he tried to organize the workers of the factory districts surrounding Philadelphia into the "Trades' Union of Pennsylvania." Despite Ferral's exhortations that the assembled delegates fight for the ten hour day and unite with the mechanics of Philadelphia in a broad organization that would also include farmers, the movement failed.[15] Thereafter, together with William English, he helped build the Trades' Union of Philadelphia. He was especially active during the ten hour strike of 1835. His speeches before non labor audiences, and the co-operation he won from workingmen's leaders of other cities, were largely responsible for the success of that strike.[16] During the summer of 1835 he managed to find time to be an agent for the distribution of Brothers' journal.[17] In 1836, following the arrest of a number of striking workmen by the mayor of Philadelphia, Ferral was one of the leaders of the Philadelphia union selected to hold

[14] See John R. Commons and Associates, *A Documentary History of American Industrial Society* (Cleveland, 1910), V, 336.

[15] *Pennsylvanian*, Dec. 24, 1833, cited in Commons, *Documentary History*, V, 336.

[16] *The Man*, June 29, 1835; *Pennsylvanian*, June 9, 1835; *National Laborer*, May 14 and Sept. 17, 1836; cited in *ibid.*, VI, 46; V, 358, 378.

[17] The *Radical Reformer* for June 27, 1835, lists (page 48) "Mr. John Ferral's Schuylkill Falls," as one of four distribution points of the paper.

discussions with leaders of other parties in order to secure the nomination of candidates friendly to labor.[18]

At the National Trades' Union's first meeting in 1834, Ferral was elected second vice-president. He was one of five men chosen "to prepare a statement of the best means to be used to prevent the reduction of wages, and ensure the reduction [of] the hours of labor." In addition, he held a number of other important assignments.[19] The following year, in recognition of his contribution to the success of the ten hour movement, Ferral was elected president of the National Trades' Union.[20] At the conventions of both 1835 and 1836 Ferral spoke eloquently in behalf of the rights of factory workers, the need to bring more journeymen's societies into the national organization, and the need for a more liberal government land policy.[21]

Ferral remained with the organized labor movement longer than did most of his contemporaries. Thus in March of 1837 he assumed the post of corresponding secretary of the Philadelphia Trades' Union. Thirteen years later he was active in the Pittsburgh Workingmen's Congress, simultaneously representing the Brooklyn Masons' Laborers at a gathering of the New York City Industrial Congress. Like others in the labor movement, he became a disciple of George Henry Evans' land reform movement in the 1840s and 1850s.[22]

Rivaling Ferral for leadership in the Philadelphia and Pennsylvania movements, although he was unlike him in important ways, was William English, who also became a celebrity in the national labor movement. English's career bears an interesting resemblance to that of Ely Moore, the well-known trades' union leader of New York.[23]

---

[18] *Pennsylvanian*, Oct. 3, 1836, cited in Commons and Associates, *History of Labour in the United States* (New York, 1918), I, 378; Philip S. Foner, *History of the Labor Movement in the United States* (2 vols.; New York, 1947 and 1955), I, 160.

[19] *The Man*, Aug. 26, 27, 28, 29, and Sept. 2, 1834.

[20] *National Trades' Union*, Oct. 10, 1835, cited in Commons, *Documentary History*, VI, 228.

[21] *Ibid.*, pp. 245–246, 269, 271, 277.

[22] *National Laborer*, March 18, 1837; New York *Daily Tribune*, July 8, and Aug. 13, 1850; cited in Commons, *Documentary History*, V, 338; VIII, 303, 333.

[23] On Moore, see Walter Hugins, "Ely Moore: The Case History of a Jacksonian Labor Leader," *Political Science Quarterly*, LXV (March, 1950), 105–

Like Moore, he was a working man who spent little time actually practicing his trade, attained prominence in the early labor movement largely because of his oratorical prowess, was a successful candidate for political office, and throughout his career, in fact, displayed more interest in politics than in anything else. And as was true of Moore, he held important posts in labor organizations.

English described himself as "a mechanic, born to toil from early childhood, [who] never . . . entered a school by the light of day." [24] Brothers, however, described him as "a journeyman shoemaker too idle to stick to his trade." [25] (This comment, it must be noted, was made during Brothers' sour period.) Before he became a union leader, English was active in the first Philadelphia Working Men's party and participated in movements criticizing monopolies, banks, lotteries, and the absence of equal education.[26] When the National Trades' Union convened in 1834, English attended as the delegate of the Philadelphia Cordwainers and was elected as the recording secretary.[27] It was to his own cordwainers' union and to the trades' union movement within Philadelphia itself, however, that he made his main labor movement contribution. He was in the forefront of the effort—premature, as it turned out—to establish a national cordwainers' society. His own organization chose him as its representative to the national convention which took place in New York City on March 7, 1836. He formulated the rules of this convention, helped draw up a plan whereby cordwainers' societies in the various states could support each others' strikes, submitted a constitution, and helped draw up an appeal to all cordwainers to increase their wages.[28]

125; and Hugins, *Jacksonian Democracy and the Working Class* (Stanford, 1960), pp. 63–68.

[24] William English, "Oration Delivered at the Trades' Union Celebration of the 4th of July," *Radical Reformer and Working Men's Advocate*, Aug. 1, 1835, p. 120.

[25] Brothers, *United States of North America*, pp. 224–225. Schlesinger thus refers to English as an "unreliable journeyman shoemaker"; Arthur M. Schlesinger, Jr., *The Age of Jackson* (Boston, 1945), p. 204.

[26] See the *Free Enquirer*, Oct. 7, 1829; Commons, *Documentary History*, VI, 317–329.

[27] *The Man*, Aug. 27, and Sept. 2, 1834. English was later given an honorary seat in the 1836 convention.

[28] *National Trades' Union*, March 26, 1836, cited in Commons, *Documentary History*, VI, 317–329.

He also was active in the "Trades' Union of the city and county of Philadelphia," an organization consisting of mechanics, factory workers, and day laborers. At its very first meeting, English was elected secretary. In this union, whose main achievement was a successful ten hour strike in 1835, English held a variety of posts, ranging from recording secretary to president. He was also the group's leading orator.[29]

In 1835 English ran on the "progressive" Democratic ticket as a candidate for the State Senate—the political split of the Democratic Party in Pennsylvania was very similar to the one which had produced the Loco Focos in New York—and thus began a somewhat checkered political career, which brought an early end to his trades' union activities.

At the center of the New England labor movement stood two unusual organizations, the New England Association of Farmers, Mechanics and Other Working Men and the short-lived body which followed it, the General Trades' Union of Boston and Vicinity. The former group was political as much as economic, representing an interesting attempt to unite agriculture and labor. The trades' union was also unique, above all for the breadth of its interests. There is fitness in the fact that the two leaders of these organizations were themselves unusual men, embodying both in their persons and their careers the uncommonness of the movement they led.

Seth Luther was the leading figure of the New England labor movement during the decade of the 1830s. Journeyman carpenter, labor orator and agitator, traveling union delegate and part-time editor, Luther was one of the busiest and undoubtedly the most colorful individuals in the labor movement of the era. He was born in Providence, Rhode Island, the son of a veteran of the American Revolution.[30] His early life was hard, since his father's income as a war pensioner was not high. Luther had little formal schooling other than that offered by a brief term in a common school, and most of

---

[29] The *Register of Pennsylvania*, Nov. 39, 1833; *The Man*, June 29, 1835; Commons, *History of Labour*, I, 389–392; *Pennsylvanian*, June 9, 1835, and March 13, 1834; *National Laborer*, May 14, and Aug. 13, 1836; Commons, *Documentary History*, V, 325, 338, 349, 358, 375–376, and VI, 44–46; *Radical Reformer and Working Man's Advocate*, Aug. 1, 1835, p. 119.

[30] See Louis Hartz, "Seth Luther: The Story of a Working Class Rebel," *New England Quarterly*, XIII (Sept., 1940), 401–418, for a useful account of Luther's life.

his early education consisted of a stint of work in the New England mills, learning the carpenter's trade, and travel across the continent.[31] His wanderings made a great impression on him, confirming his early belief in the equality of man, including the much maligned Negro and Indian.[32] When he returned from the wilderness he began on a career consisting of a new kind of travel: he became a missionary of the workingmen.

Luther first appears on the labor scene during the ten hour strike of March, 1832, in Boston.[33] He launched his career as the leading unionist in New England by delivering an address to the striking workers.[34] His remarks, spotlighting the conditions of factory workers here and abroad, evoked an instantaneous and enthusiastic response from the workers. He was asked to repeat the lecture by the second convention of the New England Association.[35] The address was published and quickly went through three editions, gaining its author immediate fame.[36]

At this time he was in close contact with Dr. Charles Douglas (sometimes spelled Douglass), the publisher of the *New England Artisan*, the official publication of the New England Association. Douglas, at this second convention of the organization, was elected its president.[37] Luther, who wrote articles and sought subscriptions for the *Artisan*, began a fruitful alliance with Douglas that lasted for

[31] Seth Luther, *An Address on the Origins and Progress of Avarice* (Boston, 1834), pp. 39, 11–12, 39–42.

[32] *Ibid.*, pp. 38–40.

[33] *Working Man's Advocate*, April 7, 1832.

[34] Seth Luther, *An Address to the Working Men of New England . . . with particular reference to the effect of manufacturing* (3rd ed.; Philadelphia, 1836).

[35] See the Boston *Post*, Oct. 9, 1832, for the resolutions of the second convention of the New England Association, thanking Luther for his efforts in behalf of the working classes.

[36] There is an interesting disparity between Louis Hartz and Arthur Schlesinger, Jr., in assessing this document. To Hartz, it was a "crucial organizing call for the whole labor movement," which "doubtless did much to inspire future efforts at national organization," and was possessed of "bitter irony and passionate earnestness" and an "evocative symbolism" which "caught up and articulated the sentiments of workers everywhere" (*op. cit.*, p. 404). To Schlesinger, "Luther's program was routine and rather harmless, and his special diagnosis of little interest" (*op. cit.*, p. 150).

[37] On Douglas, see below.

several years. Together, they helped organize a trades' union in Boston in March of 1834.[38]

The house carpenters of Boston, one of the sixteen trades represented in the union, sent Luther as one of their two delegates to its first convention. He was elected secretary of the union and immediately became influential in its councils.[39] By June, the organization was said by sympathizers to have forty thousand members—an eightfold exaggeration, as it happened! [40] Bitter attacks on it as a secret society practicing unusual cruelties on its members evidently did not succeed very well in frightening off adherents.[41] As has been noted in an earlier chapter, the Boston union sponsored many activities, the most significant of which undoubtedly was the great ten hour strike in 1835. This lost cause served as a backdrop for one of Luther's most successful efforts, the *Ten Hour Circular,* which he drew up with the collaboration of two other unionists. As has been shown, although the circular had spectacular results elsewhere, it did not succeed in Boston. Nor could Luther's indefatigable efforts in behalf of the strike—his tour of the eastern seaboard cities, for example—turn the tide.[42]

That Luther was not thriving, either financially or physically, because of his many labor activities, is indicated by the following advertisement which appeared in a labor paper of the time:

A CARD. The undersigned being in a precarious state of health, earnestly requests all persons who are indebted to him for books to forward the amount by mail immediately. The amount due from each person may be considered small, but the aggregate would be, under present circumstances, of great benefit to me. . . . I return my sincere thanks to those who have promptly fulfilled their agreement in sending *cash* for what they have been pleased to order—those *gentlemen* who have taken books

---

[38] *The Man,* Feb. 20, 1834, contains the call to the first meeting, evidently drawn up by Luther and Douglas.

[39] *The Man,* March 7, 12, 1834.

[40] *The Man,* June 11, 1834.

[41] *New England Artisan,* May 31, June 21, and Oct. 25, 1834.

[42] All during this period Luther was busy repeating his address on factory conditions, as well as making new addresses, such as: *An Address on the Right of Free Suffrage* (Providence, 1833); *An Address Delivered Before the Mechanics and Workingmen of the City of Brooklyn* (Brooklyn, 1836).

from me and sold them and retained the money, I leave to the enjoyment of their own conscience.

Seth Luther [43]

The following year, despite his poor health, Luther attended the New York convention of the National Trades' Union, served on the ways and means committee, and spoke in favor of the ten hour day and improving the conditions of factory workers. He remained in the movement for labor and reform to the end of his life, suffering a prison sentence as a result of his participation in the free suffrage struggle in Rhode Island in the 1840s. We hear of him in 1846 still fighting for the ten hour day at a conference in New Hampshire.[44]

Charles Douglas was the other outstanding figure of the New England labor movement. Unlike Luther, Douglas had never himself been a worker. This did not prevent him from aligning himself with labor and holding prominent posts in the labor movement of the era.

Born in New London, Connecticut, Douglas spent many years in traveling around the globe, championing humane causes.[45] In 1831 he founded the weekly *New England Artisan* of Pawtucket, Rhode Island, and for three years used the columns of this journal to promote the cause of labor.[46] When he began publication of a new labor paper, the New London *Political Observer and Working Man's Friend*, in the spring of 1831, the editor of the New York *Working Man's Advocate* expressed his complete agreement with the new paper's opinions, and his admiration for "the great personal worth and editorial ability of the editors of the new paper." [47]

Douglas had become sufficiently well known to be elected the first president of the New England Association by the assembled "mechanics and workingmen" at the Boston convention in February, 1832.[48] In this organization, he urged that workers play an independent political role and that they organize factory operatives into

[43] *New England Artisan,* Sept. 6, 1834.

[44] Hartz, *loc. cit., passim;* Commons, *Documentary History,* VI, 233, 242, 245, and VIII, 122.

[45] See letter from a "Boston Correspondent," in the New York *Evening Journal,* Feb. 28, 1832; *Working Man's Advocate,* March 3, 1832.

[46] *The Man,* March 12, 1834.

[47] *Working Man's Advocate,* May 14, 1831.

[48] *Columbian Centinel,* Feb. 16, 1832.

unions. His nomination by the Democrats, in that same year, for senator from the Seventh District of Connecticut was greeted with approval by the *Working Man's Advocate*, as the nomination of "a firm friend of the workingmen and of the workingmen's measures." [49]

As has been noted, Douglas also played a leading part in the formation of a "Trades' Union of Boston and Vicinity." According to the "Proceedings of a General Convention of the Trades of Boston, March 6, 1834," Douglas presided at the formative meeting, was granted all the privileges of regular membership by the passage of a special resolution, was appointed to help draft a constitution for the union, and delivered a major address. His *New England Artisan* was voted the "official publication" of the union.[50]

When later that year the Boston union sent delegates to the first convention of the National Trades' Union, Douglas was one of three men selected. At this first convention, Douglas helped prepare an "address to the mechanics and laboring classes of the United States," and performed a number of administrative jobs.[51] During the 1836 convention of the national union, despite the fact that the Boston trades' union no longer existed, Douglas was elected to a special seat in the convention and subsequently to committees on education and the factory system.[52]

After the Panic of 1837 and the ensuing decline of the labor movement, Douglas continued to sympathize with the cause of labor and reform. In 1845 he attended the gathering of the New York Industrial Congress as an "interested person," [53] and in 1850 addressed a meeting in Boston of the state convention of the Friends of Industrial Reform, making the old point that workers should "arouse themselves to their true interests." [54]

One classic type associated with the early labor movement did not himself labor, organized no unions, and had no direct ties with any

[49] *Working Man's Advocate*, March 3, 1832.

[50] *The Man*, March 12, 1834. On Nov. 3, 1834, Douglas began to publish the Boston *Daily Reformer;* see the *Working Man's Advocate*, Nov. 8, 1834.

[51] *The Man*, Aug. 26, and Sept. 2, 1834.

[52] *National Laborer*, Oct. 29, 1836, cited in Commons, *Documentary History*, VI, 265–266.

[53] New York *Daily Tribune*, Oct. 15, 1845.

[54] *Ibid.*, Oct. 26, 1850.

group purporting to be a labor organization. His involvement in the movement consisted essentially of pro labor oratory and the general recognition accordingly conferred on him as a "friend of labor." Such a figure was Theophilus Fisk of New England. Even during that phase of his varied career when he addressed labor audiences and edited labor journals, Fisk, who evidently was a man of great energy, devoted himself to numerous other causes which had little or nothing to do with labor.[55]

Fisk was born in New England just after the turn of the nineteenth century. After training in his youth for the Universalist ministry, he gave up this career to become a vehement critic of organized religion in the late 1820s and early 1830s, as the publisher of the journals *Priestcraft Unmasked* and the *New Haven Examiner*.[56] Before long he became a critic of social abuses, delivering a series of hard-hitting lectures before Boston unionists during the winter of 1834–1835. One of his lectures, "Capital Against Labor," delivered in Boston at Julien Hall in May, 1835, was especially favorably received and reprinted in pro labor newspapers.[57]

He now became co-editor of the Boston *Reformer*, previously edited by Douglas, continuing its policy of supporting the labor movement.[58] In October of 1835, during the second convention of the National Trades' Union at New York City, Fisk, who had been voted an honorary membership in the group, delivered a special address to the delegates.[59] After giving up the editorship of the *Reformer*, Fisk went south in 1836 to lecture in behalf of labor's rights as against capital. He so antagonized one audience as to provoke a demonstration of physical violence against him. Not all southern audiences resented his remarks, however, for he opposed abolition quite as much as he did the exploitation of labor. In fact, during the last years of his life, although he continued to edit newspapers,

[55] See Joseph Dorfman, "The Jackson Wage-Earner Thesis," p. 298.

[56] Arthur Schlesinger, Jr., *op. cit.*, p. 169.

[57] *Working Man's Advocate*, July 25, 1835; New York *Evening Post*, Aug. 6, 1835.

[58] Schlesinger thinks that Fisk was a more effective editor than Douglas, and that the paper became much livelier under his direction (*op. cit.*, p. 170).

[59] *National Trades' Union*, Oct. 10, 1835, cited in Commons, *Documentary History*, VI, 238.

these were now preoccupied with the issue of slavery, denouncing extremists on both sides of the issue.[60]

The New York City labor movement was unique in that its trades' union leaders, whatever their faults or questionable traits, were in fact men who had spent some time in the ranks as craftsmen or journeymen workers. Probably the best known labor leader not only in New York but in the nation was Ely Moore. Since his career has been carefully examined by Walter Hugins, there is no need here to do more than indicate briefly the character of Moore's activities.[61]

Moore was elected the first president of the "General Trades' Union of New York City" that developed in August, 1833, out of the strike of the journeymen carpenters for higher wages.[62] He also was elected the first president of the National Trades' Union. When he was elected to the House of Representatives in the fall of 1834, as the candidate of the Democratic party, it was thus generally believed that labor had succeeded in sending its leading figure to the United States Congress.[63]

Moore was born July 4, 1798, in rural New Jersey. He early had learned the printer's trade, although his opponents charged that he actually had spent little time in it.[64] He married well, taking "advantage of his fortunate connection" to speculate in land and rise in the hierarchy of the Democratic party. According to Hugins, he was far more interested in politics than in trade unionism, as was evidenced by his failure to organize a union or lead a strike. In fact, Hugins' conclusion is that "Moore's success story tells, not of a worker's rise to a position of leadership through trade-union activity, but rather of an ambitious middle-class politician who, by capitalizing upon a brief early history as a journeyman printer, endeavored to advance his

---

[60] See the Boston *Reformer*, Aug. 4, 1837, cited in Schlesinger, *op. cit.*, p. 236.

[61] When he was a graduate student at Columbia in 1947, Hugins wrote as his master's essay, "Ely Moore the Case History of a Jacksonian Labor Leader." For his later writings on Moore, see note 23, above.

[62] See New York *Morning Courier and Enquirer*, May, June, 1833; John Finch, *Rise and Progress of the General Trades Union of the City of New York and its Vicinity* (New York, 1833).

[63] *The Man*, Aug. 27, and Sept. 26, 1834.

[64] *Daily Whig*, June 7, 1839, and *Evening Star*, Oct. 31, 1839, cited in Hugins, "Ely Moore: The Case History . . . ," *Political Science Quarterly*, LXV (March, 1950), 111.

own and his party's political fortunes." [65] There is no question that Moore's prominence was due in large part to his flamboyant oratory.

During his period of labor leadership, he edited the *National Trades' Union*, a leading labor journal. But it was his speeches on labor issues which accounted for his popularity. It was this popularity which enabled him to escape with reputation almost unscathed from the one storm which threatened his position, early in 1835—the controversy about his role in the prison-labor issue.[66] After his election to Congress and his re-election in 1837, he relinquished his direct ties with the labor movement. Over the last twenty years of his life he served as surveyor of the Port of New York, a United States Marshal, publisher of a rural journal, agent for Indian tribes, and a registrar for the government land office at Lecompton, Kansas.[67]

Even more of a political opportunist than Moore was another leader of the New York trades' union movement, Levi D. Slamm, who was born in New York City at the beginning of the nineteenth century. Slamm was a controversial figure well hated both within and without the labor movement, whose enemies effectively blackened his reputation with many of his contemporaries and with many later students.[68] Although Slamm may not have been undeserving of his bad reputation, some evidence can be interpreted as presenting him in a decent light. And, likable or no, he was indubitably a leader of the labor movement. Doubts raised as to how long he really was a journeyman in the society he led do not affect the fact that he was a leader and one selected for such a role by journeymen workers.

A leader of the Journeymen Locksmith's society, Slamm represented his organization in the General Trades' Union of New York

---

[65] *Ibid.*, pp. 107, 108–113.

[66] Moore, who late in 1834 and been appointed by the state of New York as one of three commissioners to report on the prison-labor question, had signed his name to a joint report which had little criticism to make of the system. The union and its supporters, to whom prison labor was an undisguised menace, were aghast, and for a time demands were raised that Moore be ousted from his positions in the New York City union, the National Trades' Union, and his seat in Congress. Eventually, Moore rode out the storm. See *The Man*, Feb. 26, and March 2, 7, 30, 1835; *Working Man's Advocate*, March 7, 1835. Later, the *Daily Plebeian* carried a "vindication" of Moore in its issue of Aug. 19, 1842.

[67] "Ely Moore," *Dictionary of American Biography*.

[68] See the treatment accorded Slamm in Hugins, *Jacksonian Democracy and the Working Class*, p. 69.

and vicinity.[69] A tireless worker, Slamm not only became the corresponding secretary of the trades' union but a member of a number of its committees, a formulator of resolutions, and one of five
directors responsible for the publication of a union journal, early in
1836.[70] He was sufficiently well known and respected to be chosen as
one of the delegates to the National Trades' Union conventions in
1835 and 1836, at which he was active in framing resolutions, writing
up proceedings, and formulating prison-labor policy. He worked on
several committees and also was corresponding secretary of the
national union for one year.[71]

The labor movement was a springboard from which Slamm cata-
pulted into New York politics in the last part of the decade. The split
of the Tammany organization that produced the Loco Focos in the
fall of 1835 also provided Slamm with a new outlet for his energies
and ambition.[72] He became active in the new reform group. Conservative opponents of the movement, anxious to implant the notion of its
Jack Cade-ish character, saw to it that his name was kept alive, by
referring to the Equal Rights party as "Slamm, Bang and Company."
In fact, one colleague believed that with any other name, his contributions to the party would have gone unnoticed.[73]

Slamm was one of thirteen candidates nominated by the Loco
Focos for the state assembly in 1837. He was evidently respected for
the part he played at the protest meeting of June 13, 1836, against the
sentencing of the journeymen tailors by Judge Edwards.[74] He had
defied the state legislature despite a threat of arrest that was held over
his head.[75] Having proved his devotion to the cause, he was rewarded accordingly. Shortly after the 1837 elections, he was elected
recording secretary of the new party, but the honor turned out to be

[69] *The Man*, March 2, 30, 1835.

[70] The *Union*, April 21, 1836.

[71] Commons, *Documentary History*, VI, 228–229, 244–245, 249–250, 258, 265,
267–269, 297–298.

[72] See FitzWilliam Byrdsall, *History of the Loco-Foco or Equal Rights Party*
(New York, 1842); Carl N. Degler, "An Inquiry into the Loco-Foco Party"
(Master's essay, Columbia University, 1947).

[73] Byrdsall, *op. cit.*, p. 134.

[74] The *Union*, June 14, 1836.

[75] Byrdsall, *op. cit.*, p. 119.

ephemeral. The panic was on, and in the ensuing wreckage was to be found the Loco Focos, together with most other labor and reform organizations of the period.[76] In the period that followed, Slamm devoted himself to Democratic party politics and to furthering his own publishing career. First, he assumed control of a liberal journal, the *New Era,* for a brief period, early in 1840, and then several years later he edited and published the *Daily Plebeian,* together with its weekend companion, the *Weekly Plebeian.* Though these papers lasted for nearly three years, and at times enjoyed wide circulation, Slamm seems to have been beset by financial worries throughout this phase of his career.[77] His efforts as an editor earned him the plaudits of Democratic stalwarts, but at the cost of the emnity of some of his earlier associates.[78] The charge was spread by enemies that Slamm was for sale to the highest bidder, unscupulous in his dealings with individuals, and altogether unprincipled.[79] It was also said that he had little ability and that his rise to whatever small eminence he had achieved was due to his intriguing and scheming, rather than to his

---

[76] Byrdsall, in fact, places the blame for the demise of the party on Slamm's shoulders, since as recording secretary he called no meetings after his election to office. But that this perhaps colored judgment—Slamm had replaced Byrdsall in the office—does explain the downfall of the insurgents is highly unlikely (*ibid.,* p. 188).

[77] See the *Weekly Plebeian,* December 7, 1844, for an account of the great increase in circulation of the *Daily Plebeian,* a growth, however, that was not accompanied by a like growth in its advertising. The last issue of the *Daily Plebeian,* May 12, 1845, describes the harrowing financial circumstances that had overtaken Slamm.

[78] In 1840 Slamm was nominated for the post of assistant alderman by a Democratic meeting in the Tenth Ward (*New Era,* April 8, 14, 1840).

[79] Mike Walsh, whose "Spartan Band" of young men with fists often dominated Democratic meetings, had a consuming hatred for Slamm. Walsh's paper, the *Subterranean,* the lecture platform, letters, the street—in short, any medium that was available—were used to pour abuse on Slamm's head. To Walsh, whose abuse was like no one else's, Slamm was full of "impudence and elastic, pliable India rubber conscience"; he was a "noxious stinkweed," a "blackmaster," also a "compound of vanity, roguery and imbecility"; a "poor devil upon whose mental soil it was impossible to cultivate an idea, as it is to raise fine apples in an iceberg." Thus, Walsh raved on through sundry other vilifications. See Mike Walsh, "Speech at County Meeting of Tammany [1841]," in Walsh, *Sketches of the Life of Mike Walsh* (New York, 1843), pp. 27–29. Slamm dragged Walsh into court for libel, but was unable to win a verdict against him (*Daily Plebeian,* September 1, and October 17, 1843). Though not resorting to abuse, Byrdsall regarded Slamm as an overrated man, attracted only to the surface of things, and interested only in his own personal advance (*op. cit.,* p. 134).

talents. Even one of his harshest critics, however, could not agree with the latter assertion.[80]

Slamm's attempts to pander first to one and then to another faction of the Democratic party in the 1840s do not make an appealing picture.[81] Yet, even during this phase of his career, his writings show that he continued as always to be an ardent champion of the labor movement.

By all odds, the most popular of the New York union leaders was John Commerford, described by Byrdsall as an honest "mechanic of considerable talent as a political speaker." [82] No snide questions were or have since been raised about this man, for he was an honest-to-goodness journeyman mechanic, who rose from the ranks in the chairmakers' trade, single-mindedly devoted his life to the cause of labor and reform, and was possessed of a manner and personality which evoked universal praise.

Commerford was one of the few leaders whose career spanned both the Working Men's party and the trades' unions, for he had been active in a Brooklyn organization which in 1830 supported the Owen and Evans' faction of the New York Working Men.[83] In the early 1830s he became the leader of the Chairmakers' and Gilders' Society, representing them in the General Trades' Union of New York. Before he was chosen as president of the New York Union in 1835, Commerford performed a wide variety of services for the organization. A list of these is suggestive: He drew up the resolution supporting a strike of Newark cordwainers; he was on the committee which expressed the union's opinion of the state prison-labor report; he helped the cabinetmakers draw up a new "book of prices"; he was on the committees to check the financial situation of the Leather Dressers' Society, to investigate the price situation of the Poughkeepsie Cordwainers, to go to Poughkeepsie to support the

[80] Byrdsall unwittingly makes a point for Slamm when he reprints an official reprimand of Slamm by the New York State legislature, which states: "You, Mr. Slamm, though younger in years [than a colleague], have exhibited before this House proof of intellectual endowment, which cannot fail to gain for your opinions and conduct, an influence which they would not otherwise carry with them (*ibid.*, p. 119).

[81] See Hugins, *Jacksonian Democracy and the Working Class*, p. 69.

[82] Byrdsall, *op. cit.*, pp. 51–52; see also Hugins, *Jacksonian Democracy and the Working Class*, pp. 72–74.

[83] *Sentinel and Working Man's Advocate*, Aug. 4, 1830; *Working Man's Advocate* Oct. 23 1830, cited in Hugins, *Jacksonian Democracy* . . . , p. 238.

strike there, to report on the union's financial status, to arrange a
second anniversary celebration, to support the oBston ten hour
strike, and to invite Seth Luther and other Boston delegates to
address the New York organization.

After his election, he was placed on the committees to draw up a
report criticizing the New York City Common Council for refusing
to provide a room to the National Trades' Union for its annual convention; to communicate with the Philadelphia labor movement
about the ten hour strike; to prepare amendments to the Union constitution; to prepare plans for a daily paper to be put out by the
Union; and to report on Judge Savage's decision against striking
New York City workingmen. He was chosen to draw up a resolution congratulating the members of a newly formed Albany trades'
union; and in 1835 he made the major address at the second anniversary celebration of the New York City trades' union.[84] He also
edited the daily newspaper of the New York union, the *Union*, a
journal designed "to advocate the social rights and interests of the
mechanics generally." [85]

His record in the National Trades' Union was also a full one. The
Proceedings tell us that "John Commerford, Journeymen Chair-
maker's Society" delegate to the convention of 1834, was elected corresponding secretary of the organization. In the following years he
served as recording secretary and treasurer.[86]

As was true of other New York labor and reform figures of the
time, Commerford was keenly interested in political activity and
played an important part in the Loco Foco movement. After the
Panic of 1837, like John Ferral and other laborites, he became a fol-
lower of Evans' land reform cause and worked in this movement for
the rest of his life.[87]

[84] *The Man*, Dec. 20, 1834; March 2, 17, 30; June 29; July 6; and Sept. 2, 1835;
also, *National Trades' Union*, May 2, 23, 30; June 13; Aug. 1, 15; Nov. 28, 1835;
Jan. 16, 30; and March 12, 1836; *Working Man's Advocate*, Sept. 19, 1835; the
Union, April, 1836.

[85] Byrdsall, *op. cit.*, p. 51; the *Union*, April 25, and May 16, 1836.

[86] *The Man*, Aug. 27, and Sept. 2, 1835; *National Trades' Union*, Oct. 10, 1835;
National Laborer, Oct. 29, and Nov. 5, 12, 1836, cited in Commons, *Documentary History*, VI, 265, 266.

[87] Byrdsall, *op. cit.*; Degler, *loc. cit.*; Masquerier, *Sociology of the Reconstruction of Society* (New York, 1877), *passim*; Schlesinger, *op. cit.*, pp. 258,
348, 492; Hugins, *Jacksonian Democracy* . . . , p. 74.

What significant generalizations are afforded by the varied labor careers of the unionists? These leaders of the early trades' union movement differ markedly from their present-day counterparts. They were not business unionists. A Luther and a Douglas were social reform agitators, as well as trades' union leaders, their interests ranging far beyond those problems directly relevant to unions. Varied types of affiliation to the labor movement could bestow leadership on an individual. A man could be an active officer, like Commerford, an editor of a sympathetic journal, like Brothers, a fiery orator or pamphleteer, like Fisk, and be accounted a leading spokesman for American labor in each case.

A number of the early leaders seemed interested primarily in political careers. Moore, Slamm, and English used their union careers as springboards from which to leap into Democratic party politics. While they did not give up their labor sympathies, it seems clear that they considered the trades' union movement a means to an end.

Most of the leaders spent only a short time in the labor movement. Luther, Commerford, and Ferral, who tried to organize workingmen and who remained active in various labor organizations for a number of years, were unusual in their staying power.

They did not lead trades' unions because they had worked up from the ranks, for the most part. Oratorical ability and power of pen, rather than long years spent in a trade, determined the parts played by Douglas, English, Slamm, Moore, and even the "carpenter," Luther.

The unique characteristics of the Jacksonian labor leaders were very much the product of the equally unique movement they led. Short-lived unions determined the brief careers of their leaders. A labor movement whose members hoped to be spared the dismal experience of a factory system or their reduction to the status of permanent wage workers, could and did easily proffer leadership to men who were not themselves workers. The time was ripe for men interested in leading labor primarily because they were convinced they knew the path to its redemption. In such an atmosphere there was room at the top of the labor movement for social reformers and relatively educated men, as well as for dedicated journeymen mechanics.

PART THREE

The Social Philosophies and Beliefs of the Leaders

7

Children of the Enlightenment

To read the many statements made by the Jacksonian labor leaders on every variety of social issue is to be back in the world, not of the nineteenth, but of the eighteenth century. For although the American Revolution had occurred more than a half-century before their time, the labor leaders continued to speak the language of the generation of Jefferson, Paine, and the Adamses, and to advocate the theories of John Locke. What gives a certain charm to their utterances is their freshness and their naïve enthusiasm, as though for all the world these doctrines were original with them or, at the least, of recent origin, put forth only yesterday or the day before. The grandiloquent rhetoric they used was undoubtedly an attempt to capture the style of the eighteenth-century political and social philosophers. This bombast sometimes obscured but did not altogether hide the kernel of ideas contained therein: the writings and speeches of the Jacksonian labor leaders show that they were children of the Enlightenment.

They were ardent believers in natural laws and natural rights. Every man, they believed, was born with these rights, and to secure them, men had forfeited the freedom of the state of nature and formed themselves into a society. Artificial social institutions too often had resulted in human misery, however, frustrating nature's benevolent designs for man. Happiness would result when society's institutions would be changed, enabling men to realize their natural rights. When they spoke of natural rights, however, the labor leaders meant something not dreamed of by Thomas Jefferson or John Adams.

Natural rights had never been given a universally approved definition. The concept had been a two-edged sword, used on the one hand both by parliamentary opponents of the Stuarts or by American opponents of the Parliament, in each case as philosophical justification for political rebellion, and on the other, by the exponents of conservative economic doctrines, who taught that movements for the redistribution of wealth, or even for social reform, were violations of the natural right to property. The labor spokesmen, in common with a small number of English thinkers, discovered different implications in Lockean doctrine.

English radicals had found hitherto unexplored riches in Locke's political treatises. In contrast to the political reformers who "took from Locke the theories of the social and political compact," the agrarians "appealed to Locke for the truth of their first principle that the land was originally held in common." Anticapitalist writers "based themselves, in addition to these self-evident truths, on Locke's theory that labour was the real title to property." [1] The harsh English poor law, for example, was attacked on the ground that it violated the natural rights of the poor. Its critics argued that "men, by renouncing their community rights, reserved to themselves, or could not have abandoned, the right to existence; the maintenance of the poor was thus guaranteed by the social compact, or by the law of nature." [2] English radicals and reformers of the early nineteenth century could base almost every call for social change in the interests of the laboring poor on the theory of natural rights. Their Jacksonian labor brethren took note.

The writings and speeches of the American labor leaders abound with references to the laws of nature or to natural rights. Despite variations in their definitions of the terms, they were as one in stressing their social or economic rather than their political implications. At one extreme stood Ely Moore. While equating the right to self-government with the right of revolution, he nevertheless stressed the right of fortunate or able men to achieve great wealth, secure against the attacks of social levelers. At the other extreme stood Thomas Skidmore. In answer to the question, "What are rights?" he replied, "the title which each of the inhabitants of this globe has to partake of and enjoy equally with his fellows, its fruits and its productions." To him natural rights meant the right of all members of society on their coming of age, whether born of the rich or the poor, to an equal share of society's property. For without property, life, liberty, and the pursuit of happiness were meaningless slogans. (Certainly one strand of Enlightenment thought can be detected in his revision of Descartes: "I am; therefore is property mine." Or in his declara-

---

[1] Max Beer, *A History of British Socialism* (2 vols.; London, 1948), I, 101–102.
[2] *Ibid.*, p. 105.

tion that man's right to property derives from the mere fact of his birth; because he exists, "rather than because of any *circumstance* attending his birth, such as the *place*, the *parties present* at his entrance into life, *particular* parents, rather than other parents, or any other parents, or any other ridiculous reason whatever.")

Being sensible men, most of the labor spokesmen went to some pains to disassociate themselves from Skidmore's "agrarian" views, as they were called.[3] Yet the fact is that their interpretation of natural rights was closer to Skidmore's than to Moore's. For although they might express, publicly and explicitly, repugnance for agrarianism, their actual beliefs were not very far removed from it. Even Skidmore's great enemy in the Working Men's movement, Robert Dale Owen, agreed that wealth derived through the labor of others was an outrage against nature, and that nature's laws proclaimed the ascendancy of the general, or community, good over that of the individual. Stephen Simpson, the Philadelphia Working Men's leader, might hold with Moore that perfect equality was impossible, in view of the unequal abilities nature had allocated to men, but he also agreed with Skidmore that it was essentially due to artificial institutions that nature's beneficent plan for the happiness of all men was upset. For that matter, while Moore himself believed that a superior individual "had a perfect right to all the advantages which result from those superior gifts" bestowed on him by nature, his central belief that an individual's own abilities should determine his fortune is close to Skidmore's view that one's wealth or status should not be the result of parental wealth or influence. John Ferral, the Pennsylvania unionist, spoke for most of the leaders when he said that the "accumulation of the wealth of society in the hands of a few individuals . . . is subversive of the rights of man."

The essential meaning of natural rights according to the Jacksonian labor leaders, however, was the right of labor to enjoy the fruits of its own work, or to what European radicals and socialists of the nineteenth century called the whole product of labor. The New England labor leader, Charles Douglas, spoke for most of his colleagues when he said that for workers to reap the fruits of their own labor "is just as it should be. It is in accordance with the laws of nature and the immutable principles of right and justice." Simp-

---

[3] See chapters ten and eleven, below.

son read into nature's laws not only the decree that labor alone is entitled to what it has produced; he interpreted the original social contract as a binding assurance that this maxim would be respected. It is true, however, that the term "labor" meant different things to different men in that era: it is not always clear precisely which groups or which activities were meant to be gathered under the rubric. What is clear, however, is the great extent to which the labor leaders relied on the doctrine of natural rights and the similarity between their interpretation of it and that of radical European contemporaries.[4]

They were also given to theorizing about human nature. Here, too, they were in the debt of the Enlightenment for their belief in the plasticity of the human personality and the dominant part played by man's environment in shaping it. Probably nothing is more responsible for the antique flavor of much of their rhetoric than its preoccupation with man's nature; and this not because their views on the matter agreed with this or that thinker, but rather because they were expressed at all, and with the seriousness, enthusiasm, and conviction that marked the discussion of man in the Age of Reason and its aftermath.

They regarded human nature as a mixed baggage, made up of a motley assortment of traits ranging from perverse to sublime. Wondrous powers combined with grievous faults in the human personality, complicating all attempts to fashion a model society. Perhaps the most serious weakness of man, in their judgment, was his selfishness. In a typical statement, Simpson wrote that man was innately

---

[4] For the views of the labor leaders on natural rights, see Seth Luther, *An Address to the Working Men of New England . . . with particular reference to the effect of manufacturing* (3rd ed.; Philadelphia, 1836), p. 5; also Luther, *An Address on the Right of Free Suffrage* (Providence, 1833); Ely Moore, *Oration Delivered before the Mechanics and Workingmen of the City of New York* (New York, 1843); also Moore, *Address on Civil Government* (New York, 1847), pp. 20, 28–29; Thomas Skidmore, *The Rights of Man to Property* (New York, 1829), pp. 32, 44, 54, 59, 60, 133, 357: Robert Dale Owen's articles in the New York *Free Enquirer*, Jan. 9, 1830, and the New York *Working Man's Advocate*, Jan. 16, 1830; also Owen, *Lectures on the Marriages of the Priesthood of the Old Immoral World* (London, 1835), p. 50; Stephen Simpson, *The Working Man's Manual* (Philadelphia, 1831), pp. 52–53, 57, 67, 136, 138, 224; John Ferral's article in *The Man*, Aug. 29, 1834; Charles Douglas' article in the Pawtucket *New England Artisan*, June 21, 1834; and Thomas Brothers' editorial in the *Radical Reformer and Working Man's Advocate*, Aug. 29, 1835, p. 178.

"selfish, ambitious, proud, avaricious, and vain, [and] delights in being superior to his fellows; and even when the desire of fortune is gratified, the habit of extortion and the ambition of riches remain." The abundance of nature is frustrated precisely by "the corrupting, the debasing passions of man." George Henry Evans believed that, apart from a few exceptional men, in general, "it is rarely that we find individuals who are disinterested enough to devote themselves to the task of ameliorating the hardships which oppress the mass of society, *particularly in opposition to their own interests.*" Seth Luther devoted a pamphlet to a study of this near fatal flaw in human character.

Greed or avarice, as he called it, was "the mainspring of crime, in all its thousand shapes and forms." Latent in all of us, it cuts across class lines "and thrives in our bosoms; its influence is felt more or less in all parts, and classes, and degrees of society." Luther's conclusion that an "insatiable appetite for gold" had "destroyed the happiness of the many, that the few may roll and riot in splendid luxury," was shared by William English and John Commerford. As a good child of the Enlightenment, however, Luther held society "accountable for all the evils produced by this hateful monster with the sting of a scorpion, and the fangs of a viper." For like most of his fellows in the labor movement, Luther was an environmentalist in his interpretation of the process of human character development.

"A child, as soon as he can put two ideas together, is taught to believe, by the example and precept of his parents, that *money* is the most valuable thing on earth," Luther wrote. Thus society not only turned man's latent flaws to bad account; it created them in the first place. Douglas felt that only bad institutions and bad laws had perverted man's character. Levi Slamm believed with Robert Dale Owen that though man was naturally weak and irresolute, he was "not by nature corrupt . . . his vices are generally the result of his poverty, the circumstances in which he is placed, the society by which he is surrounded." Crime, according to Slamm, was due primarily not to man's natural depravity but rather to the maldistribution of wealth.

Not that man was totally depraved, even in a class society. Some of the leaders agreed with the classical economists that egotism was a valuable force for promoting both the individual's and the community's welfare. According to Moore, if self-love stimulated man "to a contest for power and dominion," "this prevailing disposition of the human heart, so far from being an evil in itself, is . . . essential to the welfare of society. The selfish generate the social feelings." Simpson remarked on the valuable consequences of man's intense curiosity, his "thirst for novelty" (an alleged thirst that was the foundation stone of the theory of the French utopian Fourier). Owen also detected a Faustian impulse, "a restless spirit of curiosity; an unsatisfied thirst after novelty; an irrepressible desire to see, to hear, to feel, to know—to discover whatever is hidden, and to approach whatever is distant." Douglas found that coexisting with selfishness was "the inherent kindness of the human heart." Perhaps there is significance in the fact that the two leaders who favored the most drastic reorganization of society, tended to see man's nature in the most favorable light. Skidmore held that if men had a failing it was only in the patience with which they accepted social evils. But he had no doubts about human decency. "No man," he wrote, "makes a greater mistake than when he supposes a vast majority of mankind are not honest. I build my system on the moral constitution of man." Ferral depicted man as an uncomplicated being whose innocent search for happiness was frustrated not by his own flaws but by society's.[5]

In no respect was their thinking more typical of the Enlightenment than in its optimism. Their environmentalism accounted for their hopefulness: since human imperfections were merely the product of a society organized in a peculiar way, all that was necessary to get rid of the blemishes was to refashion society. "As he is treated in society, so will he rise or fall in the scale of human excellence," Simpson said of man. Despite differences in their interpretations of human nature or society's laws, his colleagues agreed with

[5] The views on human nature that have been used in the discussion are taken from the following: Simpson, *Working Man's Manual*, pp. 26, 66, 223; George Henry Evans in the *Working Man's Advocate*, Jan. 23, 1830; Luther, *An Address on the Origins and Progress of Avarice* (Boston, 1834), pp. 6, 7, 19–21, 26; William English, "Oration Delivered at the Trades' Union Celebration of the 4th of July," *Radical Reformer and Working Man's Advocate*, Aug. 1, 1835, p. 126; John Commerford, "Address Delivered Before the General Trades' Union," the *Union*, April 26; May 26, and June 10, 1836; Douglas, "Address to the Mechanics," *New England Artisan*, Sept. 6, 1833; Owen, *A Lecture on Consistency* (London, 1841), p. 3; and Owen, *Lectures on the Marriages of the Priesthood. . .*, p. 47; Levi D. Slamm, in the *Daily Plebeian*, Feb. 9, 1844; Moore, *Address Delivered Before the General Trades' Union of the City of New York* (New York, Dec. 2, 1833), pp. 7–8; Skidmore, *Rights of Man to Property*, pp. 10–11, 345–346; Ferral, in *The Man*, Aug. 29, 1834.

him that the good society was close at hand. The course of working-men, wrote their good friend Theophilus Fisk, has been "upward and onward until now they are enabled from the proud eminence to which they have attained to look forward and behold the promised land."

As a good child of the eighteenth century, Skidmore believed that the cure of society's ills would simply follow a rational explanation of the disease. An attentive mankind, once cognizant of the true condition of things, would act to set them right. "Henceforward," he wrote, "let a writer advance views that will benefit the great mass of the community; and there will be found no powers adequate to stay their adoption." Skidmore's early success in the New York Working Men's movement undoubtedly strengthened his naïve conviction that a high-minded, logical treatise would change the world and that he, Thomas Skidmore, would be its author.

If other labor leaders offered different explanations as to why utopia was within sight, they nevertheless saw the future through the same rose-colored glasses. Owen believed that an improved technology was the good fairy that would make possible a system of equality and a race of happy and magnificently educated men. The young Owen was overcome with emotion at the thought of a community educated in accordance with his principles: "Who can even imagine the change it will produce throughout society? The world has never yet seen a republic of cultivated freemen, but the next generation will see it. I would I might live to witness such a spectacle, afterwards, I could die contented and happy." (Owen lived more than fifty years after he wrote these words, but if he never saw his predictions come to pass, he doubtless bore up well, since in his riper years he discarded his belief both in technology and education, for the solace of "spiritual religion.")

Simpson, Slamm, and Moore agreed not only that a happy future was at hand but that the main reason it would be achieved here, rather than in Europe, was the greater abundance of this country and therefore the relatively superior situation of the American worker. American workingmen would of course have to exercise much wisdom in translating potential abundance into actual. But if Moore had some doubts as to whether the necessary good sense would be displayed, Slamm had few, and Simpson seemed to have none whatever.

Some of the more aggressive leaders based their optimism concerning the future of the working class on the growing militance of labor. To Douglas, labor's independent political action was the main source of hope. In his rhetoric, the laboring class would shortly achieve that station "to which it is entitled by the laws of nature," while "at no former time . . . has their prospect of final success appeared so flattering," because and since "the working class first dared to act on the all-important subject of selecting agents from among themselves to transact their legislative business." Ferral, on the other hand, was struck by labor's economic activity and power. The successful ten hour strike of Pennsylvania workers in 1835 moved him to exclaim: "How bright and cheering are the future prospects of the human family—what is there of happiness that may not be hoped from this auspicious commencement of reform, which, if radically carried out, must in the end, annihilate the various inequality [sic] that now pervades society." Commerford's vision of the future included a grim scene in which workers, who had "followed their oppressors like shadows," paid them back tenfold, "for their many aggressions on the rights and happiness of their fellow men." If this happy day of retribution was at hand, it was due in part to the fact that workingmen were seeing things in a clearer light, as well as to the refusal of such leaders as Commerford to relapse into a "hopeless fatalism" that was "destructive to the well being of mankind." In this sense, optimism was not merely a pleasant emotional state; it was a necessary weapon in the struggle for social justice.

A hasty reading of the Jacksonian labor leaders' description of their contemporary society, marked, as we shall see it was, by a preoccupation with misery and squalor, might suggest that their optimism was in some way paradoxical or that it contradicted a gloomier bent of mind. Actually there was no contradiction. As is the case with such realists as Zola or Daumier, it was because they were social reformers that they were drawn to the unlovely aspects of society. And it is because as *social* reformers they regarded human problems as ephemeral—due to temporary societal maladjustments rather than to man's innate shortcomings or the nature of things—that they were optimistic.[6]

[6] The quotations and allusions to the optimism of the labor leaders are taken from the following: Skidmore, *op. cit.,* pp. 10–11, 14; Owen, in the New Harmony *Gazette*, Dec. 6, 1826, p. 79; Owen, in the *Free Enquirer*, May 8, 1830, and also Owen, *An Address on Free Inquiry* (London, 1840), p. 3; Simpson, *The*

A few of the intellectuals in the labor movement subscribed enthusiastically to the hostility shown by one strand of Enlightenment thought toward organized religion. Owen and Fisk, for example, denounced religion's justification of the status quo, its tendency to rationalize the oppression of the laboring poor.[7] Most of their colleagues, however, confined their discussion to secular matters. What made them children of the Enlightenment was not their denunciation of superstition, but their disingenuous beliefs in natural law, natural rights, and the plasticity—and therefore perfectibility—both of human nature and human society.

Working Man's Manual, pp. 71, 89; Slamm, in the *Daily Plebeian*, July 24, and Oct. 12, 1844; Moore, *Address Delivered Before the General Trades' Union*, p. 30; and also Moore, *Oration Delivered Before the Mechanics and Workingmen*, p. 15; Douglas, in the *New England Artisan*, Dec. 6, 1833, and May 31, 1834; Ferral, to the editor of the *Radical Reformer and Working Man's Advocate*, July 4, 1835, p. 62; and Commerford, "Address Delivered Before the General Trades' Union," *The Man*, May 25, 1836.

[7] For Owen's early criticism of religion, see Owen, *A Sermon on Loyalty* (London, n.d.), p. 3; and the *Free Enquirer*, April 10, and June 26, 1830. After he became converted to religion, Owen held that the main shortcoming in his father's work as a reformer was the lack of a spiritual element in his program. "He limited his view of man to the first three score and ten years of his life, ignoring the illimitable future beyond. But the Secular school can never prevail against the Spiritual. It has nothing to offer but this world, and that is insufficient for man"; (Owen, *Threading My Way* [New York, 1874], p. 296). For Fisk's view, see *Priesthood Unmasked*.

8

American Society in Their Eyes:
A Study in Bleakness

The picture of American society painted by the Jacksonian labor leaders was a grim one indeed, preoccupied as they were with the nation's discordant and unlovely elements. It was very much a minority viewpoint, since most of their eminent contemporaries saw a very different social landscape, marked by comparative equality and widespread abundance. The favorable reputation enjoyed by the decade prior to the Panic of 1837 as years of social and economic growth and opportunity rather than of unrelieved gloom, points to the greater persuasiveness of the more roseate picture depicted by such Americans as Henry Carey, Philip Hone, or Edward Everett, and such European visitors to our shores as Michael Chevalier and Harriet Martineau.[1] As is true of all but statistical comments about society, the words of the labor reformers tell us more about the men who said them than of the conditions they describe— but this generalization applies equally to their yea-saying contemporaries. The available evidence concerning social and economic conditions in the late 1820s and the 1830s is neither massive nor conclusive, and has in fact been interpreted quite differently by different modern authorities.[2] Fortunately, the concern of this chapter is less

[1] For a view that nearly all was well in America, see Henry Carey, *Essay on the Rate of Wages* (Philadelphia, 1835), pp. 89–90; Allan Nevins, ed., *The Diary of Philip Hone 1828–1851* (2 vols.; New York, 1927), I, 41; Edward Everett, in a speech before the Friends of Domestic Industry, reported in the (Boston) *Columbian Centinel*, Oct. 29, 1831; Michael Chevalier, *Society, Manners and Politics in the United States* (Boston, 1839), *passim;* Harriet Martineau, *Society in America* (New York, 1837), vol. II, pp. 53–60; and the editorials of such journals as the New York *Commercial Advertiser* and the Boston *Columbian Centinel.*

[2] Cf. Ernest L. Bogart and Charles M. Thompson, *Readings in the Economic History of the United States* (New York, 1916), pp. 524–525; Harold U. Faulkner, *American Economic History* (New York, 1943), p. 310; Alvin H. Hansen, "Factors Affecting the Trend of Real Wages," *American Economic Review,* XV (March, 1925), 32; John R. Commons and Associates, *History of Labour in the United States* (New York, 1918), I, 348–350. See also Chapter 2 above.

with what in fact *was*—or history as actuality—than with what certain men, the Jacksonian labor leaders, *believed* to be the case. Right or wrong, their description of society provides us with an invaluable Rohrshach into the social consciousness, and perhaps the unconscious, as well, of a significant group of Americans.

It may well be that they were drawn to the seamy side of things because of inner drives characteristic of the psychic patterns of social malcontents, rather than because of the objective existence of glaring wrongs. There seems no question but that certain Enlightenment principles concerning man and society had hardened into fixed convictions which colored the observations a number of them made of their surroundings. The wish was the father to the thought of others; and I suppose it could be said of all of them that they saw what they wanted to see. All of which suggests that like the rest of the species, when the Jacksonian labor leaders turned their gaze on society, they saw with more than their eyes.

One feature of the American scene fixed their attention and emerged as the pervasive theme of their canvas: Poverty. For as they saw it, not a minority but rather the mass of Americans lived under appalling material conditions. As good idealists who believed that men lived by more than bread alone, the labor leaders found the physical want experienced by the poor less galling than the bleak emotional and intellectual lives that the poverty-stricken were doomed to lead. For as all good environmentalists knew, the material conditions of men determined their thought and feeling.

Almost all of the leaders saw the same scene, regardless of how they might differ in personality or background. George Henry Evans, who would prove to be a durable fighter in the reform cause; the aristocratic Robert Dale Owen, a doctrinaire dilettante of sorts in the workers' political movement; the irate pro labor small capitalist Thomas Brothers; the opportunistic Stephen Simpson; the ubiquitous Charles Douglas; the dedicated trade unionist John Commerford— these and their colleagues all agreed that the lives of thousands in the cities were so precarious that "perhaps their very existence depends upon a turn in the weather"; that daily it became "more difficult to procure employment"; that despite the "boasted prosperity" living conditions had deteriorated; that "the condition of the working people gets worse every day"; that the major cities abounded with "dark alleys," the "abodes of the miserable objects of grinding poverty"; and that the plight of most people was a desperate one in which if "sickness or want of employment should intervene for any length of time," hunger and ruin would result.[3]

When the labor leaders referred to the misery of the masses, it was the "laboring poor" whom they had in mind. For the most part of the middle class themselves, the articulate spokesmen of workingmen were bitter at what they believed to be labor's plight in this country. Where the conservative Henry Carey held the situation of the laborer to be excellent, and even his philanthropic father, Mathew Carey, believed many workers here to be so well off as not to be discountenanced even by a fairly long illness, the laborites saw a very different picture. According to them, labor everywhere in America was overworked and underpaid, receiving a pittance in return for its gigantic contribution to society's well being. Completely dependent on their capitalistic employers for their livelihood, workers were brutally exploited, in many cases even cheated or victimized by extortion. As a result labor lived in an intolerable atmosphere of want and hunger. Despite "equal rights" and "charters of liberty," labor's condition was akin to that of the feudal serf. Victimized by the "most unequal and unjustifiable distribution of wealth," workingmen tried ineffectually to maintain large families, though one step removed from total want. And bad as things were, they showed signs of further deterioration. In contrast to the cheerful view of the optimists, this was the bleak and forbidding scene depicted by the labor reformers.

As galling as its miserable material condition was the status of labor, the low opinion in which it was held in this country. Good society not only exploited workers but it regarded them with contempt. In a typical outburst, the cordwainers' leader, William English, said: "If we [the workers] ask for time for innocent recreation or for intellectual improvement, we are answered that we will

[3] The above quotations on the prevalence of misery in Jacksonian America are taken from the *Working Man's Advocate,* Jan. 29, 1831; and a series by Robert Dale Owen, entitled "Wealth and Misery," which first appeared in the New Harmony *Gazette,* Nov. 8, 15, 22, 29, and Dec. 6, 13, 1826, and was later reproduced with only a few modifications in its conclusions, made by Owen, in the *Working Man's Advocate* of May 1, 8, 15, 1830; the *Radical Reformer and Working Man's Advocate,* June 13, 1835; Stephen Simpson, *The Working Man's Manual . . . ,* (Philadelphia, 1831), pp. 127–128; *New England Artisan,* June 7, 1834; the *Union,* June 9, 1836; John Commerford, "Address Delivered Before the General Trades' Union of New York and Vicinity," reported in the *Working Man's Advocate,* Sept. 19, 1835.

spend it in drunkenness and debauchery. If we ask for the dollar we have earned, we are met again with a ready answer, 'You only want to spend it in some useless extravagance.' " It was time workingmen no longer submitted to being called the "swinish multitude," "the lower classes," "the mob," and "all the baser epithets." Luther was perturbed that the fair sex too often preferred "a perfumed dandy to a hard-headed, honest mechanic; a poor fool with an empty skull, to an honest, intelligent, useful, hard-working man; and this merely because the dandy looks more like a monkey than a man." Simpson observed that there was nothing new in the low reputation enjoyed by labor; he traced it back to antiquity and the identification of labor with slavery and servility. But whatever the causes, labor in Jacksonian America was a degraded group.

Several of the leaders believed that workers were too abject, that their miserable state was in part due to their docility. Luther criticized the too-patient bearing of a mountain of abuses. Moore told a labor audience that "you have by your servility—by your want of self-respect—by your lack of confidence in yourselves, and in each other, courted your present standing." If some of his co-workers could not agree, there was no argument that the condition of American labor was one of misery.[4]

[4] Mathew Carey, *Appeal to the Wealthy of the Land* (2nd ed., Philadelphia, 1833), p. 5; Henry Carey, *op. cit.*, pp. 89–90; the addresses of Charles Douglas and others to the workingmen of Massachusetts, reported in the *New England Artisan* for Oct. 25, 1834; also see the *New England Artisan* of Sept. 6, 1834; see George Henry Evans in the *Working Man's Advocate* through the years of 1832 and 1833; and also Evans in *The Man*, Feb. 18, 1834; Levi D. Slamm, in his "Address to the Workingmen," in the *Daily Plebeian*, Oct. 19, 1842; Thomas Brothers, in *Radical Reformer and Working Man's Advocate*, July 11, 1835; Simpson, *op. cit.*, pp. 86, 14, 16–17; William English, "An Address to the Mechanics and Working Men of the Trades' Union of the City and County of Philadelphia," in the *Pennsylvanian*, Jan. 9, 1834, cited in Commons, *Documentary History*, V, 339; the *Union*, July 1, 1836; Thomas Skidmore, *The Rights of Man to Property* (New York, 1829), pp. 4, 15; see the *Radical*, January, March, and August, 1841, for George Evans' comments on labor conditions during the 1830s; *Radical Reformer*, June 13, Aug. 29, 1835; Seth Luther, *An Address on the Origins and Progress of Avarice* (Boston, 1834), pp. 10, 12–13; Theophilus Fisk, *The Bulwark of Freedom* (Charleston, 1836), p. 14; also Fisk, *Capital Against Labor;* Commerford, "Address Delivered Before the General Trades' Union of New York and Vicinity," reported in the *Working Man's Advocate*, Sept. 19, 1835; John Ferral, "Report of the Resolutions Committee to the first Convention of the National Trades' Union," in *The Man*, Aug. 29, 1834; William English, "Oration Delivered at the Trades' Union Celebration of the 4th of July," *Radical Reformer and Working Man's Advo-*

What was especially frustrating was the fact that this misery prevailed in a society whose productivity was expanding at a rapid rate, and which therefore should have been able, if not to stamp out poverty altogether, certainly to reduce it substantially. But, if anything, the lot of the poor was worsening. The labor reformers anticipated both the ideas and the language of Henry George, a half-century later, in their attack on the paradox of want amidst plenty. Owen noted that it now prevailed here as in Great Britain, and for the same reasons. His fellow publisher and collaborator, George Henry Evans, who during the Working Men's phase of his career tended to see things as Owen did, was dismayed at the existence of poverty "in an age of the world . . . when labor is able to create . . . more than ten times the amount of wealth which it could a hundred years ago! when every man and woman, if labor were only as fairly rewarded as it was then, would be rendered not independent only, but affluent, by eight hours daily employment." Thomas Skidmore agreed with his opponents. Fifteen years later the New York politician and unionist, the opportunistic Levi Slamm, noted that this country and England were societies which made "too many hats, shoes, shirts, etc., yet thousands have not hats for their heads, shoes for their feet, or comfortable shirts for their backs! In the midst of plenty there is destitution!" [5]

A number of the leaders attributed almost every problem plaguing the country to the existence of poverty. Drunkenness, social aberrations of every kind, crime, even disease, were on the increase precisely because poverty, too, was spreading. When in 1832 a cholera epidemic raged over the eastern seaboard, Evans wrote, "it may be

---

cate, Sept. 1, 1835, pp. 122–123; Seth Luther, *Address to the Working Men of New England* (3rd ed., Philadelphia, 1836), p. 31; Ely Moore, *Address Delivered Before the General Trades' Union of the City of New York* (New York, 1833), pp. 20, 27.

[5] Owen, "Wealth and Misery"; George Henry Evans, in the *Working Man's Advocate,* Jan. 29, 1831. More than a decade later, when he had commenced his career as a land reformer, Evans would write that, despite a "superabundance of wealth in our country, there is every variety of misery among those who produce"; the *Radical,* Jan., March, and Aug. 1841, 1, 8, 33, 129. Poverty amidst wealth is a basic theme of Skidmore's *Rights of Man to Property;* Simpson, *op. cit.,* and Thomas Brothers, *The United States of North America as They Really Are* (London, 1840); the *Daily Plebeian,* Feb. 17, 1845.

heretical . . . but we firmly believe that the cholera so far from being a scourge of the Almighty [as some said it was] is a scourge which mankind have brought upon themselves by their own bad arrangements which produce poverty among many, while abundance is in existence for all." [6]

Evans also believed that not only diseased bodies but deformed personalities resulted from poverty. In common with other contemporaries in and out of the labor movement, he attributed crime to poverty. The labor movement, of course, had more than an academic interest in this issue, since the convict labor that some employers relied on was regarded by the unions as a threat to the mechanics' welfare. Evans' advice was that the best way to deal with the matter was not by the passing of resolutions but "to remove the causes which produce convicts: to prevent poverty and ignorance." Brothers professed to believe that a great proliferation of prisons had taken place in the early 1830s, and that the "horrid cause" which had produced "this state of things" was obvious. According to Luther, the main crime in the eyes of good society was poverty. Prisons were filled with "men guilty of no crime but being poor." If their inmates were treated callously it was because of this fact. Luther comes close to arguing that in view of the class nature of crime and punishment, the duty of the just man is to "open prison doors." Probably the Enlightenment's influence on labor thought in this matter is best shown in Slamm's words a decade later, when he states that crime is not caused by the "natural depravity of man," but "by the unequal distribution of wealth." "Give to every man a competency," he urges, "and nine-tenths of the poverty and crime now existing would disappear." [7]

In detecting a connection between crime and poverty, the Americans placed themselves in a mainstream whose best-known member was to be Charles Dickens. In view of later findings by criminologists and other authorities, their viewpoint was more than merely an emo-

---

[6] *Working Man's Advocate*, July 21, 1832. For a later scientific analysis that in part confirms Evans' stab in the dark, see Edgar Sydenstricker, *Health and Environment* (New York, 1933).

[7] *Working Man's Advocate*, June 14, 1834; *Radical Reformer and Working Man's Advocate*, Aug. 29, 1835; Luther, *Origins of Avarice*, p. 30; *Daily Plebeian*, Feb. 6, 17, 1845, and March 6, 1844.

tional outburst along predictable lines: it had a fair degree of merit as a sociological analysis.[8]

Though their canvas was done almost entirely in the bleak tones of poverty, the labor leaders left a small but significant part for another motif: the riches enjoyed by the few. In grotesque contrast to the misery of the masses, a small number of Americans lived in "lofty mansions," surrounded by "lawns, orchards, pleasure grounds . . . outhouses, and all the concomitants of wealth and grandeur." There was no democracy of want in America. Here as elsewhere inequality was the rule. According to Owen, if the many were doomed "by fraud and by force" to misery, it was due to the unjust appropriation by the few of more than their share of man's wordly goods. Variations on this theme were developed by Simpson, Slamm, Douglas, and the others, that "no man can become rich, without making another one poor, and that all accumulation of great fortunes, unnecessarily begets pauperism"; that "wealth concentrated, cannot exist, unless accompanied with surrounding poverty." Finally, "while the ownership of the world is by law vested in the few . . . what else," they asked, "but inequality, poverty, and crime must be the inevitable lot of the greatest part of its inhabitants?" [9] Other Americans might regard riches as the reward of virtue, but to the labor

[8] Dickens' *Hard Times* and *Great Expectations* are representative of his view that crime and social injustice are interrelated. As for later scholarly findings, the authorities naturally differ with perhaps no one going so far as to attribute crime to poverty alone. A typical conclusion is the following: "Economic insecurity, undernourishment, inadequate clothing, and lack of necessary medical care are bound to create attitudes dangerously close to recalcitrance and incorrigibility. There is little wonder, then, that delinquency and crime are so frequently associated with poverty" (Harry Elmer Barnes and Negley K. Teeters, *New Horizons in Criminology* [New York, 1951], p. 177). Also see William A. Bonger, *Criminality and Economic Conditions* (Boston, 1916), pp. 564–571; Cyril Burt, *The Young Delinquent* (London, 1938), pp. 68–69; L. Radzinowicz and J. W. C. Turner, eds., *The Modern Approach to Criminal Law* (London, 1948), pp. 17–18; Edwin H. Sutherland, *Principles of Criminology* (Chicago, 1939), p. 51; Mabel A. Elliott, *Crime in Modern Society* (New York, 1952), pp. 359–360, 375–377; Frederick H. Wines, *Punishment and Reformation* (New York, 1919), pp. 417–418; Blake McKelvey, *American Prisons* (Chicago, 1936), pp. 24–25; S. B. Warren, *Crime and Criminal Statistics in Boston* (Boston, 1934), p. 34; Max Grünhut, *Penal Reform* (Oxford, 1948), pp. 138–143; Gilbert Slater, *Poverty and the State* (London, 1930), *passim*.

[9] *Working Man's Advocate*, Jan. 16, 1830; Simpson, *Working Man's Manual*, pp. 127–128; *Daily Plebeian*, April 8, 1844; *Political Observer and Working Man's Friend*, June, 1832, quoted in *Working Man's Advocate*, June 30, 1832.

leaders wealth was only the unfailing corollary of the misery of the masses.

Not their own industry but the toil of others accounted for the accumulations of the rich. Skidmore believed that rich men must renounce their wealth, since they "live on the labor of others, and themselves perform none, or if any, a very disproportionate share." It is not clear what occupational group Evans had in mind, but it is clear that he advised workers not to co-operate with "persons not engaged in any *useful* occupation, but [who are] living on the labor of others." This imprecision in referring to "the rich" or "the idle" was not confined to Evans. Brothers, himself a small capitalist, scorned what he called the "tribe of usurers and idlers of all sorts, not one of whom would be able to live for a week if it were not for the help derived from the [working] men." In his characteristic rhetoric, Luther denounced those "who toil not, neither do they spin, but who are nevertheless clothed in purple and fine linen, and fare sumptuously every day" because of the labor of others. Ferral referred at one time to idlers, at another to plunderers, in neither case making altogether clear what groups he had in mind, but leaving no doubt whatever that both groups "abstracted the fruits" of the honest toil of the laboring poor. In an equally purple passage, English asks workers, Are not the rich "provided by our labour with beds of down . . . ? Do they not . . . riot and dissipate upon the proceeds of our industry?" On the other hand, when Simpson refers to those who "live and grow rich by the labour of others," he means capitalists; as does Fisk in his indictment of "the indolent drones" (who are) "clothed in purple and fine linen" by the endless toil of labour. Imbedded in the lavish rhetoric of the latter two, was the thought that the rich and the capitalists were one and the same.[10]

As these labor spokesmen depicted him, the rich man's characteristic trait was not industriousness but greed. Perhaps they felt there was poetic justice in the alleged tendency of the wealthy to corner the market not only in the world's material things but also in the

[10] Skidmore, *op. cit.*, pp. 3, 4; *Working Man's Advocate*, April 3, 1830; *Radical Reformer and Working Man's Advocate*, July 11, 1835; Luther, *Origins of Avarice*, p. 3; John Ferral in a letter to the editor of the *Radical Reformer and Working Man's Advocate*, July 25, 1835; English, "Oration at the Trades' Union Celebration"; Simpson, *op. cit.*, p. 70; Fisk, in address delivered in Boston, May 20, 1835, in the *Working Man's Advocate*, July 25, 1835.

most unattractive features of human nature. If the greed of the rich made them unlovely, it also made them frightening and oppressive to the poor. It also assured the failure of all plans for reform that depended on the beneficence or sympathy of the wealthy. For according to Luther, their "insatiable appetite for gold" made the rich impervious to human misery. Their constant motive, wrote Simpson, was to "fatten the few of the high privileged classes." They were motivated by an unenlightened self-interest, according to Evans and Brothers. No one was more critical than English and Moore of the "unbounded ambition and insatiable avarice," and "the heartless cupidity of the privileged few." In his newspaper, Commerford warned working men that "it is idle to look for anything from them [the rich]—all that we must look for is that which is narrow, mean and contracted." In a well-received address to labor, he asked, would not their insatiable avarice drive them, "if they possessed the power [to] reduce us to the level of the most miserable of the laboring classes of Europe?" [11] The unattractive portrait they painted of the rich indicates that the labor leaders' belief in the perfectibility of the human race was modified by misgivings concerning its most fortunate members.

If the rich were selfish, they also were clever, certainly clever enough to know both their own interests and how to advance them. They sought—and through the influence of their wealth they had achieved—power over American society. Skidmore explained the inevitability of this in the good logic that was invariably used by doctrinaire radicals: "He who commands the property of a state or even an inordinate portion of it, has the liberty and the happiness of its citizens in his own keeping." When his colleagues, ostensibly guided not by a preconceived social philosophy but by the facts of life, directed their gaze upon American society, they saw the same thing.

Gold was running the country. If anything, the rich were more arrogant and powerful here than elsewhere. They controlled every device and institution which might possibly further their own wealth and influence. Their power enforced low wages, the terrible work-

[11] Luther, *Origins of Avarice;* Simpson, *op. cit.,* pp. 40–41; *Working Man's Advocate,* Jan. 23, 1830; *Radical Reformer and Working Man's Advocate,* July 18, 1835, pp. 86–87, and June 20, 1835; English, "Oration at the Trades' Union Celebration," p. 120; Ely Moore, *Speech in Reply to the Hon. Waddy Thompson,* in the House of Representatives, May, 5, 1836 (Washington, 1836), p. 7; the *Union,* May 26, 1836; John Commerford, *loc. cit.*

ing conditions of women and children, the ignorance of the poor, and social inequality. They controlled the press, which "with a very few exceptions is listed on the side of wealth, strongly attached to the aristocracy of the country, always ready to do their bidding and advocate their interests." Such journals enabled them to shape the thinking of the people along favorable lines.[12] They were able to manipulate every part of American society, because above all they had control of government. For the labor leaders subscribed to the view, increasingly popular with the radicals of the early nineteenth century, that economic power determined political power. Wealth pulled the strings of government.

Charles Douglas, the New England leader, on the one hand followed in an old medieval tradition, while on the other he anticipated Dickens and other European radicals when he denounced the class bias of the law, lawyers, and courts. It was "by the force of unjust laws, which the people have not made, which they never consented to, and can never comprehend, that property is gradually passing into a few hands, and is made sure to a few rich families while the mass of the people are fleeced, and made to pass their lives in toil." If the legal system was expensive—as well as rotten and corrupt—and if the laws were incomprehensible, that was in accord with the design to make them so. By this view, lawyers were the tools of the rich, the laws they wrote "wicked instruments of oppression." The sentencing by the court of striking journeymen tailors in 1836 confirmed the belief of Fisk and Commerford that in this country "a distinction of justice" prevailed, under which workingmen could never receive fair treatment from "tribunals where men set themselves up as the lawful organs of keeping one class as the mere slaves of the other." [13]

[12] Skidmore, *op. cit.*, p. 388; Luther, *Origins of Avarice*, pp. 9, 12, 14, 16; English, "Oration at the Trades' Union Celebration," pp. 122, 120; John Commerford, "Address Before the General Trades' Union," in the *Union*, April 26, May 17, and May 28, 1836; *Radical Reformer*, June 15, 20, 1836; *Daily Plebeian*, Sept. 2, 23, 1842; Simpson, *The Working Man's Manual*, pp. 85, 87, 46; editorial in *Working Man's Advocate*, Oct. 31, 1829; Charles Douglas, "Proposals for publishing a weekly newspaper to be called, the Female Advocate and Factory Girl's Friend," in *New England Artisan*, June 7, 1834. Also see the *New England Artisan* for Sept. 6, 1834.

[13] Douglas, in the *Political Observer and Working Man's Friend*, cited in the *Working Man's Advocate*, June 30, 1832; and in *New England Artisan*, March 22, Sept. 6, and Oct. 11, 1834. See Fisk, *Capital Against Labor;* the *Union*, May 31, and June 8, 11, 1836.

No part of the labor leaders' American portrait was more hetero-dox than their view of the nation's politics. At a time when Jack-sonians both referred to themselves and were widely referred to as the party of the common man—in contrast to their aristocratic foes, the Whigs—the leaders of labor stigmatized both the political system in general and its major parties as "humbug." That in certain places and for certain issues labor groups might see eye-to-eye with the Democrats did not blind the leaders of the workingmen to what they believed to be an essential truth about American politics: the Democrats, like their opponents, were a party dedicated to serving the rich and the capitalists. For that matter, labor had occasionally aligned itself with the National Republicans, with the Antimasons, and with other parties as well. Tactical maneuvering that temporarily brought unlike groups together was not to be confused with ide-ological harmony.

One of the major arguments used to justify the organization of separate Working Men's parties in the late 1820s was the alleged domination of the major parties by the rich. And well after the Working Men had disappeared and the trades' unions had emerged as the leading labor organizations, the labor spokesmen continued to attack the two major parties in terms that had hardly changed. Arthur M. Schlesinger, Jr., has written that a major reason for the fall of the Working Men was the switching of the workers' allegiance to the Democrats. As has been pointed out earlier, the decline of the Working Men was due to altogether different causes.[14] But what is of special interest was the tendency of labor leaders not only *not* to affiliate with the Democrats but, if anything, to attack that party with special vindictiveness, as though to counteract the belief in-culcated by some Jacksonians that their party was peculiarly close to the laboring man. According to Thomas Brothers, the Democrats differed from the Whigs only in trying to mask a connection with bankers and monopolists that the Whigs openly proclaimed.

Nor was such criticism atypical. Evans held the major parties re-sponsible for the privileges of the few, on the one hand, and the misery of the masses, on the other. To Luther, most elected officers were men who picked the pockets of the poor. For workers to sup-port such parties was to "kiss the hand which gives the blow." Fisk

[14] *The Age of Jackson* (Boston, 1945), p. 143. Cf. chapter two above.

believed that "overwhelming monied influence" explained why "so great a portion of the laws are made for the interest of a few rich men, in favour of wealth, instead of honest industry." Simpson warns workers about the "fallacious structure and pernicious tendency of the parties now in vogue" to cater to the interests of the few. Douglas might approve the Democratic war on the second Bank of the United States, but he simultaneously characterizes Democrats and Whigs as those who "fleece the people and are . . . bent on leading an idle life at the expense of other men's labor." Commerford saw the major parties alike in one important respect: both had contempt for the rights of workingmen and trade unionists.

The reason the people had not seen through the sham nature of the major parties lay in the shrewdness and cunning of the latter. Since the people had the vote in this country, it was necessary for the leading parties to exercise all their wiles if they were to maintain the delusion that they were concerned with the problems of working people. Whigs and Democrats alike had proved equal to the task, with the latter if anything showing the greater mastery of the art of political deception. Prior to the formation of the Working Men's party, the workers had been "kept in leading strings by aspiring demagogues, who . . . had no one feeling—no interests in common" with them, Evans told the new party. "As to the Whig members [of the government], I find no fault with them," wrote Brothers, during the height of the trade union upsurge; "they were sent to make the rich richer and the poor poorer, and they obeyed the will of their constituents. But the Democrats, what shall we say of them?" Douglas advised workingmen not to permit themselves "to be gulled by mere names or mere professions, from whatever quarter they may chance to come." Moore, himself an aspiring politician, nonetheless reminded the workers that they had "been too often flattered and betrayed by politicians! Too often deceived by those who caressed and bepraised them!" In a letter to Seth Luther, John Ferral wrote that the "parties . . . tried to lure [labor] into the meshes of their nets." Probably nothing better illustrates the skeptical attitude of labor toward the "humbugs" than the following comments made by the politically ambitious William English to a labor audience:

. . . once a year they call us *men;* once a year we receive the proud appellation of freemen; once a year we are the *intelligent, virtuous, orderly working men.* But then they want our *votes,* and they flatter us; they want our interest, and they fawn upon us; and it grinds them to the very soul, to have their delicate fingers clenched in the friendly gripe [sic] of an honest hand, but they dare not avow it then. There is contamination in the very touch of a man who labours for his bread; but it will not do to say so on the election ground, for that would lose them our votes. They know our strength; although it would seem we do not; and hence they resort to every stratagem to distract and divide us; to cut us up into parties and fragments of parties; to set each man against his neighbor; to turn, almost, our very brains with political excitement; and all for what? To elevate themselves!!!

Without exception the labor leaders regarded the American political system as a hoax, and the turbulent party struggles of the era as full of much sound and fury, signifying little for workingmen.[15]

They further argued that political rights were of minor significance in the face of the domination of society by the rich. These views led Arthur M. Schlesinger, Jr. to state that "George H. Evans, John Commerford, John Ferral, and the early labor leaders seemed to regard democracy as more protective doctrine than good in itself. In power they might have acted little differently—if toward different ends—from Daniel Webster and Nicholas Biddle." [16] In my opinion, Mr. Schlesinger has misinterpreted the beliefs of the labor leaders. Far from being some species of Stalinist or authoritarian-leftist critics of "bourgeois democracy," or anything like it, these men were supporters of democracy, reserving their criticism for those men and practices which they believed abused and perverted it. With the possible exception of Thomas Brothers, who returned to England after the Panic of 1837, convinced that democracy, fraud, and poverty were inevitably intertwined, they never lost their faith in self-government, certainly not during that phase of their careers when they were active in the labor movement.

Clearly the social canvas the labor leaders painted was featured by glaring inequality, not only of condition, but of power, status, and

[15] See the *Union*, June 29, 1836; *Radical Reformer*, June 27, 1835; *Working Man's Advocate*, Nov. 21, and Oct. 31, 1829; Luther, *Origins and Progress of Avarice*, p. 16; Seth Luther, A. H. Wood, and Levi Abell, to John Ferral, July 20, 1835, in *Working Man's Advocate*, July 25, 1835; Theophilus Fisk, *The Banking Bubble Burst* (Charleston, 1837), p. 7; and Fisk, *Capital Against Labor*; *New England Artisan*, Aug. 16, and June 21, 1834; the *Union*, May 21, 1836; Ely Moore, *Speech in Reply to the Hon. Waddy Thompson*, p. 4; John Ferral to Seth Luther, June 22, 1835, in *The Man*, June 29, 1835; English, "Oration at the Trades's Union Celebration," p. 123.

[16] *Age of Jackson*, p. 318.

opportunity. If they had had to give a title to their handiwork, it might have been: "America—the land of class conflict." For as they saw it, classes existed here, the lives and minds of their members separated by an unbridgeable gulf. Skidmore's entire theory rested on a premise which he convinced himself was a fact, that in society are "two distinct classes, proprietors and non-proprietors; those who own the world and those who own no part of it." The mild Evans not only believed that the interests of workers differed from those of other classes but that essentially society was a jungle in which the powerful preyed on the weak. His colleagues sounded variations on this theme. Simpson believed "there exists so great a separation in all the social duties and associations, as almost to constitute them [labor and capital] different species." Luther questioned the significance of political freedom in a society based on class distinctions. Fisk spoke bombastically of the war between the capitalist and the pro-ducer—though it is not always clear what he meant by the latter term. English, however, defines his terms clearly when he pontificates that "the war waged by capital against labour is co-existent with capital itself." By labor he means employers as well as journeymen, distinguishing both from merchant capitalists.

Some of the trade unionists detected, in addition to class conflict, an alleged attempt on the part of the rich and the capitalists to camouflage or to deny the existence of the struggle, on the one hand, or to blame labor agitators for its continuation, on the other. Both points are sharply made by Commerford. According to him, American labor's attempt to improve its lot was met by the capitalists as follows: "Why, you ungrateful wretches, look at your fellows in other countries, and observe how miserably they fare, and then acknowledge our humanity; shut your turbulent mouths." In his view, precisely those men who charged reformers with stirring up class strife were the ones "straining every nerve to draw the cords of oppression and want to the greatest stretch of elasticity." They were simply "wily intriguers." Ferral asked the question, where idle rich live off the laboring poor, "who is there that can term such a mon-strous state of things, a community considered as one family?" Only those who profited from class conflict would deny its existence.[17]

[17] Skidmore, *op. cit.*, p. 125; *Working Man's Advocate*, April 3, 1830; the *Radical*, Jan., March, and Aug., 1841, pp. 1, 8, 33, 129; Simpson, *The Work-ing Man's Manual*, p. 211; Luther, *Address to the Working Men of New Eng-land*, p. 5; Luther, Wood, and Abell, "The Ten-Hour Circular," in *The Man*,

The labor leaders were aware their charge of a class antagonism rending American society was attacked by their critics as either a glaring distortion or, if their picture were conceded to be accurate, as an evil of their own creation. The leaders for their part denied that class conflict was something they either fabricated or advocated. It was simply a fact of American life. They were by no means impartial toward the matter, however; nor did they delude themselves into believing that they were objective about the evils in American society. They were not—not even in their own minds—engaged only in presenting a clinically accurate version of contemporary America. Rather, they painted with passion, convinced that their version of life was true, but certain also as to which portions of the social scene were evil and would have to be done over in the future. Not one of them, for example, was neutral toward the class conflict he found raging in this country.

A minority among them would do what they could to soften the clash, to reduce, if not altogether to remove, the tension between the classes. Owen was opposed to radical measures of reform because of the rancor and bitter hatreds they engendered, while Slamm hoped that the prevailing hostility might be lessened through more responsible behavior by the rich. The opportunistic Moore, who could thunder as righteously as any man, when it suited him, sought to assure the public that the trades' union movement worked toward reducing class strife; "to allay the jealousies, and abate the asperities, which now unhappily exist between employers and the employed." Moore's writings and speeches for this period indicate that here he expressed, not what was politic, but what he truly believed. He feared extremes. In fact, as he made clear, if his sympathies were not with the "affluent and the powerful," neither were they with the "breadless and the impotent," but rather with what he called the "intermediate classes," ostensibly caught between the two warring factions. His goal was an even balance.

Most of the leaders, however, reacted very differently. Instead of trying to harmonize the relations between the classes, they would,

May 13, 1835; Fisk, *The Banking Bubble Burst,* p. 49; Fisk, *Capital Against Labor;* English, "Oration at the Trades' Union Celebration," pp. 121, 127; the *Union,* June 9, 1836; John Ferral, letter in the *Radical Reformer and Working Man's Advocate,* July 28, 1835.

if anything, exacerbate the situation. Skidmore, for example, was accused of being "in favor of drawing a line between rich and poor." The charge had merit. Were it up to him, employers, or "the rich," would have been kept out of the Working Men's party. His more conservative colleague, George Henry Evans, put the argument for this approach neatly: "While these divisions in society exist," it would be his object "to draw the line as distinctly as possible between them, in order to prevent any further encroachments." Luther called on workers to form a "front" of their own, while the hat manufacturer Thomas Brothers failed to see the humor in his advice to "working people" that they "should never admit into their [war] council one who does not belong to them." Fisk and English also used intransigent language, though at times with the imprecision of Brothers, whose rhetoric seems almost revolutionary, as when he calls for "a continuous warfare . . . between the workers and the idlers." (Closer examination in this case indicates that he is talking about higher prices!) References abound to "unholy apostles of Mammon," or to "bloated wealth." But rhetorical devices or no, the purple language, more often than not, only exaggerated rather than deceived.

For the leaders agreed with John Ferral that "whilst the robbers [of labor] have been, and are still despoiling the community . . . in every way that knavish cunning can devise, what sane mind, if intentionally honest, would attempt to amalgamate these two parties, and call them one family?" Labor had not created the division in society, but according to most of its spokesmen, there was no alternative to recognizing, even emphasizing, its existence. To do otherwise was to play the game of those who denied the existence of class conflict only to perpetuate and continue to profit from it.[18]

[18] For attitudes toward class division, see Robert Dale Owen, *Republican Government and National Education* (London, n.d.), p. 5; Owen, *Situations* (London, 1839), pp. 8–9; *Working Man's Advocate*, Jan. 16, and Feb. 13, 1830; *Free Enquirer*, June 12, and Oct. 16, 1830; Moore, *Address Delivered Before the General Trades' Union of the City of New York*, p. 13; Moore, *Remarks in the House of Representatives*, Feb., 1839, p. 16; Moore, *Address on Civil Government* (New York, 1847), pp. 6–7, 23–24; Moore, *Address Delivered Before the General Trades' Union . . .* , p. 10. Moore did imply, however, that society would be based on common interests and mutual assistance only after signficant changes had been made in its structure. Also see Thomas Skidmore's publication *Friend of Equal Rights*, for April 14, 1830, cited in *Working Man's Advocate*, April 17, 1830; *Free Enquirer*, March 20, 1830; the *Radical*, Jan., 1842, p. 8; Luther, *Address to the Working Men of New England*,

The Jacksonian labor leaders analyzed American society at the same time that they described it. They knew the causes of its ills, and they also knew what was needed to correct them. An evaluation of their thinking and its significance is best attempted after their diagnoses and prognoses have been examined. But it seems clear enough from their *description* of American society, alone, that these were nay-sayers of the first order. The political and social landscape they drew of America bears a remarkable resemblance to the dismal English social landscape painted by William Cobbett and their radical socialist contemporaries in old England. Of course it was a distorted view, in both cases; the political, economic and social facts on which it was based, are arguable. But what is not in dispute—and particularly is this so if the facts are indeed distorted—is the social philosophy of the men capable of viewing a happy society so grimly. If times were, in fact, good, then disgruntled radicals indeed were the Jacksonian labor leaders, who depicted them in so harsh a light.*

---

p. 31; Luther, *Origins and Progress of Avarice*, pp. 12–13; Fisk, *Capital Against Labor;* English, "Oration at the Trades' Union Celebration," p. 127; *Radical Reformer,* July 18, 1835; John Ferral, letter to the editor, *ibid.,* July 25, 1835.

* For a discussion of the actual condition of American society during the era, see Edward Pessen, *Jacksonian America: Society, Personality and Politics* (Homewood, 1969), ch. 3.

9

The Poor Not the Authors of Their Own Misery: The Attack on Malthusianism

Many Americans refused to believe that the searing portrait of Jacksonian society painted by the labor leaders was a true one. For if there are some men who see misery and discord even where their traces are faint or nonexistent, there are others who can see only harmony and well-being around them. Yet it was not only radical dissenters who accepted the harsh labor version of the state of things. There were advocates of the status quo who conceded the prevalence of want and inequality. These persons differed from social critics, not in their picture of social conditions, but rather in their *explanation* or in their discussion of its causes. Where the reformer was invariably an environmentalist, fixing responsibility on one or another social institution, the fatalistic conservative gloomily concluded that misfortune was grounded in the nature of things or in the nature of man and was therefore inevitable in human life. In the Jacksonian era pessimists had a powerful and seemingly scientific explanation to justify acquiescence in the face of social distress. This of course was the theory developed by Thomas Malthus in his *Essay on Population*.[1]

Malthus' famous work had appeared in 1798, as a refutation of the perfectionist theories of the English radical William Godwin.[2] Where Godwin had held out the hope of a perfect society based on plenty and equality for all, Malthus tried to prove that such a hope

[1] T. R. Malthus, *An Essay on the Principles of Population* (2 vols.; 6th ed.; London, 1826). Unless otherwise noted our allusions to Malthus' *Essay* will be to the sixth edition, a point which takes on special significance in the case of Malthus' classic, with its many additions, omissions, and new shadings, from edition to edition.

[2] Godwin had written *Political Justice* in 1793.

was a dream. Basing his conclusions on the alleged "constant tendency in all animated life to increase beyond the nourishment prepared for it," or the principle that "population had the constant tendency to increase beyond the means of subsistence," Malthus taught that in the absence of sexual restraint misery rather than equality was the inevitable lot of the many. It was this principle, buttressed by arithmetic ratios and references to population developments in various nations of the earth, which, according to Malthus, accounted for "that poverty and misery observable among the lower classes of people in every nation." [3] It was not long before Malthusianism was accepted as gospel both here and in England.[4]

If anything was inevitable it was that some of the labor leaders would attack the theory. For to environmentalists its doctrines were pernicious, both for their persuasiveness and their actual popularity. So long as it stood unchallenged, the wretchedness of the masses was tacitly conceded to be necessary and proper. This intellectual fortress had to be assaulted.

The argument of the American labor thinkers was for the most part directed against the conservative social implications of Malthus' doctrine. In a sense Malthus' essay could be said to have two aspects. On the one hand it was a work of "pure science," purporting to contain principles and proofs based on an objective observation of men and nature which had reached inescapable conclusions about the relationship of population to the means of subsistence. On the other, it was a social analysis, tortuously stretching its skimpy "scientific evidence" to justify conservative pronouncements on society, which criticized the status quo only for its disposal of crumbs to the destitute.[5] Malthus, his followers, and even most of his contemporary critics, treated these two aspects as though they were intimately,

---

[3] Malthus, *Essay*, I, 2; books one and two; preface to the second edition, *ibid.*, p. iv.

[4] Kenneth Smith reveals the growing popularity of Malthus' doctrine, especially in England. As early as 1807, it was being praised in the House of Commons for its signal effect in influencing thought in salutary, i.e., laissez-faire, directions. See Smith, *The Malthusian Controversy* (London, 1951), pp. 36, 37, 275, 296–297; also see James Bonar, *Malthus and His Work* (London, 1885), p. 363; Joseph Dorfman, *The Economic Mind in American Civilization* (New York, 1946), vol. II, *passim.*

[5] See Kenneth Smith for an attack on the alleged scientific and logical flaws in the doctrine (*op. cit.*, book three, "Critical Analysis").

even necessarily, related.[6] Once accept the validity of the "ratios" and the grim social conclusions had to follow.

The American labor reformers generally said little about the "proofs," reserving their fire for the pessimistic conclusions of the doctrine, as well as the conservative social theory on which they rested. Of course they were not the first to undertake this attack. From the time of the appearance of the first edition of the *Essay* in 1798 to Malthus' death in 1834, England was bombarded with polemical broadsides on the issues it raised. Critics questioned the ratios, asserted that the earth's potential had barely been tapped, that increased population tended to reflect social advance as well as produce more food, predicted an era of magnificent agricultural advance based on the application of chemistry to food growing, and in some cases voiced doubts as to both the justice and the practicality of the remedial method of "moral restraint." [7] They also condemned the doctrines that the poor were primarily responsible for their own misery, that society's structure had little effect on the welfare of the masses, that nature compelled social inequality, and that social reforms were both hopeless and vicious.[8]

In America Alexander H. Everett was one of the few to challenge the *Essay's* pessimistic conclusions. He argued that the industrious workingmen of this country would register gains simultaneously with their population growth, were not subject to an iron law of wages, and that an increase in our population would result in greater wealth and productivity, thus improving rather than weakening the ratio between population and subsistence.[9] But prior to the attack

[6] The English reformers Francis Place and William Thompson were notable among the early critics of the doctrine, in that, though impressed with the necessity for a "preventive check" on human procreation, they rejected Malthus' social arguments.

[7] See the summaries and analyses of the writing of Simon Gray (1816), John Weyland (1816), James Grahame (1817), William Godwin (1820), David Booth (1820), Piercy Ravenstone (1821), Francis Place (1822), Alexander Everett (1823), William Thompson (1824), Michael Sadler (1830), and Thomas Rowe Edmonds (1832), in Kenneth Smith, *op. cit.*, pp. 86–91, 91–96, 101–110, 121–131, 131–141, 142–152, 153–159, 159–164, 164–169, 190, 198–202.

[8] See the views expressed by Charles Hall (1805), Thomas Jarrold (1806), William Hazlitt (1807), George Ensor (1818), William Cobbett (1819), W. F. Lloyd (1833), in *ibid.*, pp. 50–56, 60, 70–78, 114–119, 120–121, 202–206.

[9] Dorfman, *Economic Mind*, II, 593–595; K. Smith, *op. cit.*, pp. 159–164.

on Malthusianism initiated by Robert Dale Owen and others in the labor movement, Everett's was a voice in the wilderness. For in the early part of the nineteenth century, as Joseph Dorfman has noted, "there was general agreement on the validity of the doctrine." Most writers on economic subjects subscribed to it, as, for that matter, they did throughout the remainder of the century.[10]

In a certain sense, then, the labor figures were pioneers in their assault on Malthusianism, and not least because the content of their critique was quite different from that of the conservative middle-class critics. Before examining the labor argument, however, it might be well to describe in more detail the intellectual edifice against which they directed their attacks. For it was often said by Malthusian sympathizers that the critics were attacking not what Malthus had written, but what they had heard about the book at second or third hand. Malthus, it was argued, did not mean nor was he responsible for what some of his disciples said and did ostensibly in the name of his principles. Let us therefore examine briefly what Malthus had in fact written.

Malthus stated that the idea of the perfectibility of man or society, was absurd. It was a great error to attribute vice and misery to human institutions; they sprang from the actions of the poor themselves. Laws of nature dictated that "some human beings will be exposed to want. These are the unhappy persons who in the great lottery of life have drawn a blank." [11]

It mattered not whether society were organized in accordance with the co-operative principle or on a system of private property; in the one as in the other, misery would soon become the lot of the many. A condition of inequality was advantageous, however, in that it offered greater incentives and was "best calculated to develop the energies and faculties of man."

"A real advance in the price of labor," was a welcome develop-

10 Dorfman, *Economic Mind*, I, 399; II, 520–521, 538, 544, 546, 558. George R. Geiger makes the point that criticisms of Malthusianism "were by no means welcome or even presentable" in the time of George (*The Philosophy of Henry George* [New York, 1933], p. 87).

11 Malthus, *op. cit.*, p. 34. This rather cold appraisal especially incensed some of his English critics, and is reminiscent of a passage appearing in the second edition (1803) but later withdrawn, which alludes to "nature's mighty feast" at which "there is no vacant cover" for the unemployed.

ment, "but the attempt to effect this object by forcibly raising the nominal price . . . every thinking man must reprobate as puerile and ineffectual." Therefore, all attempts by laborers to organize or to strike in order to better their conditions were doomed to failure. In fact it was absurd to believe that workers were at all times deserving of good wages. The poor must learn that the way to improvement lay not in social reforms nor in immediate advantages, but in prudence and restraint or sexual abstinence. One of the great dangers was that the "lower classes of people," led on by irresponsible demagogues, were too impatient and "too frequently in the habit" of looking forward to "direct and immediate relief." They did not realize that such improvements were ephemeral, that the only solid mode of permanent improvement depended on their use of the "preventive check." In certain cases, however, emigration of the poor was a "both useful and proper" supplementary means of achieving the proper ratio.

In any case, the situation of the poor was worsened by the application of relief to them in the form of poor laws. These laws rewarded the undeserving, "diminished the shares" of the industrious, encouraged the depravity of the laboring poor, and destroyed that necessary stimulus to mankind, i.e., that "dependent poverty ought to be held disgraceful." The product of a misguided benevolence, these laws contradicted the imperatives of nature. In their own way they were almost as dangerous as the notions often spread by "dissatisfied [men] of talents" among "the lower classes of people, that all of their poverty and distress arise solely from the iniquity of the government." Nothing was worse than "these general disclaimers, who attribute the distresses of the poor, and almost all the evils to which society is subject, to human institutions and the iniquity of governments." They must be strongly resisted, both because of the falsity as well as the dread consequences of their views. Even a tyranny must be supported against such revolutionaries, whose notions lead only to violence and turmoil. Lately their views had gained in popularity among the masses, spreading the false idea that all were deserving of equality.

In view of this danger, it was time that steps be taken to educate the people to their "true situation," i.e., teach them "what is really true," or simply all the ideas taught by Malthus. What is more, proper education would have the happy effect on the poor of "making them bear with patience the evils which they suffer, from being aware of the folly and inefficacy of turbulence." This last point is underlined again toward the close of the work.

Even if the remedies he suggested are not acted on by the poor—a failure which might be mistakenly interpreted as the failure of Malthus' entire plan—all would not be lost. So long as they believed its judgments to be true, the

lower classes . . . would become more peaceable and orderly, would be less inclined to tumultuous proceedings in seasons of scarcity, and would at all times be less influenced by inflammatory and seditious publications. . . . The mere knowledge of these truths . . . would still have a most beneficial effect on their conduct in a political light; and undoubtedly, one of the most valuable of these effects would be the power that would result to the higher and middle classes of society, of gradually improving their governments, without the apprehension of . . . revolutionary extremes. . . .

In effect, Malthus concludes that whether his system works or not, the acceptance of its arguments would have the salutary effect of weakening the movement for social reform.[12]

These were the conservative social implications of Malthusianism against which the Americans directed their fire.

Although he believed that society was responsible for the misery of the poor, Owen nevertheless agreed with certain aspects of the theory. As a youth he had blamed what he called careless or selfish or even depraved parents for the misery endured by youthful factory workers.[13] In maturity, he did not completely discard the notion that though the poor were not the authors of their own misery, they yet contributed heavily to it by their own irresponsibility. In late 1829 and early 1830 he wrote a number of articles urging birth control as a partial solution to the problems of the poor.[14] In December of 1830 he published a book, *Moral Physiology*, on the same theme. Despite the fact that he not only rejected Malthus' social judgments but advocated a "check" that was unaccept-

[12] *Ibid.*, II, 16, 20, 218, 291, 36, 42, 330, 441, 76, 110, 95, 112–113, 326, 425, 228, 60; see book three, chapters v, vi, and vii, pp. 63, 82, 83, 309, 312, 322–323, 40, 320, 337, 399, 356–358, 438–439.

[13] See Chapter 4 above.

[14] See the *Free Enquirer* for the years 1829 and 1830.

able to him—Malthus favored abstinence, not birth control—Owen was given the name "Malthusian" for his troubles.[15]

He began the discussion by proclaiming the criminality of child-raising by the poor:

> The intelligent and unprejudiced portion of society will agree . . . that it is in any human beings, an unprincipled act to become the parents of those to whom they cannot afford sustenance and care. Such an act is . . . criminal. . . . The murderer deprives of life, in cases where the law regards life a blessing; the thoughtless parent often gives life, where ignorance and penury render it a curse. If wilfully to deprive of enjoyment be a criminal act, is it not also criminal wilfully to create wretchedness?[16]

"I think we have no right," he continued, "to bring young beings into existence, for whose future welfare, both physical and mental, we have not a fair prospect of amply providing."[17] This was actually more in the spirit of the English reformer Francis Place than it was of Malthus.

To Owen, the effects of large families among the underprivileged were terrible to behold. Hard-working fathers were turned into slaves of toil. But the poor women suffered even more, he felt:

> How often is the health of the mother, giving birth every year to an infant—happy if it be not twins!—and compelled to toil on, even at those times when nature imperiously calls for some relief from daily drudgery—how often is the mother's comfort, health, nay, sometimes her life thus sacrificed! Or, if care and toil have weighed down the spirits and at last broken the health of the father, how often is the widow left, unable, with the most virtuous intentions, to save her fatherless offspring from becoming degraded objects of charity, or profligate votaries of vice!

No man could feel more strongly than he, he assured the workingmen, the terrible injustice of "the system of laws and the present order of things." But it remained true "that the pressure of a large family not a little aggravates the evil."[18]

---

[15] Skidmore applied the term as an epithet; *Free Enquirer*, Aug. 7, 1830. Norman E. Himes also describes Owen that way, but approvingly ("Robert Dale Owen, the Pioneer of American Neo-Malthusianism," *American Journal of Sociology*, XXXV [Jan., 1930], 529–547).

[16] *Free Enquirer*, Dec. 5, 1829.

[17] *Working Man's Advocate*, Feb. 13, 1830.

[18] *Free Enquirer*, Oct. 23, 1830.

He could not but agree with Malthus, that "population unrestrained, *must* increase beyond the possibility of the earth and its
produce to support," and that "at present it is restrained by vice
and misery," precisely as viewed by Malthus. In defense of Malthus,
Owen points out that he "did not choose to be considered the apolo-
gist of vice and misery," much preferring the practice of celibacy; it
was not his fault that his readers were too immoral to be moved by
his appeal, while some of his disciples were too quick to absolve
society of all responsibility in the matter. In the long run, Malthus'
principle is right, for population "cannot be suffered to increase
unrestrained for more than every few hundred years, and . . . if the
checks which poverty, vice and misery now place upon it were
removed, some others must sooner or later, come into play." If mankind would only heed the advice, and accept the preventive check,

the effect would be salutary, moral, civilizing; . . . it would prevent
many crimes, and more unhappiness; . . . it would lessen intemperance
and profligacy; . . . it would polish the manners and improve the moral
feelings; . . . it would relieve the burden of the poor and the cares of the
rich; it would most essentially benefit the rising generation, by enabling
the parents generally more carefully to educate and more comfortably to
provide for, their offspring.[19]

It was idle, however, to expect mankind, as now constituted, to
embrace abstinence. "To tell the poor they must not marry, and
thereby expect to lessen the number of mouths to be fed, and check
the increase of poverty, is a utopian scheme of reform," said Owen.[20]
That was precisely the weakness in Malthus' position. The method
he prescribes is unrealistic. It does not account sufficiently for the
perverted human nature of man, a nature too licentious and selfish
to tolerate abstinence. Owen, however, who believes he understands
men, has something more practical to offer. In his *Moral Physiology*
he argued not for abstinence but for contraceptive methods and the
education of the poor in their use. Such techniques were known in
educated and enlightened circles everywhere in Europe, were used
by the wealthy, and it was time that the plain people adopted them.[21]

[19] Robert Dale Owen, *Moral Physiology* (London, 1841), pp. 17, 20; *Free
Enquirer*, Oct. 16, Oct. 23, 1830.

[20] *Free Enquirer*, Dec. 5, 1829.

[21] Owen expected abuse from prudes for this position; he was not disappointed
(*Moral Physiology, passim*).

The advocacy of birth control was not Owen's only attack on Malthusianism; nor was it the most important one.[22] In contradistinction to the Malthusians, he wanted it distinctly understood that "a solution of the population question is offered, as an *alleviation* of existing evils, not as a *cure* for them—as a palliative, not as a remedy for the disease." Further, the alleviation offered through a reduction of population was slight and superficial: that "the distress which labor-saving machinery is producing, or that the evils now resulting from overpopulation may be cured, or *essentially* alleviated, by any repression of population—that is what I cannot perceive, and do not believe to be a fact," he wrote. Alluding to the more happily organized insects, he asked, "Who ever heard of a hive being over-supplied with bees, so long as room remained in its cells to receive them?" And if conditions grew bad among them, because of an irrational and inequitable internal organization, "would they recommend to each other prudential restraints on population lest the young bees should be unable to obtain employment, and thus die for want of honey?" [23]

To ask the question was to answer it. What evidently confused some Malthusians was the fact that "iniquitous laws, false education, and a vicious order of things are continually producing effects which are erroneously attributed to over-population." According to Owen, the

effect springs not from absolute number, but from the ignorance of men. Monopolies favour the rich—imposts impress the poor. Commercial rivalry grinds to the dust the victims of an overgrown system of competition. To these and similar causes, and not to positive excess of people at the time being, is distress felt over the . . . world. . . . Population might be a tenth part of what it is, and unjust legislation and vicious customs would still give birth, as they do now, to extravagance and want.

For the present, then, population was not the main problem: "Americans, surely, will have room enough for a few generations to come. And when their millions of acres of forests have yielded to the woodman's axe, and their towns and villages cluster along the shores of the Pacific, it will be time enough to talk of population being the cause of want." [24]

[22] Himes' summary of the anti-Malthusianism elements in Owen's thinking is significantly incomplete (*op. cit.*, pp. 542–543).

[23] *Moral Physiology*, p. 19; *Working Man's Advocate*, Feb. 13, 1830.

[24] *Moral Physiology*, p. 19; *Working Man's Advocate*, Feb. 13, 1830.

Owen's severest criticism was directed against the tendency of the Malthusian theory to act as a bulwark for the status quo, as though for all the world it was a crime against nature and God to stand for reform of social conditions. In this respect, said Owen, regarding the work of Malthus:

His book . . . has done infinite mischief. I have heard his disciples declare openly, that they considered the crimes and wretchedness of society to be *necessary*—to be the express ordainings of Providence. . . . I have heard it argued by men of rank, wealth and influence, that the distinctions of rich and poor, and even of morality and unmorality, of luxury and want, will and must exist to the end of the world; that he who attempts to remove them fights against God and nature; and, if he partially succeed, will but afford the human race an opportunity to increase, until the earth shall no longer suffice to contain them. . . . It must be confessed, that this is a comfortable doctrine for the rich idler; it is a healing salve to the luxurious conscience; an opiate to drown the still small voice of truth and humanity which calls to every man to be up and do his part toward the alleviation of the human suffering that everywhere stares him in the face.[25]

Owen disagreed completely with Malthusianism as to the fundamental causes of human misery, just as he rejected its assumptions about the inevitability of poverty. Where Malthus called for abstinence as the only path to progress, Owen advocated birth control, regarding it only as one commonsense method, to be supplemented by other more important ones, by which the poor could fend off complete degradation.

Skidmore naturally had no patience with a doctrine which denied not only the value of reform, but the validity of all his ideas about property. Before 1831 he had written an occasional note criticizing Malthusianism,[26] but it was the appearance of Owen's book praising birth control, which moved him to deal with the theory at length. In 1831 he wrote *Moral Physiology Exposed and Refuted*,[27] a work consisting of his critical comments, printed alongside the text of Owen's *Moral Physiology*. In this tract Skidmore denounced the

[25] *Free Enquirer*, Oct. 16, 1830. That *Moral Physiology* is made up in good part of earlier writings of Owen is confirmed by the appearance of this passage.

[26] See the *Free Enquirer*, Aug. 7, 1830.

[27] Thomas Skidmore, *Moral Physiology Exposed and Refuted* (New York, 1831), pp. 76, 39.

ideas of both Malthus and Owen, if anything reserving the harsher criticism for the latter. As a dogmatic social critic, he would not tolerate ideas—even radical ideas—that deviated from his own. As a strident champion of the poor, he could neither forget nor forgive Owen the material comfort he had always enjoyed. As an unbending extremist, he found concessions of any sort to Malthusianism altogether unpalatable. As a banished Working Men's leader, he leaped to attack his onetime nemesis, perhaps on any pretext. Whatever the reasons, Skidmore acted in the best tradition of doctrinaire radicalism, by vilifying and pouring scorn on a fellow critic of conservatism, whose ideas—in differing from his own—were not only wrong but wicked, corrupt, and dangerous.

If their plight was not caused by their own deeds, why should the poor have to forego the pleasure of raising a normal family? Skidmore asks, at the outset. Owen and his supporters, in favoring birth control as a reform measure, were "guilty of the . . . crime of throwing out false lights to decoy the wretched from the discovery of the true remedy of their distresses. . . ." What was needed was not fewer but more people. To Owen and the advocates of birth control, Skidmore retorts:

[Instead of devoting themselves to securing means to diminish the number of mouths] better, far better, it seems to me, it would be to seek the means of filling them, and of increasing their number, and thus to make the great aggregate of human enjoyment as great as possible. Better, far better, it appears to me, it would be, to set about discovering the means of preventing the existence of enormous incomes, derived from the labor of others, such as that of half a million or a million of dollars annually, whereby half a million or a million of bushels of wheat for example are or can be annually monopolized by a single person; and the laborers, who produce it, along with their children, are made to hunger and perish. It is *this* power of thus monopolizing immense quantities or the results of the annual labor, no matter whether it be through rents of land or houses, through interest on money, through profits on speculations or through inadequate compensations for labor, that fills society with the evils of scarcity and famine. Destroy this, and it will be a long time before Robert Dale Owen, or any other man will have any cause to complain of the number of mouths. So far then as he succeeds in turning public attention from the object of discovering the means of destroying these unequal and enormous incomes thus derived from the labor of others, he effectually serves the cause of oppression, injuring those for whose benefit he affects to write.

A "vicious organization of government" rather than large families was the cause of the untold misery suffered by the mass of mankind. Not an excess of population but an excess of the poor was what was wrong; and this disease was to be cured neither by moral restraint nor birth control. To Owen's point that large families brought great suffering to poor women, Skidmore replied:

If it has been that women have been the victims of very great sufferings in society, let us say, and say it in truth, that it is owing to other causes than that of reproducing our race. . . . Let us say it is owing to the fact that Miss [Frances] Wright, that Mr. Owen, and ten thousand other Aristocrats possess in their hands, that wealth which the labor of others has created and those materials of nature, which are alike the property of all; thus placing a great mass of women, as well as men, in circumstances of the most afflicting, degrading, and oppressive poverty.[28]

In his *Working Man's Manual*, published in 1831, Stephen Simpson, the intellectual leader of the Philadelphia Working Men, also dissected Malthusianism. While sharing some of the basic views of Owen and Skidmore, he manages, in addition, to make some original points. To Simpson, Malthusianism is a spurious attempt to justify social inequity and disharmony. Its main significance is in the unwitting testimony it offers to "the mercenary degeneracy of the age," in the fact that such a doctrine can be respected. Only "class bias prevents its adherents from noting its fallacies." Simpson's simple view of the historical origins and the social utility of the Malthusian argument is neatly summed up in the following purple passage from his *Working Man's Manual:*

In the midst of plenty, avarice, power, ambition, extortion—all start up to monopolize the bounties of nature, and create a famine for seven-eighths of mankind, in order that the remaining fraction may riot in gluttony, and luxuriate in excess. And the famine thus caused by the diabolical passions of man, is attempted to be ascribed to nature; whilst the pampered scribes of a voluptuous nobility coolly sit down, and under the pretence of philosophy, attempt to calculate that nature has not provided subsistence for her children.[29]

Were the proponents of this doctrine slightly objective, they could

[28] *Ibid.,* pp. 21, 27, 35. Owen dismissed Skidmore's charges as "vulgar sneers." See the *Free Enquirer,* June 25, 1831.
[29] Stephen Simpson, *The Working Man's Manual* (Philadelphia, 1831), pp. 229, 48.

not fail to note the fallacy of their argument. For "the slightest observation will satisfy the most prejudiced and skeptical mind, that nature has superabundantly supplied the industry of man with the means of universal comfort." [30]

Pauperism is not the product of an iron law of nature but of an inequitable social system. Nor is it the wages of high living. True, "the cant of capital has ascribed pauperism to prodigality; but the voice of science refers it to avarice. The class of paupers seldom have a chance of wasting a patrimony; their only inheritance being misery and rags. A thousand are born paupers for one who becomes so by waste and extravagance." As for the notion that pauperism is the inevitable consequence of the insufficiency of nature, Simpson offers a vivid refutation:

The whole order of nature, the economy of the world, physical as well as moral, and the beneficence of Providence, all proclaim that pauperism is the child of luxury, monopoly and avarice. The superabundant fruits of the earth, the o'erteeming womb of nature in its spontaneous productions, the superfluity of labour, from the hand of industry, the immense mountains of wealth, accumulated by avaricious extortion, and legal fraud, the satiety of luxury, palled into disease by surfeited appetite, idleness pampered into the tomb by voluptuous enjoyment, one man in the possession of millions, and thousands rioting in over abundance, clearly demonstrate that the perversions and vices of man, and not the order of nature, have generated the excrescence of pauperism, upon the face of the earth.

It is clear that by "vices of man" Simpson meant something altogether different than did the Malthusians.

His concluding attacks on the scheme are written from the point of view, not of a moralist outraged by the hint at restricting population, but of a rational optimist who will not accept such confession of human inadequacy. He concludes:

In addition to the cruelty of the scheme, it is unwise, impolitic, and oppressive. It is unwise, because it assumes the first principle, that poverty must exist, and must increase: it is impolitic, because it tends to add to the burdens of society, by inculcating the necessity and growth of pauperism, and depressing the poor into lethargy, as well as urging them to vice. It is oppressive because it seeks to close up, by a dismal fatality, the door of enterprise, exertion, emulation, competition, pride, independence, and industry. . . .[31]

[30] *Ibid.*, pp. 225, 8.
[31] *Ibid.*, pp. 127, 227.

Malthusianism is purely negative:

In place . . . of depriving the poor of the solace of matrimony, because
they may not be able to support themselves, we are bound by every consideration of sound policy, religion, morality and benevolence, to devise
means to diminish their poverty, by seeking out and removing the causes
of so unequal a distribution of labor, and encourage both marriage and
population, as the means of national wealth, as well as individual happiness.

Simpson's critique is not simply that of the environmentalist radical.
He also speaks for a dynamic rather than a static business outlook.

Thomas Brothers, the hatmaker and publisher who played so lively
a part in the Pennsylvania union movement of the 1830s, also
attacked Malthusianism. By his evaluation it was simply a scheme
justifying severer exploitation of labor. He attacked it largely on
moral grounds. In England, capitalists hoped to "do with less
hands." They already had reduced the workers

from bread, bacon, beef and ale, to bread and water; and a law has been
recently passed to reduce them to still coarser food . . . and this is to be
the food for the men that are needful to keep the "improvements" in
good order; while the rest, if Parson Malthus' doctrine be carried into
effect, are to be cleared off the land, and transported to the swamps and
sands of other countries.[32]

Similar things are in store for America if the principles of Malthusianism are observed:

The money manufacturers and improvement men, with Parson Malthus
at their head (no, I believe it has pleased God to call him to give an
account of his stewardship) . . . talk of making a law to *"drive the poor
to the law of nature,"* and that law is to be construed to mean, that they,
the poor, shall shift for themselves, and shall not be allowed to partake of
the fruits of the earth, which is, under the new order of things, said to be
exclusively the property of the improvers and bankers; those greedy
wretches forget that, to be driven to the law of nature, is to be driven to
the dividing of the land, or rather to the ranging at will, and to the taking
of food where it is to be found, according to the word of God.[33]

[32] He refers to the Poor Law of 1834, which superseded the old system of
parish relief that had been attacked by Malthus. The new law provided for
workhouses, or *bastilles*, as they came to be known, for the unemployed.

[33] *Radical Reformer and Working Man's Advocate*, July 4, 11, 1835, pp. 52, 65.

The fruits of the application of the Malthusian doctrine would be the exact opposite of those dreamed of by its initiator.

The labor attacks on Malthusianism foreshadowed the line taken by social reformers of a later day. Henry George, for example, in his *Progress and Poverty*, also explained the success of Malthus as due to "the fact that he furnished a plausible reason for the assumption that some have a better right to existence than others. . . ." Justifying the greed of the rich, as it did, the theory's popularity was assured. "Prudential restraint" was not a cure but a false road, inasmuch as misery was due not to the habits of the poor but to society's inequitable organization. In language very much like that of Skidmore before him, George denounced the doctrine for parrying the "demand for reform," and sheltering

selfishness from question and from conscience by the interposition of an inevitable necessity. It furnishes a philosophy by which Dives as he feasts can shut out the image of Lazarus who faints with hunger at his door; by which wealth may complacently button up its pocket when poverty asks alms, and the rich Christian bend on Sundays in a nicely upholstered pew to implore the good gifts of the Allmighty Father without any feeling of responsibility for the squalid misery that is festering but a square away. For poverty, want, and starvation are by this theory not chargeable either to individual greed or to social maladjustments; they are the inevitable results of universal laws, with which, if it were not impious, it were as hopeless to quarrel as with the law of gravitation.[34]

Actually, George, like the Jacksonian labor critics, had no quarrel with the general concept of universal social laws, which he here dismisses sarcastically. So long as they are *true* laws—that is, laws he agrees with—they are to be accepted. The trouble with the Malthusian principles is not that they purport to be law but that they are wrong.

Optimists that they were, the labor spokesmen would not accept the gloomy pronouncements of the Malthusian theory. Nor, as inveterate environmentalists, would they accept its attempt to fix the blame for the human plight on the misbehavior or the instincts of the people themselves. Even those who, like Frances Wright and Robert Dale Owen, found certain human traits deserving of criti-

[34] Henry George, *Progress and Poverty*, Modern Library Edition (New York, 1939), pp. 338–339, 299–300, 99–100.

cism, blamed social misery—and to a large extent these same personal imperfections—on asocial institutions.[35] As we shall see in the next chapter, opinions invariably differed in attributing responsibility to this or that institution as the cause of the evil. But on one point there was agreement: the poor were not the authors of their own misery.

[35] See Owen, *Lectures on the Marriages of the Priesthood of the Old Immoral World* (London, 1835), p. 54; and also Owen, *Republican Government and National Education*, p. 11; the *Working Man's Advocate*, Jan. 16, and May 15, 1830; *New Era*, May 1, 1840; Seth Luther, *An Address on the Origins and Progress of Avarice* (Boston, 1834), pp. 19–21, 26, 34–35; John Commerford, in the *Union*, May 23, 1836.

10
The Causes of Social Distress

The Jacksonian labor leaders were quite aware of human imperfections—some of them more than others—and recognized the negative social consequences of such unattractive traits as selfishness or laziness. Criticizing Malthusianism from the standpoint of a realist, Robert Dale Owen noted that, in urging people to curb their passion, the doctrine asked what weak humans were incapable of giving. Owen's criticism seems directed more against a human weakness than at a social institution. Yet if Owen and the other leaders were aware of flaws in man's character, it is also true that neither Owen nor any of his colleagues saw these blemishes as major causes of social wretchedness. In their judgment, hunger, inequality, lack of opportunity, were caused neither by man's sexual instincts nor by his emotional deficiencies, but rather by a number of artificial social institutions.

Many things in American life were blamed, some of these implied in the leaders' caustic criticism of American life. For their picture of American society was in a number of particulars as interpretive as it was descriptive. Thus domination of the major parties by wealth was both a *feature* and an *explanation* of the American scene. This would explain why so little was done to ease the burden of the poor. The alleged avarice of the rich, also, was an example of a manifestation that was a cause, and a cause that was a manifestation. The leaders themselves sensibly made no hard and fast distinction between cause and effect. They painted a damning picture; in some cases at the same time, in other cases at a different time they offered their interpretation of it.

A list of all the causes they mentioned would be a long one. It would show, however, that only a few institutions were emphasized as truly important. Nor is it accidental that these were essentially economic. The leaders were realists, in the sense that they looked to wealth—the system of producing it, distributing it throughout the society, transmitting it across the generations—for the source of power within society. Very much concerned with morality and morale, they believed, as did social reformers before and after, that the state of the spiritual life very much depended on the material. Though man might not live by bread alone, nevertheless, his enjoyment of higher things depended in the first place on the satisfaction of the stomach.

The system of private property was widely criticized as the fundamental evil, responsible for countless other evils. With regard to other issues, the rhetoric of the labor spokesmen often seemed more radical than the actual content of their ideas; but this was not true in the case of their condemnation of private property. For here they spoke very softly; so softly, in fact, that oftentimes the critical idea has to be patiently dug out of the mass of words, so deeply imbedded, so carefully hidden is it. This was so for one essential reason: the bad reputation enjoyed by Thomas Skidmore and his ideas. Known above all for his radical views on private property, Skidmore had been denounced as an "agrarian," abused by conservatives outside the Working Men's movement and scorned by his enemies within.[1]

In view of the notoriety of his views, most of Skidmore's colleagues went to some pains to detach themselves from "agrarianism," to make clear their non-association with, even their opposition to, the stigmatized doctrine. Ely Moore assures his congressional audience that workingmen abhor the idea of equality of possessions; Seth Luther informs his readers that property is a good thing. Robert Dale Owen, himself placed under a cloud by the commercial press of New York City as a terrible radical in his own right, tries to assure this same press that even though he, Owen, had been elected secretary by a party which unanimously endorsed Skidmore's ideas on property, things were not what they seemed: neither Owen nor the workingmen had fully understood the resolutions they voted for; Owen had only "casually attended" the meeting, "ignorant of what were the objects of those who called it, what were the measures to be proposed, or who the individuals who were to propose these measures; and . . . heard the resolutions at the meeting for the first time." Stephen Simpson describes himself as an "anti-agrarian." And even George Henry Evans, later to be the founder of the "New Agrarianism," as the movement to have every man vote himself a

[1] See Chapter 4 above.

farm came to be known, had found it necessary to delete from the third issue of his *Working Man's Advocate* the tainted phrase, "all adults [entitled] to equal property," which had been on the masthead of the journal's first two issues: "All children are entitled to equal education; all adults to equal property, and all mankind to equal privileges." [2]

After making these disclaimers, however, the leaders generally went on to attack private property in their own right. Their substantive ideas, it turned out, were quite similar to Skidmore's. Now this may be hard for some modern readers to accept, not only because of the explicit renunciations of Skidmore, cited above, but also because of the interpretations that appear in modern scholarly works. For it was not only Robert Dale Owen who held that New York workers voting in support of Skidmore's ideas did not understand what they were doing. The modern radical labor historian Philip S. Foner agrees, as did Helen Sumner, when in making her substantial contribution to the first volume of Commons' *History*, she wrote that Skidmore's program was foisted upon the workingmen and was not actually understood by them. Modern scholars have thus accepted the interpretation of the editorial writer for the New York *Commercial Advertiser*, that "the people at the meeting" "could not have understood their own resolutions." [3] Once accept the idea, however, that ordinary rank and file workingmen could approve attacks on private property, with full knowledge of what they were approving—as is sometimes true of men in a state of consciousness—it becomes easier to understand that leaders of these workingmen could also make such attacks.

[2] See Ely Moore, *Speech in Reply to the Hon. Waddy Thompson*, given in the House of Representatives, May 5, 1836 (Washington, 1836), p. 6. Later, Moore was to defend the right to slave property (*Remarks in the House of Representatives*, Feb., 1839, pp. 10-11. See Seth Luther, *An Address on the Origins and Progress of Avarice* (Boston, 1834), p. 40; Louis Hartz, "Seth Luther: The Story of a Working-Class Rebel," *New England Quarterly*, XIII (Sept., 1940), 411; Robert Dale Owen to the editors of the New York Commercial Advertisers, Oct. 26, 1829; the *Free Enquirer*, Oct. 31, and Nov. 7, 14, 28, 1829; Simpson, *The Working Man's Manual* (Philadelphia, 1831), pp. 53–55; *Working Man's Advocate*, Oct. 31, and Nov. 7, 14, 1829.

[3] John R. Commons and Associates, *History of Labour in the United States* (2 vols.; New York, 1918), I, 245; Philip S. Foner, *History of the Labor Movement in the United States* (2 vols.; New York, 1947 and 1955), I, 134–135; New York *Commercial Advertiser*, April 25, 1829.

There is reason to believe that during the age of Jackson, attacks on private property were at times acceptable to workingmen. For example, in the very act of pulling down the slogan of equal property to adults, Evans went to great lengths to demonstrate that he continued to believe essentially in the same goals and was modifying his journal's masthead only because it had been "misunderstood." In his lengthy explanation, he argues that not only children are entitled to equal means to pursue happiness but that "all, on arriving at an adult age, are entitled to equal property." [4] He gives the impression of a man required by practical exigencies to do something he finds distasteful, trying very hard to convince not only himself and his own conscience that he is not retrogressing but also a group of hard-eyed friends—in this case, the readers of his labor journal. Possibly the best evidence of all that attacks on private property were occasionally politic is that they were at first overwhelmingly supported by the New York Working Men, and that it was only due to his identification with such views that Thomas Skidmore was made a leader of that party and came within a hair's breadth of election to the New York State Assembly.

In their discussion, certainly the labor leaders made no great contributions to the theory of the subject. Their comments appear to be derivative, very much influenced by such English writers as John Gray, Charles Hall, Minter Morgan, William Thompson, and, of course, Robert Owen.[5] The most original of the American critics without a doubt was Skidmore; although it is clear that he, too, was very much influenced by others. When asked about the origins of his beliefs, Skidmore referred to his reading of radical journals when he was a boy.[6] He kept reading as he grew up; and from both the language and the ideas he used in the volume in which he fully stated his theory, it seems reasonably certain that he had been influenced by the writing of earlier English agrarians: such as Thomas Spence,

[4] See the editorial in the *Working Man's Advocate*, Nov. 14, 1829.

[5] For the best-known versions of the antiprivate property view, see Anton Menger, *The Right to the Whole Product of Labour* (London, 1889); Beatrice and Sidney Webb, *History of Trade Unionism* (New York, 1920); Max Beer, *A History of British Socialism* (London, 1948); G. D. H. Cole, *A Short History of the British Working Class* (London, 1926).

[6] See Amos Gilbert, "A Sketch of the Life of Thomas Skidmore," serialized in the New York *Free Enquirer*, in issues for March 30, April 6, and April 13, 1834.

who argued that people of a later day should not be bound by the property arrangements agreed to by earlier generations; William Ogilvie, who saw workers cheated out of what was properly theirs, in value added to the land, by the system of private property; and, not least, by Thomas Paine, who called attention to society's tendency to confuse the land itself, properly the property of all, with improvements made on it, the fruits of which should go to the individuals responsble for them.[7] Where these eighteenth-century writers attacked private property in land, however, Skidmore went further and denounced private property in general. (Some of Skidmore's contemporaries in the American labor movement were not so fastidious in their usage, leaving somewhat obscure whether it is private land ownership or private ownership, per se, that they question.)

Skidmore's own effect on others was greater than has generally been credited. A negative influence has of course been conceded, as when Miss Sumner wrote of his activity, that it "furnished the opponents of the labor movement during many . . . decades with a telling catchword whereby to deprive it of a hearing before the public."[8] On the other hand, Evans' prediction that future generations would admire and reprint Skidmore's work "in spite of its errors, when thousands of the popular publications of the day shall be forgotten." came to pass.[9] It is of more than minor significance that according to Evans it was Skidmore's program that caused him, Evans, to reflect on the inequity of the system by which land was owned.[10] Out of these reflections inspired by Skidmore, came the

[7] See Thomas Spence's "Lecture Before the Newcastle Philosophical Society," in 1735, outlining his plan of land reform; William Ogilvie's *Essay on the Right of Property in Land*, 1781; and Thomas Paine's *Agrarian Justice Opposed to Agrarian Law and Agrarian Monopoly*, first published in 1795–1796— all to be found in Max Beer, ed., *The Pioneers of Land Reform*, (New York, 1920).

[8] Commons, *History of Labour*, I, 245; Foner, *op. cit.*, pp. 135–136.

[9] The *Radical*, April, 1841, p. 52. A number of works by modern authorities contain excerpts from Skidmore's *The Rights of Man to Property*. See, for example, Joseph L. Blau, ed., *Social Theories of Jacksonian Democracy* (New York, 1947), XXV, 355–364; Willard Thorp, Merle Curti, and Carlos Baker, eds., *American Issues* (Chicago, 1944), I, 233–241; Irving Mark and Eugene L. Schwab, eds., *The Faith of Our Fathers* (New York, 1952), pp. 51–55.

[10] See the *Working Man's Advocate*, March 6, and May 22, 1830; the *Radical*, April, 1841, p. 52, and April, 1843, pp. 51–52.

land reform movement of the 1840s and 1850s that played so great a
role in winning passage of the Homestead Act during the Civil War.
There is also a striking similarity between the thought and language
of Skidmore in 1829 and that of Henry George, a half-century later.

George's *Progress and Poverty* rejected redistribution of land or
wealth, calling instead for a single tax to accomplish necessary reforms. Yet George made clear that this scheme of reform was
selected by him for tactical considerations; he hoped it would achieve
results similar to those which would flow from confiscation, but with
less friction and at less social cost.[11] Like Skidmore he believed that
"the wide-spreading social evils which everywhere oppress men amid
an advancing civilization spring from a great primary wrong—the
appropriation, as the exclusive property of some men, of the land on
which and from which all must live." It was because land was treated
as private property that humanity had to suffer "vice and misery,
poverty and pauperism."

The pages of George's classic abound with concepts and language
that bring to mind Skidmore. In one passage George asks: "Has the
first comer at a banquet the right to turn back all the chairs and claim
that none of the other guests shall partake of the food provided,
except as they make terms with him?" Fifty years earlier Skidmore
had written that the prevalent inequality reminded him of a

large party of gentlemen, who should have a common right to dine at
one and the same public table; a part of whom should arrive first, sit
down and eat what they chose; and then, because the remaining part came
later to dinner, should undertake to monopolize the whole; and deprive
them of the opportunity of satisfying their hunger, but upon terms such
as those who had feasted, should be pleased to prescribe. Such now is the
actual condition of the whole human race.[12]

Skidmore attacked private property in pamphlets, in newspaper
columns, in letters to the editor, and at public meetings, in the form

[11] Henry George, *Progress and Poverty*, Modern Library Edition (New
York, 1939), pp. 328, 403–405; George R. Geiger, *The Philosophy of Henry
George* (New York, 1933), pp. 130–131.

[12] George, *op. cit.*, pp. 340–341, 133–134, 328, 338, 345, 346–347, 358; cf. Skidmore's *Rights of Man to Property*, p. 355. It is not unlikely that both Skidmore
and George were influenced by that passage from the second edition of Malthus' *Essay on Population* which alludes to "nature's mighty feast" at which
"there is no vacant cover" for the late comers.

of speeches and resolutions. There is no question, however, that the most comprehensive statement of his views was his opus *The Rights of Man to Property!* (with a subtitle that went on for more than four lines of close, small print, in the fashion typical of the time) that he published in New York City in 1829. In it he charges that private property is the great source of human misery, as well as a violation of each man's right to wealth. Original sin consisted in the early disposition of vast grants to a few landed proprietors and the failure of society to have provided for the descent of property—"if property must descend in a family line"—in an equal manner, instead of having been placed at the disposal or caprice of testators. Like Ogilvie before him, he argued that the value of property derived from labor. In view of this fact, it could not be regarded as a saleable commodity belonging to this or that owner. In a characteristic peroration, he asks:

Why not sell the winds of heaven, that man might not breathe without price? Why not sell the light of the sun, that a man should not see, without making another rich? Why not appropriate the ocean, that man should not find space for his existence, without paying his fellow being for it? All these things could be done if it were practicable, with as much propriety, as the present exclusive and eternal appropriation is made, of the land and all that belongs to it.

The terrible irony was that precisely those whose labor conferred on property whatever value it had were doomed by the system of private property to a nightmare existence of endless toil. The fortunate under this system "are born, only to enjoy." Equally unjust was the system's insistence that original disproportions in wealth be preserved among the sons, the son's sons, and all later generations, by the process of private inheritance. The vicious instrument through which inequality was perpetuated from one generation to another was the will. Skidmore attacked wills with special force.

As a young man Skidmore had experienced bitter scenes with his father over the disbursal of the first income he earned. Those drawn to psychoanalytic interpretations should find interest in the fact that, in his treatise, one of the main grounds of Skidmore's criticism of wills is the tyrannical power they place in the hands of fathers.

How often do parents in possession of property, while living, employ it as the instrument of the most revolting tyranny? How often is the son, under the fear of being disinherited, compelled to comply with the unjust and iniquitous desires of the father? How often is the happiness of the daughter sacrificed, by being compelled to marry a man . . . whom she regards with disgust?

And what is the latter case but "legalized prostitution?" The worst fault of wills, however, is the power they give the dead over the living.

To the argument that men who had amassed their property through their own efforts should have the right to dispose of what was their own as they saw fit, Skidmore counters, "what is the *purpose* of this posthumous dominion over property? Is it to give pleasure to the dead? They cannot feel. . . . Is it to gratify vanity by enabling him [the testator] to say, 'Such is the property I leave you'? Generous man! I would reply, who leave behind you, what you cannot carry away with you!" Dead men, according to Skidmore, as to Jefferson, have no rights that living society must honor, least of all "rights" whose effect is to provide misery and oppression for most of the people. Wills are madness.

Why do they persist, nevertheless? Because like the system, private property, whose instrument they are, their absurdity—control over the fate of unborn generations as well as over the living—is masked. "The injustice . . . is not so visible [as in the case of other wrongs] . . . because the line which separates one generation from another, is not distinctly seen." But once mankind discovers the actual workings of the system, its time will come. It is clear that Skidmore regarded his treatise and his various polemical broadsides as precisely that stream of light which would first penetrate and then dissolve the fog obscuring the true nature of private property, the first cause of human suffering.[13]

Few were so much preoccupied with private property, so explicit in rating it on a list of evils, or so vehement in denouncing it. Yet fewer still of the labor leaders had a good word for it. While they might not go so far as did Skidmore, most of them also regarded private property as an important wrong in American society, and

[13] See the letter from Skidmore to Amos Gilbert in the *Free Enquirer*, Dec. 17, 1831; Skidmore and others, "Report of the Committee of Fifty," in the *Working Man's Advocate*, Oct. 31, 1829; Thomas Skidmore, *Moral Physiology Exposed and Refuted* (New York, 1831), *passim*; and Skidmore, *Rights of Man to Property* (New York, 1829), pp. 116, 3–4, 55, 244, 355, 388, 154, 226–227, 239, 336, 86, 90, 235, 112.

they criticized it accordingly. As befitted the son of Robert Owen, Robert Dale Owen was an arch critic of the institution. Although strongly opposed to the Skidmore program, he saw some value in its denunciation of private property. His own short treatise "Wealth and Misery," which was published first in the New Harmony *Gazette* in 1826 and, with very slight changes, four years later in the *Working Man's Advocate*, held that private wealth was unjustly accumulated in this society. His program for the reform of society, as we shall see, was based on a transformation of the system. As has already been shown, Evans, for all of his removal of the embarrassing phrase about property from the masthead of the *Working Man's Advocate*, continued to hold private property responsible for the lack of opportunity facing most people. Despite their internal bickering about program, tactics, and personality, the first leaders of the New York Working Men shared a common repugnance for the institution of private property.

Stephen Simpson may have been the "American Cobbett" to some of his Philadelphia admirers, but he describes himself as an "anti-agrarian." A close reading of his treatise in political economy, however, suggests that his own designation of himself was self-serving rather than an accurate description. Despite his attempts in this case to play down his radicalism, his ideas sound very much like Skidmore's and his agrarian predecessors. Thus he writes that labor alone gives meaning, not to mention value, to property. "Without labor there can be no property"; and again, "if an ancestor bequeathes me a thousand acres, unless labor converts them to a useful purpose, they are without value." Yet in contrast to the principle of justice, according to which those responsible for the creation of something should reap the fruits resulting from their efforts, labor is wronged. For "when we come to the primitive source of property—land, all this apparent sense of justice vanishes, and fraud and force stare us in the face." The Philadelphia Working Men's leader thus joined his New York colleagues in attacking the system of private ownership of wealth.

The trade unionists also joined the attack. Charles Douglas speaks of the few stealing power from the many,

until the earth and the fulness thereof is no longer the equal property of all God's creatures, but is possessed by a very small part of them, who lord it over their fellow men, and by virtue of these unjust regulations, not only destroy that noble equality stamped by nature on her words [sic], but reduce their fellow creatures . . . to poverty, hunger, and starvation.

John Ferral's words could easily be interchanged with those of Skidmore: "The accumulation of the wealth of society in the hands of a few individuals (which has been abstracted from the producers thereof by means of the erroneous customs, usages, and laws of society) is subversive of the rights of men." John Commerford speaks the language of the pre-Skidmore agrarians when he tells workers that one of the gravest problems facing them stems from the fact that the lands "have become the property of the few." Working people and mankind in general suffered because in violation of the Creator's obvious intention that the wants of all be satisfied, a system prevailed wherein a few monopolized the earth's riches and undeserved wealth was transmitted to equally undeserving offspring.

It is true that some of the leaders had a good word to say for private property, but the institution would have been in a very bad way indeed had it depended for its survival on their faint or mixed praise. In fact, a good case might be made for the thesis that the hostility of labor to private property in the Jacksonian era is in no wise better illustrated than in the kind of defense the institution got from some of its friends in the house of labor. The changeable Levi Slamm turns from admiration to scorn for American Fourierists, who used the columns of his journals to proclaim their views. Competition must be maintained; no drastic revision of society should be attempted, he admonishes. But on the other hand, "too great an inequality in the ownership of property—some having what would suffice for thousands, and others having none at all—is productive of nearly all the ills of society." Ely Moore gives Skidmorism short shrift. But he warns against exaggerating the menace it allegedly poses: "where there is one instance where the rights of property have been violated by the people, . . . there are five thousand instances where the people have been plundered and beggared by the heartless cupidity of the privileged few." And if Seth Luther thinks property is a good thing, he also thinks it should not be based on exploitation and inequality, nor should it rest on force. If explosions take place here and in England in the future, it will be due not to the strictures of the agrarians but to the suppression of the aspirations of the propertyless.[14]

In the spectrum of labor views about private property, if Skidmore's ideas are represented by the darkest tones at one extreme and, let us say, Moore's by the lightest, at the other, the preponderence of shades—for all the denials by the men who painted them—was toward the dark side.

A second great cause of misery, according to the leaders of labor, was the new machinery and the factory system it was in process of creating. That they could accord such treatment to a development that was essentially in its infancy during the Jacksonian era, confined to a few locales in the Northeastern states and New England, and that employed a small proportion of the nation's labor force,[15] is a nice example of the leaders' ability, if not to see that which was not there, then certainly to make bold interpretive stabs, based largely on projection, imagination, and what was happening somewhere else. In view of their harping on the subject, it might appear surprising that the labor movement *did* so little about it. Even the New England Association of Farmers, Mechanics and Other Working Men, which unlike both the labor parties and most of the

---

[14] The *Working Man's Advocate*, May 1, 8, 15, 1830; Robert Dale Owen, *Lectures on the Marriages of the Priesthood of the Old Immoral World* (London, 1835), pp. 32, 36, 47; *Free Enquirer*, Nov. 7, 14, 1829; New Harmony *Gazette*, November and December, 1826. See editorials in *Working Man's Advocate*, Nov. 14, 1829; Jan. 29, 1831; July 21, 1832; and June 14, 1834. Also see *The Man*, Feb. 18, 1834; Simpson, *Working Man's Manual*, pp. 53–55, 135; Charles Douglas' editorial in the *Political Observer and Working Man's Friend*, cited in the *Working Man's Advocate*, June 30, 1832; "Report of the Resolutions Committee to the First Convention of the National Trades' Union," in *The Man*, Aug. 29, 1834; the *Union*, April 28, 1836. See Levi D. Slamm's editorials in the *Daily Plebeian*, Jan. 27, and Nov. 27, 1844; Feb. 6, 17, and March 27, 1845; and the *Weekly Plebeian*, March 30, 1844. See again the speech of Ely Moore in the House of Representatives on May 5, 1836, p. 7; and Luther's *Origins and Progress of Avarice*.

[15] See Victor S. Clark, *History of Manufactures in the United States* (New York, 1929), I, 448–455; Louis McLane, *Documents Relative to the Manufactures in the United States* (House Document No. 308, Washington, 1833); Norman Ware, *The Industrial Worker 1840–1860* (Boston, 1924), *passim;* George R. Taylor, *The Transportation Revolution* (New York, 1951), chap. xi; Thomas Cochran and William Miller, *The Age of Enterprise* (New York, 1949), chap. ii; Arthur H. Cole, *The American Woolen Manufacture* (Cambridge, 1926, *passim.*

unions of the era, formally concerned itself with the problems raised by industrialization, essentially confined itself to discussion of the issue.[16]

Talk there was in abundance. The near incessant discussion of what in quantitative terms was yet a small factor in the American economy was not, however, a form of escapism. In addition to demonstrating the leaders' powers of imagination, it also indicated their good sense in recognizing an issue of great and increasing significance, at a time when its dimensions were only faintly discernible. For that matter, it was not only the leaders who saw the handwriting on the wall. I find something poignant in an advertisement placed in a New England labor journal in 1834 by the Journeymen Rope Makers of Boston. In response to a previous ad, proclaiming the superiority of the machine-made product, the union called for a public contest to decide the comparative durability of yarn spun by machinery with yarn spun by hand.[17] The spectre of technological unemployment was beginning to haunt American labor.

There were other good reasons for concern. America was not England, true, but there was good sense in paying close attention to the features of industrialization there, since, as John Commerford put it, "like causes produce like effects." In our own day the discussion of the social consequences of the Industrial Revolution in England in the nineteenth century has taken—as has the discussion, I suppose, of everything else—a new, sophisticated turn. On the one hand, R. M. Hartswell and his supporters argue that the misery of the masses and the alleged deterioration of their lot has been overdone and has no foundation in fact. On the other, E. J. Hobsbawm and his adherents are still fighting the good fight—on the literary level—in behalf of the viciously exploited English proletariat, in the spirit of John and Barbara Hammond and other sympathetic English social historians. The last word on this issue, of course, has not yet been said.[18]

---

[16] Boston *Columbian Centinel*, Sept. 8, 1832; Boston *Post*, Oct. 9, 1832; *New England Artisan*, Oct. 4, 25, 1832; *Working Man's Advocate*, March 3, and Sept. 15, 1832.

[17] See the *New England Artisan*, Oct. 4, 1834.

[18] On the recent controversy concerning conditions of English factory labor during the early phase of the Industrial Revolution, see R. M. Hartwell, "Interpretations of the Industrial Revolution in England: a Methodological Inquiry," *Journal of Economic History*, June, 1959; and also Hartwell, "The

The American laborites made no pretension to scholarly objectivity. The version of the factory system they accepted—and it was a version well known and believed by many Englishmen who were very far removed from socialism or radicalism—was that drawn by Charles Dickens and Thomas Carlyle, by Friedrich Engels' *Condition of the English Working Classes,* and by the Parliamentary investigations of the Sadler Committee and Lord Shaftsbury. It viewed the factories as "dark, satanic mills," in which labor of all ages and both sexes was shamelessly overworked and underpaid under abysmal working conditions. Fully convinced not only that this grim situation obtained in England but also that its development was an inevitable consequence of industrialism, wherever it might spread, most of the leaders naturally believed that a like result would occur in this country. At times, what is ostensibly a discussion of conditions in Lowell, Waltham, or Fall River, seems rather to be a description of Leeds, Brimingham, or Sheffield, by men who when they talk of America can never seem to get Great Britain out of their minds.

But whether on a small scale or not, there were factories in this country, they were organized around machine production, and there was no question that the system was growing in significance. Not to have paid close attention to the phenomenon would have been the true escapism. And in view of their numerous advantages to the capitalist, the "substantial economies [which] resulted from the mechanical power and integration of processes," their potential of mass production of cheap fabrics, the cheap and unskilled labor

---

Rising Standard of Living in England, 1800–1850," *Economic History Review,* April, 1961; and see also E. J. Hobsbawn, "The British Standard of Living, 1790–1850," *Economic History Review,* August, 1957. For earlier accounts of the new system, the following titles are still very useful: Paul Mantoux, *The Industrial Revolution in the Eighteenth Century in England* (New York, 1928); Arnold Toynbee, *The Industrial Revolution of the Eighteenth Century in England* (London, 1884), Edward Baines, *History of the Cotton Manufactures in Great Britain* (London, 1885); R. Whately Cooke-Taylor, *Introduction to a History of the Factory System* (London, 1886); Herbert Heaton, *The Yorkshire Woollen and Worsted Industries* (Oxford, 1920); L. C. A. Knowles, *The Industrial and Commercial Revolutions in Great Britain During the Nineteenth Century* (London, 1921); Erich Roll, *An Early Experiment in Industrial Organization* (London, 1930); George Unwin, *Studies in Economic History* (London, 1927). And, above all, the following works of John L. and Barbara Hammond: *The Village Labourer 1760–1832* (London, 1911); *The Town Labourer 1760–1832* (London, 1917); *The Rise of Modern Industry* (London, 1926); and *The Skilled Labourer 1760–1832* (London, 1927).

they required, and the lure of their great future prospects, factories were clearly the workshops of the future for this country. There was good reason to expect that the great merchant princes of Boston, the Cabots, the Lowells, the Appletons, the Jacksons, who had invested fortunes made in commerce, in the creation of factories and factory towns in New England, would soon have a host of imitators elsewhere in the country.[19]

The American discussion of the factory system was a lively and in some respects an original one. The labor spokesmen did not simply ape their British colleagues. No one, for example, seriously advocated Luddism, as the movement to destroy machines, was known. But the laborites did emphasize the dismal side, as illustrated by Charles Douglas' description of a famous New England factory town. He observed that in the single village of Lowell, there were about 4000 females of various ages, "now dragging out a life of slavery and wretchedness." And he continued mournfully: "It is enough to make one's heart ache . . . to behold these degraded females, as they pass out of the factory—to mark their countenances . . . their woe-stricken appearance. These establishments are the present abode of wretchedness, disease and misery; and are inevitably calculated to perpetuate them—if not to destroy liberty itself." [20] This is a very different picture from the one painted by such observers as Harriet Martineau and Michael Chevalier, whose version featured spic-and-span houses of quaint charm, paternalism of a highminded responsible sort, pleasant work which even had an aesthetic component, what with the swift, dexterous action required of nimble fingers, and much spare time for wholesome activity such as the publishing by the girls of a newspaper, the Lowell *Offering*, whose columns were oddly enough dedicated to propagating this version of the Lowell scene. (The Rogers and Hammerstein *Carousel* takes place in a charming factory setting staged by someone who obviously accepted the Martineau version as the true one.)

[19] Justin Winsor ed., *Memorial History of Boston* (Boston, 1881), chap. iii, "The Industries of the Last Hundred Years," by Carroll D. Wright and Horace G. Wadlin; Caroline Ware, *The Early New England Cotton Manufactures* (Boston, 1931); Vera Shlakman, "Economic History of a Factory Town: A Study of Chicopee, Massachusetts," *Smith College Studies in History*, XX (Oct., 1934; Jan., April, July, 1935), Nos. 1–4, *passim*.

[20] "Sketch of the Discussion on the Condition of Females in the Manufacturing Establishments in this Country," in *The Man*, Sept. 17, 1834.

It seems obvious that subjective observers looking at the same evidence, but with different eyes, and inspired by opposing convictions, have given us something other than final truth. Some factory girls had happy reminiscences of days they spent in the mills. Others did not. According to one of the latter group, "six girls often slept in one room, in three double beds. . . . Among the appurtenances of the back yard . . . was a conventional line of pig pens operated by each boarding house in the interests of economy. Near these were the wells. When the ground became properly saturated . . . there was an epidemic of typhoid fever that was a record breaker." [21] Modern scholars have noted that the hours of work were extremely long, over seventy hours in many cases, wages were low, conditions of work were oftentimes oppressive, and attempts on the part of the young women to organize in order to improve conditions, were opposed brusquely and ruthlessly.[22] Douglas' view, in other words, was by no means a wild exaggeration.

Labor's opinion of the future or even of the immediate worth of machinery and the factory system was more complex than seems to be the case at first glance. Yet no labor spokesman comes close to matching the business viewpoint as it was expressed by contemporary economists. Joseph Dorfman reveals that the latter were serenely optimistic about practically every aspect of the new system. The Rev. John McVickar of Columbia University, the southern journalist and publisher Jacob Newton Cardozo, and the eminent Charlestonian Hugh Legaré anticipated great benefits from the new machinery. Machines might cause some unemployment, but in the long run they improved the lot of labor, since by lowering prices they increased demand, stimulated production and reabsorbed the temporarily displaced labor into the economy. A small minority of men would become very rich through this development, but on the other hand, the "standard of living of the mass" would rise simultaneously.[23] The labor spokesmen saw matters differently.

[21] Shlakman, *op. cit.*, pp. 53–54.

[22] Certainly this is the judgment of Shlakman, *ibid.*; Carolina Ware, *op. cit.*; Hannah Josephson, *The Golden Threads* (New York, 1949); George R. Taylor, *op. cit.*, pp. 272–273, 275–277. Also see the *Voice of Industry*, the journal published by militant Lowell working girls in the 1840s.

[23] Joseph Dorfman, *The Economic Mind in American Civilization* (New York, 1946), II, 520, 557, 626.

What seemed to be outright rejection of machines and the factory system, however, oftentimes on close analysis turns out to be something very different. For on this issue, too, the rhetoric used by the leaders sometimes obscured more than it clarified. Denunciation of the new system's harsher aspects could take on so savage a tone as to give an impression that the speaker had no use whatever for any part of the system—a misleading impression in some cases. A sharp split in labor thought is suggested by the balanced, even sympathetic, language used by some leaders, as though their judgments are diametrically opposed to those of the harsh critics. A split there was, but it was confined essentially to choice of words. The comments of the New England labor agitator Seth Luther are a case in point.

Perhaps because in New England industrialism was already an issue, as well as a harbinger of things to come, a leader of that geographical locale had the most to say on the matter. Luther's *Address to the Working Men of New England*, the first edition of which was published in 1832, won wide support from labor audiences and earned for its author a reputation as labor's foremost thinker on the issue of factories and the new machines. Whether the reputation was justified or not is another matter, but Luther's views were used as a point of departure by a number of his colleagues.

Many of his listeners concluded that he was an undeviating enemy of the new system; certainly most of his words justified their belief. He accuses politicians and factory owners of "using all means to keep out of sight the evils growing up" under the system. But the truth will out, concerning "cotton mills, where cruelties are practiced, excessive labor required, education neglected, and vice, as a matter of course [is] on the increase." These so-called "palaces of the poor" have "produced directly" "a great proportion of the misery and degradation of the starving population" of England. Much of his address is devoted to showing that the development of the factory system here will have similarly dire consequences for this country.

Already the system was producing ignorance, vice and misery here. Unspeakable cruelties were practised in the mills by hypocritical owners whose "wives and daughters," while paying lip-service to their admiration and respect for the female employees, "would no more associate with a 'factory girl,' than they would with a Negro slave." Although physical conditions in American factories were quite as bad as those in their English counterparts, the worst feature of our mills was their long hours of work, since with "thirteen hours actual labor . . . required each day, it is impossible to attend to education among children, or even to improvement among adults." The methods of the system are vicious, its purpose selfish: "the whole system of labour in New England, more especially in cotton mills, is a cruel system of exaction on the bodies and minds of the producing classes, destroying the energies of both, and for no other object than to enable the 'rich' to 'take care of themselves' while the poor must work or starve." It would be hard to find a more severe indictment of the factory system of the Jackson era.

And yet Luther is not an inveterate foe of industrialism and all its works. True, he believes the social cost to date has been exorbitant, but he reminds workers that machinery had made possible quicker and cheaper transportation, as well as great material progress. He points out that "it is impossible to do without manufactures," and that the clock will not be turned back to a time when they were produced in less volume, more expensively. Not factories as such, but the present conditions disgracing them, must be eradicated, for "he has yet to learn that it is necessary . . . that manufactures must be sustained by injustice, cruelty, ignorance, vice and misery; which is now the fact to a startling degree." Despite the intransigent tone of many of his remarks, Luther was actually a realist with regard to the factory system. His counsel is not that it be torn down but that it be improved.[24]

The comments of Luther's fellow leaders seem to fall into two distinct categories. One group seemingly stands for total opposition to factories, to machines, or to both. The adherents to this position—let us call them the rejectionists—bristle at the mention of the evils. George Henry Evans is aware that the system has its supporters, but "let them dignify the factory system by any title they please, it is still the factory system which can destroy the dearest rights of freemen and convert their offspring into mere machines." No appreciation whatever of hypothetical future benefits is suggested by his definition:

[24] A clear statement of Luther's recognition of the inevitability of the system appears in his letter to the editor of the Portland *Courier and Mechanic's Advocate*, cited in *Working Man's Advocate*, Sept. 1, 1832; cf. Luther, *Origins and Progress of Avarice*, pp. 10–11. The bulk of his comments are found in his *Address to the Working Men of New England* (3rd. ed.; Philadelphia, 1836), pp. 17, 8, 14, 15, 19, 20, 28, 31.

The Factory System is that system by which, with the aid of machinery, a small company of men . . . are enabled to avail themselves of the labor of hundreds, and frequently thousands . . . to increase the wealth of the company, while the men, women, and children are generally worked to the utmost possible number of hours a day, and paid for their work the smallest possible compensation which will enable them to keep life in the body and sufficient strength to return to their daily task.

Charles Douglas' retort to praise of the system's economic advantages, was that "the cheapness and facility of procuring the manufactured articles, are in recompense for their injury to the health and the morals of the rising generation." To Harriet Martineau and others like her, who extolled its virtues, he replied, "the factory business which presents so fair an outside show, is perhaps the most alarming evil that afflicts our country." John Commerford regarded the factory system simply as "one of the machines which has been introduced to jeopardize our liberties"; while William English joined Douglas in bemoaning its terrible effect on the poor working girl: Who but a tyrant could drag her, "the pride and ornament of our race," forth from "domestic retirement to the performance of manual labor? What but grasping avarice could tempt a being bearing the form of man, to enter the happy circle of the fireside and bear away its bright ornament to toil, poverty, and degradation?" As for the new technology, Theophilus Fisk's view was that it was "labor-saving machines by which drones are enabled to grow rich without honest industry."

Criticism of the new system in several cases seemed to be motivated at least partially by personal considerations having nothing to do with the interests of labor in general. After he became a publisher of partisan Democratic journals, Slamm attacked the factory system for having brought misery to English workers. In this country, too, it ground the faces of laborers into the earth, turning workers into "white slaves to black hearted tyrants." By this time, however, Slamm was a supporter of slavery, as well as a free-trade Democrat, strongly opposed to all aspects of the American System. Thomas Brothers' denunciation of the new machines is the plaintive outcry of a small manufacturer unable to meet the prices set by larger operators who could afford expensive machinery for making the bodies of hats. Of course he was unhappy that half the workingmen were thrown out of work by the new processes, for was he not a friend to labor? But he is equally unhappy that the owners of the new machinery were enabled "to undersell and to ruin the rest of the trade, both bosses and journeymen."

John Ferral's comments seem typical of those of the arch critics of the new system. He joins the chorus who hold it responsible for starvation of "about three-fourths of the nation" in England. In this country the system was "subversive of liberty," the factories were "gaols, where the dependent inmates are confined." Yet, like Luther, he believed the growth of the system inevitable. What was needed was not the overthrow but "the entire reformation of the system." Ferral was only being somewhat more explicit than a number of his seemingly critical co-workers, a patient reading of whose diatribes reveal that like him, what they find offensive is not so much the system itself as its present form.

A number of the leaders, while never striking a note quite so affirmative as that registered by business or academic enthusiasts for the factory system, nevertheless stressed its positive implications, above all, for the future. They sound very much like the nineteenth-century socialists who praise capitalism's productivity. The best example of this approach is provided by Robert Dale Owen. He is sympathetic to those workers who having been displaced by machines would like to abolish them, but he urges that they follow the voice of reason rather than emotion. Luddism was impractical because it was impotent. As he saw the question, it was simply this: "Must we, to save the laborer from starvation, curtail the means of producing the necessaries and comforts of life?" The answer was obviously No. In his essay "Wealth and Misery" he develops an argument based on logical reason and historical experience in support of improved technology. In the postscript he wrote to this essay in 1830, he puts his position more clearly than before. It is "under the *present commercial arrangements*" that "machines, the people's legitimate servants, have become their masters." Not labor-saving machinery, per se, but "labor-saving machinery, *as at present directed and controlled*, works against the poor man." The proper approach to the issue is summed up in Owen's recasting of his original question: "How can labor-saving machinery be made to lessen the toil and increase the comforts of the working man?"

Machines did have a harmful effect on the conditions of labor, according to Slamm, but only because labor was currently treated as merchandise. The implication is clear that under arrangements which properly value labor the curse can become a blessing. Simpson's advice that workers reject Luddism is based on his similar estimate, that despite their bad immediate effects, machines will be a source of much future good.

John Commerford advocates an interesting scheme whereby Congress should step in and assure that the worker in danger of being replaced by a new machine would be secured "from want, until he could obtain a situation at least as good as that from which he was about to be driven." This is not only a call for job retraining: it would have the government act *prior* to the falling of the ax, thus assuring continued income to the worker threatened with technological unemployment. Although he was no doctrinaire, being blissfully unaware of any theoretical implications in his thought, Commerford comes close to predicting that the inevitable technical progress and perfecting of machinery will in the future create a kind of communism, marked by plenty for all in the realm of material goods, and political equality and justice in the realm of government. "Machinery must be viewed as one of the most energetic agents in hastening the political millennium," he writes. Eventually,

even capital itself must . . . abandon its power over machinery, for when machinery arrives at the point, which will give to the world those necessary commodities for consumption . . . the contest of capital will cease, because the supply will be furnished in such vast quantities, that competition between individuals will be destroyed. Machinery will not then be used, as it is now, for the benefit of the few, but for the mass. Governments will become the legitimate guardians of its improvements; and they will be compelled to keep machinery in operation for the comfort and convenience of the people!

By this reasoning, the *level* of production determined both the system of production and the character of government.

Skidmore's blunt advice, that the way for the laboring poor to remedy present ills caused by factories and machines was to "lay hold of" them for their own purposes, was of course rejected by the labor leaders. His central idea, however, that the problem essentially was not machine production but rather the larger system within which it operated, was shared by most of his colleagues in the labor movement.[25] For what the labor historian Norman Ware has said of industrial workers of the period 1840 to 1860 applies to the earlier leaders as well: "The American worker was not actively opposed to machinery. He was opposed to the method of its introduction, for exploitive purposes, as he conceived it, in the hands of a group alien to the producer." [26]

The third great evil of the day, according to the labor spokesmen—the very "root of evil," said Charles Douglas—was monopoly. Almost in the same breath they condemned banks as the nastiest form monopoly took in actual practice, and denounced the paper money—"rag money" to its critics—the banks issued. As the term was commonly understood in the Jackson era, a monopoly was a corporate charter granted a group of individuals by a special legislative enactment. Opposition to this system was by no means confined to workers or radicals.

Economic liberals, small businessmen, wealthy merchants, even southern planters, could also be heard castigating monopolies, though the loudest criticisms probably came from such journalists and middle-class figures as Theodore Sedgwick, Jr., Dr. John Vethake, William Leggett, and William Gouge. Joseph Blau has provided the following useful summary of the antimonopoly position of liberal Jacksonians:

[25] *Working Man's Advocate,* March 24, 1832, and Sept. 20, 1834; Charles Douglas and others, "Address to the Workingmen of Massachusetts," *New England Artisan,* Oct. 25, 1834; John Commerford's remarks to the convention of the National Trades' Union, in *The Man,* Sept. 17, 1834; William English, "Oration Delivered at the Trades' Union Celebration of the 4th of July," in *Radical Reformer and Working Man's Advocate,* Sept. 1, 1835; Frederic Byrdsall, *History of the Loco-Foco or Equal Rights Party* (New York, 1842), p. 20; the *New Era,* May 22, and June 17, 1840; *Daily Plebeian,* Feb. 11, 1843; *Radical Reformer and Working Man's Advocate,* July 4, 11, 1835; Thomas Brothers to William Atwood, cited in Brothers, *The United States of North America as They Really Are* (London, 1840), p. 70; *The Man,* Aug. 29, and Sept. 17, 20, 1834; Robert Dale Owen, "Wealth and Misery," serially in New Harmony *Gazette,* Nov. 8 through Dec. 13, 1826, and slightly revised in *Working Man's Advocate,* May 1, 8, 15, 1830; *Free Enquirer,* Feb. 13, 1830; Owen, in *Working Man's Advocate,* Feb. 13, 20, and March 13, 1830; Simpson, *Working Man's Manual,* pp. 132–133; Commerford, "Address Delivered Before the General Trades' Union," *Working Man's Advocate,* Sept. 19, 1835; Skidmore, *Rights of Man to Property,* pp. 383–384.

[26] Ware, *op. cit.,* p. xi.

Stated very generally, the position taken was that any corporate charter was a grant of privilege, tantamount to a monopoly. To obviate the problems thus created, either no such charters should be granted or all who applied should be given charters. That is, either no one or everyone should be granted a monopoly. If no one were to be granted a corporate charter, the disadvantages would be great. . . . Corporate charters . . . provide a desirable limitation of liability. The alternative was then to issue corporate charters as a matter of routine to all applicants. Thus every man would be his own monopolist and all would be equal.[27]

It was the easiest thing in the world for antimonopoly rhetoric to take on a radical tone. The fact remains, however, that substantial businessmen, including such a representative of their interests as Daniel Webster—who has been interpreted in some quarters as an ideological enemy of radical Jacksonian Democracy—found no difficulty whatever in attacking special legislative grants. Approval of general incorporation acts was eagerly supported by the many Jacksonians who favored expanding opportunities within capitalism for the small investor or businessman.[28] The decisions of the Taney Court, particularly in the Charles River Bridge case, gave legal impetus to this same, hardly anticapitalist, tendency.

The labor spokesmen attacked monopolies well before the issue was taken up by Jacksonians and others. The Jacksonian labor leaders managed not only to say but also to mean very different things, in their discussion of the issue, than was meant by Equal Rights Democrats or those who favored a freer or more competitive capitalism. Where the latter critics were concerned that the system of special grants discriminated against some entrepreneurs in favor of others, labor's concern was that the system defrauded labor. At least so went their argument. There is no good reason to suspect that most of the labor spokesmen did not mean what they said: the system rewarded the idle, the speculative, the parasitic, all at the expense of labor.

To Skidmore, the effect of private charters was to take "property

[27] Blau, ed., *op. cit.*, intro., p. xxiv. Also see Richard Hofstadter, "William Leggett, Spokesman of Jacksonian Democracy," *Political Science Quarterly*, LVIII (Dec. 1943), 581–594, for a discussion of the antimonopoly views of the Friends of Equal Rights.

[28] See Joseph Dorfman, *The Economic Mind*, II, 653–655; Richard B. Morris, "Andrew Jackson, Strikebreaker," *American Historical Review*, LV (Oct., 1949), 68; Hofstadter, *The American Political Tradition* (New York, 1948), p. 56.

from some . . . giving it to others." In the first issue of the *Working Man's Advocate*, Evans promised to oppose "the establishment of all exclusive privilege; [and] all monopolies" as oppressive burdens on labor. The promise was honored. Simpson and Luther defined monopoly as a system designed to permit capital to live off labor. Monopolies "grow rich without being industrious"; "they do labor to be sure," satirized Fisk, "but it is laboring to collect that which others have earned." "To the effects of monopolies . . . may the useful look to find the . . . cancer that is slowly consuming the vitals of their industry," wrote Douglas. His language is both vague and broad enough to leave room for the hard-working—in contrast to the parasitic—businessman as one of the "useful." On the other hand, Douglas explicitly states that a principal effect of monopolies is that "those who do all the work can barely subsist."

Another nice example of the concern expressed by some labor leaders, especially those with political ambitions, over monopoly's bad effect on business or "honest industry," as well as on labor, is a purple passage from English's exhortation to labor:

> The powers and privileges granted to a few wealthy individuals, have caused a superabundance of money to flow into their coffers, while, in the same ratio, we [labor] have become impoverished. *Speculation has superseded industry;* and each one who can, leaves his honest vocation to run riot upon the spoils of legislative favor. [The system] is sure to add another rivet to the chains which bind the working man." [Italics mine.]

Present here, too, is a characteristic aversion not simply to capitalistic profit as such but for such profit when it results from manipulation, be it of stocks or legislatures, rather than through efficient business enterprise. Essentially, however, labor's antimonopoly stand was based on the view that special charters facilitated the mistreatment of labor, in contrast to the more characteristic Jacksonian aversion to monopoly's restraints on the soaring ambitions of that army of restless, "venturous" souls, who sought not social justice but equal opportunity for profit-making.[29]

[29] See Skidmore, *The Rights of Man to Property,* p. 146; *Working Man's Advocate,* Oct. 31, 1829, and *passim;* Simpson, *Working Man's Manual,* p. 69; Luther, *Address to the Working Men of New England,* p. 6; Theophilus Fisk, *Capital Against Labor* (cited in *Working Man's Advocate,* July 25, 1835; Charles Douglas, "Proposals for Extending the Circulation of the *New England Artisan,*" in *New England Artisan,* March 22, 1834; *Political Observer and*

As with monopoly in general, the critical attitude of Jacksonian labor leaders with regard to banks and paper money, was shared by many men, both in and out of the business community. The notion that essentially it was only radicals, liberals or reformers who opposed the second Bank of the United States, for example, has been pretty effectively demolished by modern economic historians, who have shown that a variety of business and speculative types joined the claque against it, some of them eager to replace the "wicked monster" bank with their own good banks, others delighted that perhaps the main obstacle to their own inflationary ambitions would be removed with the national bank's destruction.[30]

Most workmen are strangers to esoteric currency matters, and it is not surprising that what purported to be labor thought was in some cases the work of middle-class individuals whose only connection with labor was their willingness, for reasons of political advantage, so to identify themselves. Joseph Dorfman, suspicious of a complex statement on currency and banking, with its "melange of erudite explanations," prepared by what was ostensibly a meeting of workingmen and their friends, shows that the fine hands of Condy Raguet and William Gouge were apparently involved in this "labor document.[31] Yet if some labor groups simply accepted the viewpoints of professional currency theorists, it is also true that a number of the labor leaders had their own ideas on the subject. These ideas, like all ideas, were somewhat influenced by the thinking of others; but they were fundamentally original, striking a unique note, and clearly different from the theorizing of middle-class critics of the banking system.

Where the liberal antimonopolists opposed "privileged" banking,

---

Working Man's Friend, cited in *Working Man's Advocate*, June 30, 1832; English, "Oration Delivered at the Trades' Union Celebration of the 4th of July."

[30] See Walter B. Smith, *Economic Aspects of the Second Bank of the United States* (Cambridge, 1953); Bray Hammond, "Jackson, Biddle and the Bank of the United States," *Journal of Economic History*, VII (May, 1947); and Hammond, *Banks and Politics in America from the Revolution to the Civil War* (Princeton, 1957). Not the least of the points made by Smith and Hammond concerns the bank's effectiveness in compelling state banks to honor their obligations and limit their outstanding debts, a policy particularly galling to Jacksonians of speculative temper.

[31] Dorfman, *Economic Mind*, II, 636–637; cf. Arthur M. Schlesinger, Jr., *The Age of Jackson* (Boston, 1945), pp. 78–79.

the labor people opposed banking as such. Most of them saw in banks and in the paper money they issued simply another means of exploiting labor and defrauding it of its proper share of income. The businessman takes out on labor the interest he must pay the banker, warned Skidmore. Evans' critique was typical. Banking "enables some men to live in splendor on the labor of operatives, without laboring themselves. [It is banking] that throws large classes of workmen out of employ." As for paper money, it was "the crying evil of the day . . . the dead weight upon industry; the clog upon useful labor; the means by which the drones obtain the honey. . . ." The others ring changes on this indictment. Banks, according to Fisk, made "the many live and labor for the benefit of the few"; while to Luther, Douglas, and Slamm, paper money brought desolation and famine to labor, by "giving them in exchange for their toil and sweat, stamped pieces of paper . . . which in reality cost the individuals who issued it, just nothing at all." Banks and their rag money were, according to English and Commerford, "one of the grand schemes which has been impoverishing the people." Moore, who said nothing original on this issue, simply represented the Thirteenth Ward, as did Commerford the Fifteenth, on the temporary General Committee of the "New York Workingmen Opposed to Paper Money and Banking and to all Licensed Monopolies."

Brothers, Slamm, and Simpson, as was often the case, mingled a concern for small business with their unhappiness at the evil effects of banking on labor. Brothers, in fact, blames bankers more than employers for making labor miserable. Undoubtedly his own experience as a small manufacturer colored his judgment that "employers are nearly as bad off as the employed and are dropping every day into the ranks" of wage workers. The evil cause was an impersonal scheme that permitted a fortunate few to manipulate currency, as well as the community's need for it, to their own advantage. While he believed that workingmen suffered more than any other class from the paper-money evil, Slamm also noted that the businessman, as well as the worker, could be hurt or even destroyed by the "sudden reverses of fortune that have taken place" as a result of our "vicious and corrupt money system."

Simpson managed to combine support for the second Bank of the United States with hostility to banking in general. Since most of the leaders supported Jackson on the bank issue, when Simpson's position became known, he was attacked by his colleagues as a renegade, a false friend to labor who had deserted his earlier convictions. Actually, Simpson's views remained as radical during the bank war as they had been before. His belief that the national bank protected the people from the paper-money depredations of the other banks was neither liberal nor conservative, but simply sensible—a view that such modern authorities as Fritz Redlich, Bray Hammond, Walter Smith, and Thomas Govan would approve. Nor was his support of the Bank unqualified. He wanted it reformed in important ways. In addition, however, to denouncing banking and paper money for robbing the workers, he also expressed concern for the effect on men of property; as when he wrote: "When the balloon of paper credit is in full expansion, an estate may cost fifty thousand dollars; and when the same balloon has collapsed, it will sell for twenty thousand dollars, and the first purchaser may be a beggar."

Another theme developed by some of the labor spokesmen was the trickery, or the "mystification," involved in the paper system, which enabled those who profited from it to fool working people and others into acquiescing to the system's continued operation. When Evans says that "the laboring classes do not see through the mystification by which bankers draw enormous interest upon the wealth which *their* labor produce, without adding a mite to the wealth of the community themselves," his grammar may be vague but his meaning is clear. Simpson describes bank bills as having a "fictitious character" that permits the defrauding of labor; while Brothers alludes to a "system that enables a man by a *trick*, to make as much in a day or two, as . . . hardworking women make in their lifetimes." [Italics mine.] Luther, too, believes workers have been "profoundly gulled and deceived" by a system which, to hear it admirers tell it, rewards bright and industrious men for their ability. The fact is, however, that "all the interest in this counterfeit money comes out of our [labor's] sweat and toil." [32]

---

[32] For the labor leaders' views on banking and paper money, see Skidmore, *Rights of Man to Property*, pp. 178–179, 188; *Working Man's Advocate*, April 23, 1831; *The Man*, March 22, May 7, 17, and Aug. 2, 1834; Fisk, *The Banking Bubble Burst* (Charleston, 1837), p. 19; Luther, *Origins and Progress of Avarice*, pp. 12, 14; the *New Era*, March 2, 20, and April 11, 1840; *Weekly Plebeian*, March 2, 1844; Levi Slamm, "Address to the Mechanics and Workingmen of New York," cited in *Daily Plebeian*, Oct. 19, 1842; John Commerford, "Address Delivered Before the General Trades' Union," *op. cit.*, English, "Oration

Suspicion concerning the alleged deceitfulness of various aspects of the American class system was a popular motif in American labor thought. Thus paper money cheated the working class; wills tricked present generations out of their rightful inheritance; the laws and the legal system obscured by their complexity their true role as servant of the rich; the major political parties—and especially the Democrats—by the artfulness of their masquerade, fooled the workers into accepting them as truly popular expressions of their will. This skepticism, in my judgment, was a revelation not of an emotional peculiarity but rather an inevitable feature of radical social thought.[33] For once accept the view that workingmen *were* exploited or wronged by this or that economic or political institution, how better explain their acquiescence in their own mistreatment than by reference to the fact that they were fooled? Vested interests, being a minority, were always cunning; they had to be to hold on to what they did not deserve. The victimized working people, the over-whelming majority, were always gullible. They had to be to put up with their lot.

Their discussion of banking also reveals the hostility some of the leaders felt toward commerce and commercial institutions. Owen describes commerce as "a destroying hydra that draws the hard-earned bread of [labor] and dooms her victims to perish for want in the very midst of wealth"; Slamm denounces it for seducing young men away from honest industry. Simpson concludes that social injustice commences "when the equivalents passed [in trade] are in the form of the symbols of wealth, money, whether gold, silver or paper. . . . Here Law begins to be substituted for fact, and the tremendous power of capital commences." These sentiments manifest an anti-commercial spirit that was common not only to certain nineteenth-century socialists and radicals but that is reminiscent of certain

Delivered at the Trades' Union Celebration," p. 123; *Radical Reformer and Working Man's Advocate,* June 13, 27, and July 18, 1835; Simpson, *The Working Man's Manual,* pp. 12–13, 69, 76–77, 101, 140, 187, 189. Simpson called for amendments in the second national bank's charter which would "divest the institution of a portion of its selfish and mercenary spirit" and place a limit upon the "grasping passion of the stockholders" for the highest possible power over management, in addition to earmarking excess profits as appropriations "to the cause of public education," *Pennsylvania Whig,* May 2, 1832).

[33] Richard Hofstadter has argued in a number of places that the Populist belief in a plutocratic conspiracy was a form of political paranoia.

medieval and even more ancient attitudes. They repeat the old notion that the merchant and the dealer in money are essentially sterile or parasitic. Only labor is creative.

Labor's analysis of the causes of Jacksonian America's ills was essentially an indictment, not so much of land, machines, or money, as of the commercial profit system within which they operated. Nothing so strikingly reveals the leaders' separation from other Jacksonians, whose main complaint against the commercial system was directed not against its wickedness but, rather, against its inaccessibility.

11

The Good Society and How to Achieve It

Every leader of the Jacksonian labor movement had a vision of the good society that, were it up to him, would replace or, at the least, drastically modify American society's existing arrangements. Although a few of them were relatively laconic on the matter, perhaps because their glimpse of utopia had been a fleeting one, most of the leaders were quite explicit, and in a few cases downright effusive. If their goals cover a wide spectrum of possibilities, it is also true that for all the seeming divergence of their views, there was much greater agreement in their thinking than even they were aware of. Their consensus tended toward what we today should call a socialist society.

No one of them used the term socialism. Perhaps the radical intellectuals who transformed American social thought early in the twentieth century, with their careful attempt to refrain from using Socialist or Marxist terminology (thus, "personalty" instead of "bourgeoisie"), were not the first to operate on the evident assumption that if the American people might be responsive to radical substantive proposals, it was politic to coin new terms for them. Of course, men so uncompromising as Thomas Skidmore or John Commerford were probably neither intimidated nor trying to be politic in not using a term which, as a matter of fact, was well known and even popular in England and on parts of the Continent.[1] But whether they used the phrase or not, the leaders' expressed hopes were for a society that in most particulars met that era's definition of socialism.

The present is by no means unique in ascribing many, sometimes conflicting, meanings to socialism. For since the term achieved popularity early in the nineteenth century, it has at one time or another been identified with programs which strive for economic freedom

[1] Max Beer, *A History of British Socialism* (2 vols.; London, 1948), I, 102.

and social solidarity; abolition of profit; a planned society; common property; realization of natural law; the total product of society to labor; distribution in accordance with the quantity and quality of work performed by the individual; individual liberty; community or democratic management of land and capital; achievement of religious ideals; the welding together of the worker and society; emancipation of the proletariat; or combinations of the above.[2] Nor is that all. In view of its chameleon qualities, there is wisdom in R. H. Tawney's reminder that "socialism is a word the connotation of which varies not only from generation to generation, but from decade to decade"; and in Thomas Kirkup's admonition that "above all things, it is essential to remember that socialism is not a stereotyped system of dogma. It is . . . living and liable to change." [3] The common feature of the labor leaders' socialism was its stress on labor.

The solid rock on which their idea of the good society rested was their belief that labor created all wealth. Those who are familiar with the history of social thought will know that the idea was not unique with them, even for the American scene. The fact is, of course, that the idea goes back to antiquity, was held by the founders of classical economics and our own Benjamin Franklin, and in their own time, had been eloquently expressed in Shelley's *Song to the Men of England*, which wrote of the workers:

> The seed ye sow, another reaps;
> The wealth ye find, another keeps;

[2] *Ibid.;* John Strachey, *Theory and Practice of Socialism* (New York, 1936), pp. 115–117, 119; J. Ramsay MacDonald, *The Socialist Movement* (London, 1911), p. xi; Harry W. Laidler, *A History of Socialist Thought* (New York, 1927); John H. Noyes, *History of American Socialisms* (Philadelphia, 1870); Morris Hillquit, *History of Socialism in the United States* (New York, 1910); Ira Kipnis, *The American Socialist Movement 1897–1912* (New York, 1952), pp. 315, 421; David A. Shannon, *The Socialist Party of America: A History* (New York, 1955), chap. iii, p. 258; Howard Quint, *The Forging of American Socialism*, 1953; C. K. Ensor, ed., *Modern Socialism* (London, 1904), p. xvii; Werner Sombart, *Socialism and the Social Movement* (London, 1909), chap. i; Thomas Kirkup, *A History of Socialism* (London, 1920), pp. 1, 8; William H. Dawson, *German Socialism and Ferdinand La Salle* (New York, 1899), p. 3; Reinhold Niebuhr, *Moral Man and Immoral Society* (New York, 1936); Oscar Jaszi, "Socialism," *Encyclopaedia of Social Sciences*.

[3] R. H. Tawney, Intro. to Beer, *A History of British Socialism*, p. vii; and Kirkup, *op. cit.*, p. 2.

> The robes ye weave, another wears;
> The arms ye forge, another bears.[4]

As was so often true of any discussion of labor, the leaders were not always precise in defining just what and whom they meant by the term. Most of them, however, meant by labor those who worked with their hands for wages. Skidmore noted that properties willed to an individual were of no value unless they "enable their possessor to live off the labor of others." Evans defined labor as

those who do the work and fight the battles; who produce the necessaries and comforts of life; who till the earth or dig for its treasures; who build the houses and the ships; who make the clothes, the books, the machinery, the clocks and watches, the musical instruments, and the thousands of things which are necessary to enable men to live and be happy.

Only Simpson, Fisk and, inevitably, English attempted to match this blaze of rhetoric.

Simpson is reminful of Evans when he writes that workers "produce all the wealth of society without sharing a thousandth part of it; . . . they do all the work . . . fight all our battles . . . cause all our enjoyments to flow upon us. . . . Without labor there can be no property," and when he concludes that "all capital is . . . produced by the working men of a nation."

Not to be outdone, Fisk asks the workers:

Who builds their [the rich] marble palaces, who covers their tables with the most costly luxuries . . . ? Who enables them to give their sumptuous entertainments, to roll through the streets in their splendid equipages, to spend hundreds and thousands upon fopperies and gee gaws . . . ? Who does all this? You! Your labor, your toil, your industry, alone produces wealth.

English's passage on the subject, if more brief, was as purple. He asks a labor audience: "Are they [the rich] not provided by our labour with beds of down, with costly furniture . . . ? Do they not live and move; riot and dissipate upon the proceeds of our industry?"

Most of the others were more prosaic, confining themselves to

[4] Thomas Hutchinson, ed., *The Complete Works of Percy Bysshe Shelley* (London, 1948), I, 572–573.

such statements as Commerford's observation that the worker was the "real producer of all the wealth and luxury possessed by the rich and powerful." [5] And as their image of American society made clear, they also shared Commerford's view that the working class, "from whose labor spring the articles of exchange, can scarcely obtain sufficient wherewith to make [their] . . . families comfortable." Clearly, a better society was needed.

Eloquent or perhaps grandiloquent a number of them were but most of the leaders were not, nor did they claim to be, theorists. For the most part their image of the good society emerges from sparse references, generally made not in the course of developing a model of their final goals, as such, but rather as they dealt with some specific problem. A small number of them, however, were nothing if not theorists. Of these, the man who had the most to say as to the shape society should assume in the future, was—as might be guessed— Thomas Skidmore. And by all odds, the man whose projection of the future was most savagely attacked—by his colleagues within the labor movement as much as by conservative publishers outside it— was the same Thomas Skidmore.

His co-workers fell on his plan, denouncing it for a variety of reasons that included its alleged ineffectiveness, its injustice, its partial tendency, its malicious falseness, and the ease with which it could

---

[5] Thomas Skidmore, *The Rights of Man to Property* (New York, 1829), pp. 154, 226–227, 239; Skidmore, *Moral Physiology Exposed and Refuted* (New York, 1831), p. 35; *Working Man's Advocate*, Oct. 31, 1829, April 3, and May 1, 15, 1830; *The Man*, Feb. 18, and June 28, 1834; Stephen Simpson, *The Working Man's Manual* (Philadelphia, 1831), pp. 43, 23, 29, 53–55, 64; Theophilus Fisk, *Capital Against Labor* (cited in *Working Man's Advocate*, July 25, 1835); Fisk, *The Banking Bubble Burst* (Charleston, 1837), pp. 3, 25, 30; William English, "Oration Delivered at the Trades' Union Celebration of the 4th of July," *Radical Reformer and Working Man's Advocate*, Sept. 1, 1835, p. 125; John Commerford, "Address Delivered Before the General Trades' Union of New York," in *Working Man's Advocate*, Sept. 19, 1835; the *Union*, April 21, 1836; *Free Enquirer*, Jan. 16, and Feb. 13, 1830; *Daily Sentinel*, April 8, 9, 10, 12, 13, 14, 1830; Seth Luther, *An Address on the Origins and Progress of Avarice* (Boston, 1834), pp. 3, 6, 10, 12, 40; Luther, *Address to the Working Men of New England* (3rd ed.; Philadelphia, 1836), p. 25; Charles Douglas, in the *New England Artisan*, May 31, and June 21, 1834; *Radical Reformer*, July 4, 11, 1835; *New Era*, June 9, 1840; "Report of the Resolutions Committee to the First Convention of the National Trades' Union," in *The Man*, Aug. 29, 1834; Ely Moore, *Address Delivered Before the General Trades' Union of the City of New York* (New York, Dec. 2, 1833), p. 20.

be used to slander the entire movement.[6] The impression I get is that what really stung them in Skidmore's plan was not so much the blueprint of society it offered—in fact, hardly that at all—but the fact that it actually called for confiscation, to be put into effect immediately. That it was to be put into effect peaceably only if the majority approved did not mollify Skidmore's frightened colleagues. There seems little question, too, that some of them were much more concerned with conservative critics' hostile reaction to Skidmore's program than with any intrinsic deficiencies in it.

Skidmore's program took the form of a plan divided into twenty sections. Its central purpose is clearly indicated in the first section:

Let a new State Convention be assembled. Let it prepare a new Constitution, and let that Constitution, after having been adopted by the people, decree an abolition of all debts; both at home and abroad, between citizen and foreigner. Let it renounce all property belonging to our citizens, without the State. Let it claim all property within the State, both real and personal, of whatever kind it may be, with the exception of that belonging to resident aliens, and with the further exception of so much personal property, as may be, in the possession of transient owners, not being citizens. Let it order an equal division of all this property among the citizens, of and over the age of maturity in manner yet to be directed. Let it order all transfers or removals of property, except so much as may belong to transient owners, to cease, until the division is accomplished.

The other nineteen sections were essentially concerned with means of implementation.[7]

[6] See the *Free Enquirer*, Oct. 31, and Nov. 7, 14, 28, 1829; also Oct. 16, 1830. See *Working Man's Advocate*, Jan. 16, 1830; Nov. 14, and Dec. 15, 1829; Aug. 11, 1832; May 8, 1830. See the *Radical*, April, 1841, p. 52; April, 1843, pp. 51–52. Simpson, *The Working Man's Manual*, pp. 27–28, 89, 137–138, 230; Luther, *Origins and Progress of Avarice*, p. 40; English, "Oration Delivered at the Trades' Union Celebration," p. 125; Ely Moore, *Speech in Reply to the Hon. Waddy Thompson*, given in the House of Representatives, May 5, 1836 (Washington, 1836), p. 5.

[7] The plan called for a census of persons and wealth; arrangement for public sale; equitable division of parcels; distribution to all of equal purchasing power; joint bids on large parcels; punishment to those who withheld information respecting their property; guardianship of the property of drunkards and the insane; distribution of the property of those who die during the transaction; annual dividends; the inclusion of residents who were citizens of states organized the same way as New York, for the purpose of sharing in the benefits; public education of all native-born persons; joint disposal of property of deceased husband or wife by the widow(er) and the state; imprisonment of those giving away property (since charity is provided for); the freedom of persons to leave the state; and the guarding of property against foreign competi-

Disingenuous in the extreme, not the least for its assumptions that a state convention might convene to do the things Skidmore wanted them to do, essentially on his say-so, or that the public, for all its economic and emotional diversity, was some kind of monolith that could not help but respond to his logic, the plan seemed to infuriate its many critics. One suspects they were overwrought.

Many years later, Henry George, who agreed with Skidmore that "to extirpate poverty, to make wages what justice commands they should be, the full earnings of the laborer, we must therefore substitute for the individual ownership of land a common ownership," profited from the lesson taught by the harsh reaction to Skidmore's call for immediate confiscation. While he, too, believed, "we must make land common property," George proposed the method of confiscation of rent rather than of land, since in his words, "great changes can best be brought about under old forms." He hoped to accomplish the same social result as would follow confiscation of wealth but by subtler methods.[8] Skidmore's own contemporaries in the American labor movement were similarly averse to anything resembling confiscation.

Without always revealing precisely how it was to be achieved, a number of the leaders looked forward to a society whose material needs would be handled through the mechanism of a common storehouse of goods. Distribution would be based on the principle that was to become a socialist maxim: "From each according to his ability, to each according to his deeds." According to Robert Dale Owen, this ideal state of things would one day replace "individual commercial competition." But first the prevailing marriage and family system, both a consequence and a cause of selfish acquisition, would have to be replaced by a more socially desirable method for uniting the sexes. That there was a transition in Owen's thought is

---

tion. Skidmore was so eager to end foreign trade that he cheerfully consented to "let the navy go down forever." Prosperity depended only on the home market. The expropriation was also to be directed against church properties, drawn as they were "from the iniquitous system which has robbed man of his rights forever." (*Rights of Man to Property*, pp. 137–144, 273–283, 342.)

8 Henry George, *Progress and Poverty*, Modern Library Edition (New York, 1939), p. 328. In view of George's clearcut position, it is hard to understand the statement of his interpreter that George did not favor common ownership in land (George R. Geiger, *The Philosophy of Henry George* [New York, 1933], pp. 130–131).

revealed by the two editions of his essay "Wealth and Misery." When first published in 1826, Owen's plan—the "federative system"—called for a common stock into which "each producer puts the articles of wealth he creates, as soon as they are created; and from which he draws articles of necessity and comfort, *as he requires them.*" (Italics mine.) The plan's underlying principle of distribution was to each according to his needs. By the time he had become a leader of the New York Working Men, Owen's scheme—now described as a "common storehouse"—would reward the individual only in proportion to his contribution in labor to its common stock, since without "some such modification . . . , each member is continually wondering whether his neighbor does as much as he; and thus there is a great temptation for each to act as a spy on the other's conduct." The beauty of this change was that it continued to give each member the advantages of "co-operative union," "without depriving him of the competitive incitements to individual industry." Other practical features of Owen's plan were its respect for "individual property or private rights," and its promise to avoid "the evils of an overstocked market." [9] Owen took no steps to put this plan into action, nor did he ever take up the question of how his program based on "competitive incitements" would manage to avoid the pitfalls of the wicked system of "individual commercial competition."

Evans' ideas, always influenced by Owen, also underwent transition. At first he favors producers' co-operatives, as a temporary remedy at the least, in which for only four hours daily labor the workingman would earn far more than he now did in fourteen. By the time he came to publish *The Man,* in 1834, he had been won over to the idea of a common stock, which rewarded labor and others solely according to how much they had contributed to it. "Such," he wrote, "*should* be the state of things, . . . and now . . . is the time to decide whether such shall be." In addition to the co-operative system of production, he also now began to advocate free land as the other solution to mankind's problems.

The basic ideas of George Henry Evans, influential land reformer

[9] Robert Dale Owen, "Wealth and Misery," serially in New Harmony *Gazette,* Nov. 8 through Dec. 13, 1826, and also in *Working Man's Advocate,* May 1, 8, 15, 1830; Owen, *Lectures on the Marriages of the Priesthood of the Old Immoral World* (London, 1835), pp. 32, 36, 47, 71–72; *Free Enquirer,* Feb. 13, 1830.

of the 1840s and 1850s, are anticipated in his writing in the 1830s, when he was active in the labor movement. Evans' mounting enthusiasm for free public lands begins to be registered during the latter period. Where in 1833 he is a mild advocate of the safety-valve theory, by the following year he writes that "three-fourths, we verily believe, of all the vice and misery existing in the United States might be eradicated by the just and practicable measure of allowing every necessitous individual to cultivate [without charge] a portion of the uncultivated land." By 1835 Evans is convinced that free public land is the panacea, besides which such a device as trade unionism, for example, pales into insignificance, whether as a temporary or lasting, partial or complete, remedy. Unlike Skidmore, however, Evans seeks no immediate redistribution; private ownership of land, evil though it is, is to be left undisturbed. The free distribution of uncultivated public land will work invincibly to overcome in the future the negative tendencies of the present system. Obviously, the main factor that accounted for the relative popularity and later success of Evans' "new agrarianism," was that, unlike the old, or Skidmore agrarianism, it did not disturb present title to property.[10]

Other admirers of the common-storehouse plan were Douglas, Ferral, and to an extent, Slamm. Douglas thought that it was "in accordance with the laws of nature and the immutable principles of right and justice" that there be a society "based upon labor, where everyone shall receive for himself the products of his own industry." Ferral asked American workers to support a system based on co-operative production, pooled savings, and a common store of all products, under which "moral justice would exact from every individual, when not incapacitated by natural imbecility or accident, a fair and full equivalent to society for that which he consumes, and also that he should contribute his due portion of labor towards the contingencies of society, for the protection and security he derives therefrom." Slamm expressed a dislike for panaceas, registering his unhappiness at the alleged tendency of Fourier's doctrine to foster free love, while it choked off scientific and artistic progress. He did, however, think that utopian projects were useful in small communities, and that the ideas of Robert Owen and like reformers, far from

[10] See the *Working Man's Advocate*, Feb. 20, 1830; April 14, 1832; Jan. 26, and March 2, 1833. Also see *The Man*, Feb. 18, Aug 29, and June 14, 1834; May 9, 1835.

being offensive, "deserved every consideration.[11] Of course Slamm's expressed approval of socialism may have been motivated by extraneous considerations rather than felt convictions, since, to hear many tell it, he was a shrewd, artful man. But if this suspicion is well founded, it would only signify the popularity of a doctrine capable of attracting not only zealous admirers but clever dissimulators.

In some cases the rhetoric used by the labor leaders suggests more drastic things than does the actual substance of their thought. For example, Stephen Simpson's discussion of his goals has led Broadus Mitchell to describe Simpson as an important anticipator of Marx.[12] Now it is true that Simpson was critical of the prevalent mode of distribution, as well as of the traditional political economy in which it was justified. He favored a new scheme, according to which the distribution of things is to be almost completely determined by their manner of production. Yet his writings seem more radical than they actually are. Mitchell misinterprets his thought when he describes it as an important anticipation of Marx, because of Simpson's alleged "contention that labor should . . . receive the whole of its production." Simpson never goes that far. What he asks for is not the total product. "As labour is the only basis of wealth," he writes, thus far in accord with the Socialists, "a just proportion of it must be given to the industrious, to enable them to rear their offspring." He thus favors a *larger* share for labor, rather than the whole of the product. This is more a simple call for higher wages than a revolutionary assault on surplus value.

He seeks a higher status as well as better working conditions for labor. "There is, there can be," in his opinion, "but one rule for estimating the value of labour—on principles of equity, benevolence and social harmony—that rule is, human happiness; general competence and as nearly as possible, an equality of the enjoyments of

---

[11] Douglas in the *New England Artisan*, June 21, 1834; John Ferral, "Report of the Resolutions Committee to the First Convention of the National Trades' Union," in *The Man*, Aug. 29, 1834; Ferral, in the *Radical Reformer*, Sept. 19, 1835, pp. 229–230. On Fourierism in America, see Arthur E. Bestor, "Albert Brisbane, Propagandist for Socialism in the 1840's," *New York History*, XXVIII (April, 1947), No. 2, 128–159. Slamm's *Daily Plebeian* carried for several months as a regular feature a column by Brisbane, explaining Fourierism (*Daily Plebeian*, Jan. 27, 1844; Feb. 6 and March 27, 1845; also *Weekly Plebeian*, March 30, 1844).

[12] Broadus Mitchell, "Stephen Simpson," *Dictionary of American Biography.*

life. The end of labour being happiness—it is self-evident that happiness must regulate the just value of labour." Evidently the precise ratio of this revised formula was to be determined by an arrangement not altogether unlike that governing the establishment of the "just price" in former days, i.e., the intervention of a rational authority guided by its own understanding of the common good.

Simpson himself attempts to forewarn those who might misread his analysis. "It is a fallacy to imagine, that we are aiming to controvert the established legitimate doctrines of political economy," he explicitly states. "Our object reaches higher—is more rational—and more laudable. It strikes at a fundamental principle in the distribution of wealth—that Labour shall share with Capital, in the profits of trade, in a more equitable ratio." It turns out that Simpson is urging not confiscation of the property of one class by another, but more equitable sharing by the two.[13]

Commerford would have society based upon "a true system of political economy," in which "those who earn all wealth of the nation [no longer] secure the least; while those who earn the least, monopolize all, by cunning and injustice." A change for the better is needed but it should be a "healthy reformation," rather than a complete alteration. Such language leaves some doubt as to what proportion of society's product labor is to get in the new society. When Moore told New York's unionists that the new system should enable "the producer to enjoy the full benefit of his productions, and thus diffuse the streams of wealth more generally, and consequently, more equally, throughout all the ramifications of society," he manages in one sentence to support the notions that labor should both receive all of the product, and that it should get a larger share. Most of his writings indicate that he meant the latter. The writings of the others justify the conclusion that the Jacksonian labor leaders looked forward to a new society in which labor's reward was at least equal to that of all other groups, both in status and income.[14] Like the

[13] Simpson, *Working Man's Manual*, pp. 82, 87–88, 89, 229.

[14] See the *Union*, April 21, and May 17, 1836; Moore, *Address Delivered Before the General Trades' Union*, p. 11; *The Man*, November 25, 1834; Luther, *Origin and Progress of Avarice*, p. 18; Luther, *Address to the Working Men of New England*, p. 5; William English, "An Address to the Mechanics and Working Men of the Trades' Union of the City and County of Philadelphia," in the *Pennsylvanian*, Jan. 9, 1834; English, "Oration Delivered at the Trades' Union Celebration"; Fisk, *Capital Against Labor;* Brothers to Lewis, July 18,

utopian Socialists abroad, they would not—with the exception of Skidmore—disturb any man's present private property, for all their inflammatory talk against the institution.

How was the good society to be brought about? It is in their discussion of this issue that in my judgment most of the leaders reveal either their lack of seriousness or their willingness simply to profess certain goals, while showing practically no concern whatever in doing anything likely to accomplish them. Certainly they supported many measures. Not being doctrinaires, they seemed willing to take various paths to heaven. The rub, however, is that although most, if not all, of these paths seemed to lead somewhere good, it was hardly to heaven—or even to their expressed idea of it. This is not to say that they were insincere; for I believe they were sincere, almost to a fault. I am only suggesting that while they evidently wanted a fundamentally different kind of society, they evaded the issue of how to achieve it, settling instead for the advocacy of reforms and solutions that, while useful and benign, had little to do with the ostensible purpose for which they were designed. They no doubt convinced themselves in the process that these measures would have no other effect than to transform American society.

The leaders were ardent champions of educational reform, most of them arguing that this, above all, was the means of correcting the wrongs in American society. Now in working to broaden the educational opportunities of the poor and to destroy the stigma attached to public schools, the labor reformers were fighting a good fight for what in fact was a most worthy reform. This was a reform, nonetheless, that a number of political conservatives also favored. That men of practically every social persuasion could find merit in public school reform indicates the universality of the issue, and explains in part this movement's success. But it also raises the question as to whether and how such a reform, no matter how ingeniously its alleged radical consequences are developed in the labor rhetoric, could bring about a completely new society based on the pre-eminence of labor. The distinct impression is given, in fact, that a number of the leaders championed the method of reform through education largely because they wished to avoid a more frontal attack

1839, in Thomas Brothers, *The United States of North America as They Really Are* (London, 1840), p. 1.

on the institutions they professed to abhor. Such motivation would be perfectly understandable, but it would also reflect on the depth of their feeling for the far-reaching changes they publicly hunger for.

For the most part, the educational opportunity they spoke of, the brave new programs to be set up, were to affect the young, and, thus, by bringing about a revolution in the thinking of the *next* generation, create the intellectual atmosphere likely to bring about the desired changes. It is hard, in view of this, to disagree with the few skeptics, such as Orestes Brownson, the Catholic reformer, who argued that to concentrate on educating the young was in effect to consign the present generation to their dismal fate. Skidmore comes off better with regard to this matter than he usually does, when in response to the proposition that the "right education of the rising generation" is "the most important and consequently has the strongest claim on adults of any question that can be proposed to them," he responds: "But who ever heard . . . so singular a doctrine as this? What! and is it to be said that the welfare of the *adults themselves* is second in importance to the right education of their offspring?" [15] Most of his colleagues seemed to feel precisely that, even if they never said it in so many words. They denounced contemporary society above all for its alleged mistreatment of adult workers, spoke eloquently of the need for something better, and proceeded to stress a reform that would admittedly have little immediate effect on the lives of the working class.

For the leaders were pragmatists. Far from being zealous devotees of a social theory, rigidly construed, they were, in fact, eclectic men, perfectly capable of making no distinction between what seemed to be an ideal society, on the one hand, and slight—if useful—reforms, on the other. They were willing to support various methods of reform, including some that seemed to have little hope of accomplishing their stated objectives. In the manner of sensible men of practical temper, they made a fetish neither of consistency nor of strict logic.

In supporting educational reforms, they showed themselves to be idealists, ready if necessary to sacrifice present well-being for future good. There is no question but that for whatever reasons, emotional or other, a number of the leaders burned with the conviction that

[15] Thomas Skidmore to Amos Gilbert, in *Free Enquirer*, Dec. 17, 1831.

education was both a means and an end; that a sound system of educating the young was not only the surest guarantee that society would be changed but, in itself, the central feature of the good society. "The only remedy commensurate with the abuses we purpose to remove," the sovereign measure that struck "at the root of things," according to Owen, was a system of equal national education.

Although almost all of the leaders stressed the importance of education, they had diverse and sometimes conflicting notions as to its values and purposes. Owen and Moore were drawn to it, at least in part, for its conservative implications. Not the least of the reasons the American people should support educational reform is that it "would save their country from the convulsions of a bloody revolution," Owen writes. With a sideward glance in the direction of Skidmore, he notes that "National Education [the particular scheme proposed by Owen] is a measure involving no dangerous revolutions to rouse the passions, and perhaps to blind the judgment of mankind. It presupposes no violent change in the structure of society. It is like the silent flowing of the rising tide, not like the impetuous whirl of the engulfing storm." Moore likewise alluded to equal educational opportunities for poor and rich alike as the means of preventing the rise of factions which "could arise to disturb the public tranquillity, or endanger the public welfare."

This reform likewise appealed to those who believed that man, as he was presently constituted, would not do: he must first purify himself of the unlovely traits fostered by a vicious society. He must first undertake his own regeneration before he could reform institutions, since social "injustice lies deeper than pecuniary inequality; it is beyond the power of money to remedy. It has its roots not in the purse, but in the minds and feelings." The platform for this viewpoint was built by Fanny Wright, when she wrote that "until equality be planted in the mind, in the habits, in the manners, in the feelings, think not it can ever be in the condition." Her thesis was echoed by Owen, when he asked, "What avails it that our present monopolies are destroyed . . . that all pecuniary inequality ceased in a moment, if the ignorance remain that first produced and would soon reproduce it?" His fellow publisher, and sometime disciple George Henry Evans agreed.

Education was the nonpareil reform because of its great and varied consequences. It not only made man more knowledgeable and more sociable, it would also remove the deformities inflicted by the piratical society. Evans believed it would make workingmen in the future more virtuous and, in general, lead the way to a new and superior morality. Simpson argued that "knowledge is the great remedy of intemperance; for in proportion as we elevate men in the scale of existence . . . so do we reclaim them from all temptations of degrading vice and ruinous crimes. A reading and intellectual people were never known to be sottish. . . . Thus sobriety and political honesty are the twin offspring of education." Luther regarded the sound early education of the child as the best antidote to avarice. In the manual-labor schools he advocated, not only would diseased minds be cured—"suicide would be a thing unknown"—but sickly bodies, as well: "then you will hear but little about dyspepsia." Slamm expected education to destroy the "base feelings" of man. Commerford thought it would "elevate the moral and intellectual character" of future generations of workingmen; while Douglas expected it to "spread sobriety and virtue" among the working class. It is clear that labor's leaders were concerned with the tendency of workers to imbibe heady beverages too freely and that in their estimate the best medicine for this disease was knowledge, rather than the strange rostrums advocated by temperance zealots.

Education would get rid of social, as well as individual, aberrations. Once adopt a sound schooling system and there would be "no need of jails and state prisons, penitentiaries and almshouses, houses of correction and popular executions."

It would also provide workers with a fuller and richer life, befitting the needs of self-respecting men and of a rational and just society. For "without education a portion of the community is cast into the shade." Fairness demanded that "children of the poor, as well as the rich, ought to be instructed both in letters and morals." According to Luther, equal education "would place the rich and the poor on a level in regard to intellectual worth," while also giving the former an interest in work.

Perhaps the most significant result of educational reform, according to a number of the more militant leaders, would be its impact on labor's self-consciousness. They believed that an educated working class would finally appreciate its own true worth. To Ferral, the beauty of the ten hour system was the opportunity it afforded workers to spend their increased leisure in the pursuit of fundamental truths about society. As important a truth as any other, of course, was the one concerning the significance and the destiny of the working class. Evans' succinct comment that a major purpose of education "was to remove the veil of ignorance by which the poor who suffer are prevented from penetrating into the mysteries of that legislation of the rich by which their sufferings are produced," accorded with the prevalent notion that the working people were gulled into subjection by wily oppressors. It goes without saying that the notion of some labor leaders that the role of education was to instill class consciousness into workers was unique with them, not dreamed of by such middle-class champions of educational reform as William Ellery Channing or Horace Mann.

Some of the leaders believed that the great obstacle to the education of the workers was the opposition of the rich and the powerful. With Simpson, they held that "the effort of capital and power, is always on the side of ignorance in the people," because there is always the fear of losing "exclusive privileges by imparting knowledge to the mass of the people." In Fisk's rhetoric, "the great fear of those who grow rich upon [labor's] industry" is that workers will "get time to improve [their] minds," and their eyes will be opened "to the monstrous frauds that have been perpetrated" upon them. "Let their worst fears be realized," he concluded. Of course, the rich did not uniformly display the attitude attributed to them by Simpson and Fisk, but the following excerpt from an edtiorial in the *National Gazette* in Philadelphia, is a nice example of what the labor critics had in mind:

The "peasant" must labour during those hours of the day, which his wealthy neighbour can give to the abstract culture of his mind; otherwise, the earth would not yield enough for the subsistence of all: the mechanic cannot abandon the operations of his trade for general studies; if he should, most of the conveniences of life and objects of exchange would be wanting; languor, decay, poverty, discontent would soon be visible among all classes. No government, no statesman, no philanthropist, can furnish what is incompatible with the very organization and being of civil society.

The fact is, of course, that democratization of educational opportunity in America was supported by men of all classes and political persuasion. Horace Mann spoke for humanitarians who sought social

justice without social convulsions, when he wrote that "education is
. . . the great equalizer of the conditions of men,—the balance-wheel
of the social machinery." According to Philip Curoe, in the early
nineteenth century men who were little concerned with equality believed that "universal education diminished crime, prevented poverty, and increased production." A developing industrial society
required a literate working class, as business leaders increasingly
realized. Another valuable feature of popular education was the
likelihood that it would counteract the radical, anticommercial doctrines so dangerously prevalent among the working class, and instill
in their place respect for the fundamental values required by a stable
society. This was the idea suggested by the conservative Thomas
Cooper:

> Education universally extended throughout the community, will tend
> moreover to disabuse the working class of people in respect of a notion
> that has crept into the minds of our mechanics, and is gradually prevail-
> ing, that manual labor is, at present, very inadequately rewarded, owing
> to combinations of the rich against the poor; that mere mental labor is
> comparatively worthless; that property or wealth, ought not to be accumu-
> lated or transmitted; that to take interest on money lent or profit on capi-
> tal employed is unjust. These are notions that tend strongly toward an
> equal division of property, and the right of the poor to plunder the rich.
> The mistaken and ignorant people who entertain these fallacies as truths,
> will learn, when they have the opportunity of learning, that the institu-
> tion of political society originated in the protection of property.

Obviously, class-conscious persons of left and right saw in educational reform the means of propagating necessary social lessons.

Since the accomplishment of a tax-supported, high quality public
education system in this country took some doing, there seems little
doubt but that the labor contribution to the cause was a significant
one, meriting the praise heaped on it by Philip Curoe, Frank Carlton,
and Sidney Jackson. Not the least of labor's contributions were the
unique educational ideas advocated by some of its leaders. If Owen's
plan for state-supported boarding schools, providing "food, clothing
and instruction, at the public expense," was not the sole remedy of
injustice he claimed it to be, it was nonetheless a provocative idea. If
little came of it in practice, the same could not be said of his plans for
a broad curriculum that would include agricultural and mechanical,
as well as intellectual, subjects. At a time when the common schools
were patently inferior, Evans stressed the importance of striving for

the highest quality of education in public schools. In curriculum, training of teachers, and pedagogy pains had to be taken to assure that standards in public schools equaled those in private; while with regard to higher education, Evans urged that the poor have equal access with the rich. Simpson was nominated to office by the Philadelphia Working Men primarily because he was known as an enthusiastic supporter of educational reform. He has been praised by Sidney Jackson for the sophistication and prescience of some of his ideas concerning teacher-training and curriculum. Commerford's ideas on the subject were hardly sophisticated, but they were clear enough. He advised the community, and above all its working-class members, constantly to scrutinize the quality of instruction, as well as the "moral character and qualifications of teachers." Underlying this advice was the belief that good schooling, administered by qualified teachers, would move society toward a form of socialism. Questionable as this assumption was, it remains true that in advocating, for whatever reasons, a democratic public-school system of the highest quality, the labor leaders played their part in achieving a reform of the highest importance.[16]

[16] For the discussion of education, see Frank T. Carlton, *Economic Influences upon Educational Progress in the United States, 1820–1850* (Univ. of Wisconsin, *Bulletin*, IV, No. 1, 1908), pp. 39, 50, 53–54; Philip R. V. Curoe, *Educational Attitudes and Policies of Organized Labor in the United States* (New York, 1926), pp. 32–33; Sidney L. Jackson, *America's Struggle for Free Schools* (Washington, D.C., 1941); Robert Dale Owen, *Address on the Hopes and Destinies of the Human Species* (London, 1836), p. 16; Owen, *Republican Government and National Education* (London, n.d.), pp. 11–12, 13–14; *Free Enquirer*, Nov. 7, 1829 and Jan. 16, 1830; Ely Moore, *Address on Civil Government* (New York, 1847), pp. 6–7. See *Working Man's Advocate*, Jan. 16, 1830; May 21, 1831; Feb. 13, March 6, and May 1, 8, 15, 1830. See George Henry Evans, "Report of the New York Association for the Promotion of Education," Sept. 30, 1829, in *Working Man's Advocate*, Nov. 14, 1829; Simpson, *The Working Man's Manual*, pp. 205, 40–41, 42, 212; Luther, *Address to the Working Men of New England*, p. 6; Luther, *Origin and Progress of Avarice*, pp. 34–35, 36; *New Era*, May 1, 1840; *National Trades' Union*, Oct. 10, 1835; Douglas, "Proposals," in *New England Artisan*, March 22 and June 7, 1834; Ferral, in *The Man*, Aug. 29, 1834; Ferral, letter to the editor, *Radical Reformer*, July 4, 1835, p. 62; Fisk, *The Banking Bubble Burst*; *National Gazette*, July 10, 1830, cited in John R. Commons and Associates, *History of Labour in the United States* (New York, 1918), I, 229; A. Kahler and E. Hamburger, *Education for an Industrial Age* (New York, 1948); for an analysis of the intellectual history of Thomas Cooper, see Joseph Dorfman, *The Economic Mind in American Civilization* (New York, 1946), II, 527–539; Thomas Cooper, *Elements of Political Economy* (2nd ed.; London, 1831), pp.

Most of the leaders believed that, whatever the means used, labor could rely only on itself to right the wrongs it suffered under. Thomas Brothers, himself a hat manufacturer, failed to see inconsistency in his advice that workers "should never admit into their councils one who does not belong to them." They did not hold with Mathew Carey and other benevolent humanitarians that misery would be overcome by appeals to "the humanity of the wealthy employers." Their views were well expressed by Evans when he wrote that how long social abuses "will be suffered to prevail must be decided by the sufferers themselves—the poor laboring classes of the community. The rich could not be expected to take any but the most superficial steps toward remedying social distress." [17] One of the obvious methods that workers had to use to change society was political action.

At times the utterances of the labor leaders convey the belief that political reform is "not enough," especially in the absence of drastic economic changes. Where this idea was expressed, it generally was directed against those who urged reform through the party of Jackson. For as has been shown, labor regarded both parties as humbugs, agreeing with Charles Douglas that "the working class . . . belonged to no party; they were neither disciples of Jacksonism nor Clayism, Van Burenism nor Websterism, nor any other *ism* but *workeyism*." It was not politics as such that they derided but rather what they believed to be the illusion that important reforms could be achieved through co-operation with the major parties. On the other hand, a number of the leaders did advocate labor's independent political action.

The leaders of the Working Men's parties showed by their behavior their belief in the importance of political action. In this case, theory and practice were one, for their words also expressed the same viewpoint. Evans advised that "the leisure hours of working men cannot be more usefully employed than by informing themselves on political

---

333–334; *Daily Sentinel*, April 8. 9, 10, 12, 13, 14, 1830. Evans criticized the plans for a new university on the grounds that "it would only extend the advantages of education to a few who could pay for it, while the large body of working men would be excluded from any participation in the benefit of it for want of means" (*Working Man's Advocate*, March 27, 1830).

[17] *Working Man's Advocate*, April 3, 1830, and May 14, 1831; *The Man*, Feb. 20, 1834; *Radical Reformer*, June 13, and July 18, 1835.

subjects—subjects which involve their dearest interests, and on which they have been so designedly kept in ignorance." The trade unionists also emphasized the importance of independent labor politics, even after the disappearance of the labor parties. Douglas never tired of warning workers that on the one hand they must avoid "throwing themselves into the arms of any of the political parties of the day," while on the other, they must take the "political business into their own hands." Only by selecting "for their candidates farmers and mechanics, men of virtue and integrity, who are not rich," would they "certainly triumph, and . . . destroy the vile system . . . which has already reduced them to poverty and degradation." Of course Douglas was an unusually ardent believer in the efficacy of political action. At the first convention of the National Trades' Union, when English, impressed by the early demise of the Philadelphia Working Men, expressed doubts as to both the wisdom and the popularity of political activity by labor, it was Douglas who offered a rebuttal. The question, he said, was not an abstract one, as to whether this or that form of reform was logical or not. If workers suffered because of class legislation, "how were they to get out but by legislating themselves out? They could only advance their interests by choosing such men for legislators as were identified with them." Fisk supported strikes, but he regarded them as half-way measures: "There must be a radical reform—and this can only be accomplished at the ballot boxes," he told workers. Ferral simply reminded labor that at present the servants of the rich controlled law and politics. "The working classes," according to him, "would never effectually remedy the evils under which they were suffering until they carried their grievances to the polls." [18]

The leaders were also fond of invoking the possibility of revolution. Although the memory of Jefferson and the Adamses was still fresh in the minds of Americans during the Jacksonian era, and the term "revolution" therefore still had positive connotations, it was also true that radicals, above all, perhaps because of their sensitivity to conservative criticism, had learned to grow circumspect about

[18] *Working Man's Advocate*, Nov. 21, 1829, and March 27, and May 1, 1830; *The Man*, Feb. 18, 1834; Douglas, "Address to the Workingmen of Massachusetts," *New England Artisan*, Oct. 25, 1834, and the *Artisan*, June 21, and Oct. 4, 11, 1834; Fisk, *The Banking Bubble Bursts;* Ferral, in *The Man*, Aug. 29, 1834; *Radical Reformer*, July 25, 1835; Ferral, "Remarks to the Convention of the National Trades' Union," in *The Man*, Sept. 6, 1834.

using it. Accordingly, only Skidmore explicitly approved of revolution as the suitable means of accomplishing the necessary transformation of society. Revolution was not only a right but a duty in a society that denied to the overwhelming majority of its members the right to property conferred on them by their creator. (Skidmore, unlike the younger Owen, was no atheist.) In his view, revolutions were caused, not by designing men, but by worsening conditions. In 1829 he not only convinced the executive committee of the New York Working Men's party that conditions in their country and state were deteriorating but that, in his words, "the fountain of your distresses is not to be dried up but by a revolution." Believing as he did in the right of revolution, he innocently believed that the people had only to indicate their pleasure, for the necessary change to occur. Of course pains had first to be taken to assure that the revolution was desired by the majority, for otherwise it would be wrong. He feared that some rich men might be inclined to violence to safeguard their wealth; but he was confident that they would easily be convinced "that it would be perfectly idle to oppose what so very large a majority should determine to adopt and enforce." But in any case, he was unalterably opposed to violence, for as a contemporary noted, "violence of action . . . did not come within the sphere of his designs;—he saw no occasion for [it] . . . ; his whole reliance was on the preference which the human mind gives to truth." What need was there for violence, when by Skidmore's naïve estimate, once the workers understood his message, would they not ask with him, concerning the prevailing system, "shall it not be overthrown now?" [19]

As might be expected, the same colleagues who denounced his attacks on private property and his concept of the good society also expressed horror at his advocacy of revolution. For even those men who believed in a co-operative society, would have it develop *alongside* the present one, rather than be imposed in its stead. Thus, although Owen hated private property, his plan for the future scrupulously safeguarded its present possessors. Skidmore, who burned with impatience, would not wait. Other of his colleagues spoke guardedly

[19] *Rights of Man to Property*, pp. 4, 5–6, 358, 15, 315–316, 17, 271, 335–336, 244; "Report of the Committee of Fifty of the Working Men's Party of New York," in *Working Man's Advocate*, October 31, 1829; Amos Gilbert, "Thomas Skidmore," in *Free Enquirer*, April 6, 1834.

of the abstract right of revolution—even the careful Moore more than once invoked what after all was a popular Enlightenment doctrine—but especially after the press succeeded in making his ideas anathema, the other leaders took pains to disavow Skidmorism and ˙ revolution. And yet a number of them also conveyed the impression that, like it or not, they believed a revolution was imminent, made so by the vicious workings of the system and the greedy men who profited from and controlled it.

A popular oratorical pastime was to indulge in a purple rhetoric that not only predicted imminent revolution—in this case bloody and violent revolution—but, by emphasis and nuance, condoned or at least acquiesced in it. When Brothers asks, in an editorial, "What moral principle will be subverted if the oppressed poor should rise in their *might* and *majesty*, and forcibly take their own, which their oppressors refuse to give up?" he is not approving revolution outright; but he justifies something approximating it: violent social behavior unsanctioned by law but based on a high moral principle. In the same vein, Evans asks: "If the national hive is full, should the bees be expelled or the drones?" Meanwhile, Luther suggests that since a class society incarcerates the weak and the innocent, the task of the decent man is to open prison doors.

No one abhors revolution more than Simpson. He dreads turbulence and disorder. Yet he professes to expect them soon, unless amelioration—about the chances for which he is hopeful but not sanguine—takes place. For he agrees with Skidmore that "all revolutions have been produced by inequality of condition." Either the rich will give in gracefully, or workers will resort to violence. And if they do, who can challenge their right? since "the power to remedy the evil is unquestionable; it resides in the producers of wealth who constitute overwhelmingly a majority of the people." Luther leaves much—but not too much—to the imagination in the following grim passage: "Amid the chilling desolation around them, they [the workers] cast an inquiring glance at their fellow sufferers, and ask the question, 'what shall be done?'" Ferral described the achievement of a shorter working day as labor's "bloodless revolution"; only this concession had interrupted the movement toward a revolution marked by "violence and blood." English reminded rich capitalists that workers had "the controlling power" in their hands and might be driven to desperation. Fisk warns exploiters of labor that "they would do well to pause. Beneath their feet an earthquake slumbers."

Commerford's views are of interest because they express so well labor's mixed attitudes toward the problem. He makes clear he has no use for the "visionist" ". . . who would endeavor to disarrange the equilibrium and order of our social arrangements." He wishes "it to be distinctly understood" that he "shall always discountenance anything which may tend to tumult and riot." Yet he sees the same causes which have fomented revolution elsewhere operating here, namely the tendency of the rich to aggrandize the laboring poor. Continued hostility to unions may yet engender a revolutionary spirit here. Already "a moral revolution is silently but steadily progressing," preparing workingmen for "the day of retribution" soon to arrive. In an allusion as vague yet inflammatory as any made by his contemporaries, Commerford writes: "It is not the wages which the laborers of our country at present receive, that stalk before our avaricious task masters like spectres, but it is the more substantial ghosts which are to come, which haunt their grovelling and self-grasping imaginations." [20]

What is one to make of this firebrand talk? Several things, in my opinion. To a large extent it was simply a kind of verbal seasoning, useful in flavoring speeches. These were men, after all, whose activities in so many cases were confined either to talk or to the most sober kind of action. They were not as frank as Skidmore, who at one point conceded that he resorted to "revolutionary language in order to frighten employers out of lengthening the working day!" [21]

---

[20] *Radical Reformer and Working Man's Advocate*, July 18, and Aug. 29, 1835; *Working Man's Advocate*, Oct. 31, 1829. Evans was later to write: "The very excesses of the priviliged classes will tend to their overthrow. It cannot be, that those who do the work will much longer allow themselves to be defrauded of so large a share of the proceeds of their labor" (*Radical*, Nov., 1841, p. 163). Luther, *Origins and Progress of Avarice*, pp. 30, 6, 18; Simpson, *The Working Man's Manual*, pp. 230, 20, 27, 17; also see the *Pennsylvania Whig*, Aug. 22, 1832; Ferral, in *Radical Reformer*, July 4, 1835; *The Man*, June 29, 1835; English, "Oration Delivered at the Trades' Union Celebration"; Fisk, *The Banking Bubble Burst*; the *Union*, April 21, June 10, May 25, May 28, June 4, and June 9, 1836.

[21] See George Henry Evans, "History of the Origin and Progress of the Working Men's Party in New York," in the *Radical*, 1842–1843; *Commercial Advertiser*, April 25, 1829; *Free Enquirer*, April 25, 1829.

Undoubtedly some of his colleagues hoped, too, that allusions to imminent social convulsions might induce a modest melioration. I think some of them said what they thought their labor audience wanted to hear, while others were simply carried away by their own language, believing every word they uttered. One thing seems clear: no one was frightened—even though some conservatives might profess great fear. Actually, anxiety seemed to be induced much more by trade unionism, with its modest but practical goals, than by revolutionary rhetoric.

It need hardly be said that every one of the labor leaders looked with favor upon trade unions and strikes. Not oddly, the most enthusiastic champions of unionism were the union leaders themselves. According to Moore, unions of journeymen defended labor against capital, neutralized the more vicious tendencies of human selfishness, prevented economic slavery, and preserved the workers' natural rights, added to their dignity, and safeguarded their welfare. Commerford emphasized their importance as defensive alliances which ensured the economically weak, protection against the economically strong. Ferral believed unions not only strengthened labor in its struggle for better hours and wages but could be used to overcome all of "the evils that exist in society." English read great significance into a trades' union movement. His dream was of a union of all the trades; such a body would enable every worker to "provide a comfortable subsistence for his family," education for his young, and a nest egg for his old age, and would gain for him the respect of the community. It would be so strong as to "resist the most formidable oppressions." [22]

Essentially, unionism and strikes were viewed by their American supporters as useful methods for securing and maintaining decent material conditions, rather than methods of changing society. Unlike their fellow English radicals, who already by this time regarded the

[22] Moore, *Address Delivered Before the General Trades' Union,* pp. 8–9, 12, 28; Moore, *Speech* given in the House, May, 5, 1836, p. 11; Commerford, "Address Delivered Before the General Trades' Union," the *Union,* July 1, 1836; John Ferral, Chairman of Committee reporting to the first meeting of the Trades' Union of Pennsylvania, in the *Pennsylvanian,* Dec. 24, 1833, cited in John R. Commons and Associates, *A Documentary History of American Industrial Society (Cleveland,* 1910), V, 336; *The Man,* Aug. 29, 1834; English, "Address to the Mechanics and Working Men of the Trades' Union of the City and County of Philadelphia."

general strike as a revolutionary political weapon designed to bring about broad and thoroughgoing changes in the social system, the American unionists expected only modest, if useful, tangible benefits from the strike, no matter how many might turn out to support it. This viewpoint of theirs, as well as any other, reveals, in my opinion, their essentially nonrevolutionary cast of mind.

Certainly they sincerely hoped for a new society based on social justice and respect for labor. If hoping would have done it, then America would have become a form of socialist community. Since other, tougher means were necessary, they turned instead to a number of practical and exemplary programs, contributing in no small measure to their contemporary reform movement's modest but significant successes. If these measures seemed on close scrutiny to have little chance of bringing about the good society they were ostensibly created to achieve, that fact caused no embarrassment to a group of men who were neither doctrinaires nor strict logicians.

12

Conclusion: An Evaluation of Their Thought

One thing seems clear. The leaders of the Jacksonian labor movement were radicals—if that much abused and misused word retains any shred of its traditional meaning. How else describe men who believed American society to be torn with social conflict, disfigured by the misery of the masses, and dominated by a greedy elite whose power over every aspect of American life was based on private property? A society whose transformation in the future depended on the independent action of labor, the class responsible for all of society's wealth? In view of the fact that American labor thought was so akin to English radicalism of the period, it would appear that the old notion of American uniqueness would have to be modified, at least for the Jackson era. The companion idea, that the American labor movement has been relatively conservative or even unideological, with the exception of fringe groups such as the Wobblies or the Chicago Socialists, would also seem to be in need of revision. For in the Jacksonian period, anticapitalist thought was characteristic not of the fringe but of the central leadership of the American labor movement.

It is true that at times the rhetoric used by the leaders conveys an impression of extremism that is actually belied by the modest meaning of the thought it embellishes. A number of them, for example, managed to make support of higher wages sound like a call to confiscation of private wealth. Denunciation of "parasitic bankers" might reflect only the unhappiness of a small businessman with the price of credit. Joseph Dorfman did a useful service in calling attention to the wide disparity between the radical or idealistic language used by some labor spokesmen and their mundane, even sordid, practices. In the case of others, if their activities were not so dubious, if they were not involved in speculation, for example, it remains true nevertheless that their radical ideas or language were very far removed from their sober and sedate labor activities.

What are we to make of this gulf between theory and practice? It would appear, harsh words they said to the contrary notwithstanding, that a number of the leaders had an inner conviction or an unspoken faith that American society was in fact flexible enough to permit significant progress to occur at a steady and encouraging rate. It is certainly true that with the exception of Thomas Skidmore none of them were revolutionists. They might speak in favor of a complete transformation of society and mean every word as they said it. But they had no interest in, let alone a heart for, doing the dirty, difficult, perhaps dangerous job of preparing for or organizing the great change. Education was enthusiastically championed because, though its advocates could convince themselves that its social consequences would be far-reaching and drastic, in fact it threatened no one immediately, as was made clear by the wide support it attracted from men of varied persuasion. Skidmore's charge that preoccupation with educational opportunity for children in effect consigned their parents to their fate, was good logic. For the fact is that most of his fellows, regardless of what they professed—and the sincerity of their professions is not here in question—had no stomach whatever for violence or social disorders. They loved stability, even as they talked up turbulence.

The fact that so many of the leaders were of the middle class perhaps explains the relative timidity of their behavior. Of course middle-class radicals in and out of the American labor movement have associated themselves with the boldest schemes. Social class by itself tells little of a man's ideas or of his affinity for conflict. Yet in the cases of such men as Robert Dale Owen or Stephen Simpson, surely moderate nuances in their reform ideas were influenced by their comfortable backgrounds.

A distinct impression given by some of the leaders is simply that they thrive on criticism of the present state of affairs. They are at home in denunciation, fiery attacks, trenchant exposé. In their case, it is not that the difficulties in fighting for the good society frighten them. Rather, they have little interest in preparing blueprints for the future. Contentment comes in attacking the present.

With regard to another gulf, that between their language and their thought, one explanation would seem to be the addiction of a number of the leaders to words. As good children of the Enlightenment they had great respect for the power of the word. Let it be loud and clear, and the masses were sure to react properly. Others loved the crackling sounds of fiery talk. Their colorful rhetoric somehow came tumbling out, leaving its spokesmen no alternative but to follow where it led and, if possessed of sufficient dexterity, to work out a rational or logical case for whatever position their lively verbiage had led them to.

At bottom, even though they often give a different impression, most of the leaders were pragmatists. Unlike doctrinaires, they delighted in the accomplishment of any reforms, no matter how slight—though a few of them found it necessary to interpret small gains as large victories. Fortunately for their peace of mind, they seemed to have the gift of convincing themselves. Thus John Ferral was capable of seeing in the ephemeral achievement of the ten-hour day in a number of cities what he called the glorious accomplishment of "our bloodless revolution."

Nor is there question, in my judgment, that in taking a radical position, the leaders said what they believed their audiences wanted to hear. This is most strikingly indicated in the case of the trade unionist Ely Moore, described by his biographer as an ambitious opportunist dedicated largely to no loftier ambition than that of furthering his own interests. That this man struck the radical poses he did, with an eye toward winning friends, seems obvious. I do not mean to challenge Moore's sincerity, since I am altogether innocent of knowledge concerning his deepest, truest convictions. Perhaps he was not aware of them himself. It goes without saying that both for him and for his colleagues there was no logical inconsistency in saying what might be deemed politic, and, at the same time, truly believing it. In fact, that is my estimate of their feelings.

If many workingmen and their friends *were* receptive to the voice of protest—and certainly this is suggested by the evidence—it would indicate a number of significant things not only about the state of mind of American labor but about the state of American society as well. Earlier I suggested the possibility that American workers felt a sense of alienation toward their society. Commons and the early twentieth-century labor historians concluded that American workers were conservative, or basically content, principally as a result of the beneficent effect of free land, social fluidity, and early possession of the suffrage. Receptivity to denunciations of the existing order indicates something other than contentment.

I do not mean to suggest that American workers in the Jacksonian era were in a restive state, ready for violent stratagems or the like. Like men of other classes, like their own leaders for that matter, workingmen had mixed emotions and attitudes, some of them seemingly out of harmony with others. As always, most workers did not join the unions, while fewer still had anything to do with the Working Men's parties. Those who did join one or another organization in the labor movement—and their numbers were not insignificant—undoubtedly did so for varied reasons. Applying to them Marvin Meyer's term "venturous conservatives" might be instructive, so long as it is clear that we are changing slightly the meaning of the phrase. Their inclination to ride along with the status quo may not unreasonably be interpreted as conservative—though these inconsistent "conservatives" applauded sharp attacks on the very system they accepted. What is "venturous" in their case is not an affinity for brazen financial speculation but rather a responsiveness to radical social analysis. If their feet sought the path of profit, their minds responded to the call of protest.

Another basis for American labor's radicalism, which should not be discounted because of its very obviousness, is the possibility that the plight of labor was simply as bad as its friends described it. For the most glaring and the widest gulf in the Jacksonian era was between the American Dream and the harsh reality experienced by the poor. The elder Arthur M. Schlesinger has argued recently that in the Declaration, Jefferson meant the pursuit, as in occupation or calling, rather than the chasing after, of happiness. In either case, dismal material conditions worked against labor's chances of realizing the noble goal. That the grimness of conditions was exaggerated by the labor leaders is doubtless true. Equally true, however, is the historical dictum that what men think is so, is often as important as what in fact is. And where only God—certainly not historians—can ever know the actuality, it is quite possible to gather evidence as to the *believed* reality. This evidence shows that laboring men believed themselves to be badly treated in American society during the age of Jackson.

The leaders displayed a keen interest in politics. It has been a commonplace, certainly since Samuel Gompers popularized the attitude, that independent political action in the form of separate labor-party organization is fatal to organized labor. It may well be that this concept is true when applied to the kind of labor organizations Mr. Gompers had in mind. Militant and idealistic unions, on the other hand, have usually been most interested in political action to achieve their diverse and far-reaching goals. Certainly the Jacksonian leaders had no aversion to independent political action by labor. Even after the decline of the Working Men's party, the position taken by William English that perhaps labor politics was a mistake was a minority viewpoint, vigorously countered at a National Trades' Union convention by Charles Douglas and others.

Perhaps their most interesting political attitude was the hostility they displayed not only toward the Whigs but toward the Democrats as well. Co-operation with Jackson on the bank issue and occasional support of the antimonopoly position taken by "Equal Rights Democrats" did not deflect the labor spokesmen from a course of unremitting criticism of the two major parties, "humbugs" both, whose only real difference, it was said, consisted in the fact that one attempted to camouflage a class bias that the other unashamedly displayed. Far from being a part of the alleged broad coalition the Old General led, the labor leaders were "Jacksonian" only in the sense that they lived during the Jackson Administrations, regularly denouncing his party and its works.

A significant characteristic of the era's labor thought was its concern with others than workingmen, with issues that only affected labor indirectly. For it is not stretching matters to view the Working Men's parties and the unions alike, as a broad reform movement rather than a movement of labor alone. The typical Working Men's program was a far-ranging one indeed, while the unions, too, were concerned with reform and humanitarian issues that interested men of other classes. Further, when these men spoke of "workingmen" it is clear that they meant many things in addition to mechanics who worked with their hands. When they used the word "class," they had in mind not only a functional group or one which differed from other classes by the kind of work it did or *how* it earned its income. They also had in mind men separated from others by quantity of income, no matter its source; that is, the poor as against the rich.

I do not think it is an indictment of the Jacksonian labor movement and its leaders to hold that they were concerned with social justice, broadly conceived, rather than with the amelioration of labor's lot alone. Their idealism gave a sense of high purpose to their efforts, a sense that not only adds a touch of charm to what is otherwise merely another interest group trying to get more for itself, but is probably the surest guarantee against the selfishness and even the corruption that often seem to go hand in hand with more narrow and practical concepts of a labor movement's purpose. The labor leaders were drawn to the labor movement essentially for two reasons. They believed that workers suffered more than did any other group in American society. And convinced as they were that labor alone was responsible for the creation of wealth, they also held that the greatest crime in society was the denial to the actual producers of wealth of the good things they had created. The labor movement was thus in the eyes of its leaders, a lofty movement dedicated to the high moral cause of ending suffering and injustice.

In recent years historians have interpreted the Jacksonian era as a period of restless speculation and widened business opportunity. For that matter, Tocqueville and his contemporaries were struck by the lust for acquisition that marked American life. In the words of the moralist, things were in the saddle riding mankind. This constant pursuit of material goals was widely noted and usually censured by reflective persons, convinced of its negative effects on traditional values. Standing apart both from the frenzied contest for gain, and from the patrician criticism of it, were the era's labor leaders. In contrast to the accumulators and their critics, the labor spokesmen challenged the assumption shared by both: that practically all Americans had or were in the process of getting their fair share of the community's products. They reserved their criticism not for an alleged moral deterioration traceable to material excess, but for the poverty of working people and for the social, intellectual, and political deprivation which they believed flowed from it.

Every man an entrepreneur! may have been the slogan of William Leggett and other antimonopoly Jacksonians. It was not theirs. In their private behavior as in their social thinking, the labor leaders were uncommon Jacksonians. On the one hand, they contradicted Chevalier's observation that Americans were ambitious but without any grand ambition. For certainly most of the leaders were not ambitious, in the ordinary sense, while they had a very grand ambition indeed—for society. On the other hand, they refuted Tocqueville's dictum that Americans loved change but dreaded revolutions. For while these Americans had little interest in the personal change for the better that the French aristocrat had in mind, they anticipated drastic social alterations with equanimity.

If, as some historians have argued, there was a Jacksonian consensus, uniting men of unlike social background, political affiliation and philosophical persuasion in unspoken adherence to similar fundamental principles and practices, then the typical Jacksonian labor leader stood outside of it. In one important way only, did he appear to be like his opportunistic contemporaries: his practice, too, conflicted with his theory. Yet both his thinking and his behavior were distinctive for their time.

Index